A.S

PDR
1986

MY NAME IS TODAY

An illustrated discussion of child health, society and poverty in less developed countries

David Morley
and
Hermione Lovel

MACMILLAN

First published 1986 by
MACMILLAN EDUCATION LTD
London and Basingstoke
Companies and representatives throughout the world

ISBN 0–333–43301–7

17 16 15 14 13 12 11 10   9   8
07 06 05 04 03 02 01 00 99 98

This book is printed on paper suitable for recycling and
made from fully managed and sustained forest sources.

Printed in Hong Kong

Published in conjunction with Teaching Aids at Low Cost, PO Box 49,
St. Albans, Hertfordshire AL1 4AX
TALC received assistance in the production of this book as a low cost
edition from the Swedish International Development Authority.

First published on Friday, May 30th 1986 to mark the honorary doctorate conferred
on David Morley by the University of Uppsala.

The majority of the illustrations were prepared by, or adjusted by Mrs Gillian Oliver,
M.M.A.A. A.I.M.B.I.

'We are guilty of many errors and many
faults, but our worst crime is abandoning the
children, neglecting the fountain of life.
Many of the things we need can wait.
The Child cannot.
Right now is the time his bones are being
formed, his blood is being made and his
senses are being developed.
To him we cannot answer "Tomorrow".
His name is "Today".'

Gabriela Mistral
Nobel Prize-winning poet from Chile

Acknowledgements

The original draft of this book was prepared for a presentation to the Institute of Child Health given on the occasion when Professor Morley was presented with the King Faisal International Health Award for his work in primary health care. We are grateful to our colleague, Duncan Guthrie, for help in bringing that version out, and to a very large number of people who gave their comments on that first draft and the layout of the present draft. The redesign of many of the illustrations arose from these comments. This book, although finally written by two authors, is a team effort and many of the ideas that it contains have arisen from discussions with colleagues, students attending our courses, and many others. Within the Institute, our first thanks must go to Eleonora Giorgi who undertook the assembly of all our illustrations and their cataloguing. Colleagues whom we particularly must thank are Zef Ebrahim, Pam Zinkin, Pat Harman, John Ranken, Maureen Wimble, Daphne Olorenshaw and Sheila Berry. As in all such work, much falls upon secretaries, and here we are grateful for all the assistance given by Marcia Wickramasinghe within the Institute, and from Gill Brown, Sue Brooker, Elizabeth Swan, Barbara Calder, Lynda Campbell, Ann Gudgeon, Rosemary van der Does and Margaret Dawson.

The major work on the illustrations has been undertaken by Gillian Oliver, who has patiently redrawn and adjusted illustrations again and again. The illustrations themselves come from many sources: these are indicated with the references at the end of the book. Patricia Morley undertook the drawings of the authors on the back cover. The photographic work on all the illustrations was undertaken by Ray Lunnon's team, including Carole Reeves, Jill Almond and Roland Brooks. They undertook the production of the illustrations in the final form for the printers. For the illustrations on the front cover, we are grateful to John and Penny Hubley giving us access to their enormous collection of photographs of children.

We have received many useful comments, often in great detail, from colleagues outside the Institute, and here we would particularly like to thank Donald Court, Paul Snell, Felicity Savage, Sara Bhattacharji, Lesley and Peter Adamson and John Adams. We are also grateful to Barbara Harvey in the organisation Teaching Aids at Low Cost and all those who work with her in the assistance they have given.

Our determination has been to make this book as low cost as possible so that many in less developed countries can afford it. We are grateful for the assistance of the Swedish International Development Authority in achieving this and the co-operation we have received from the publishers, Macmillan. As other writers will appreciate, the assembly of a book such as this involves many hours of work, and we are particularly grateful to our families.

CONTENTS

INTRODUCTION

CHAPTER 1: OUR CHILDREN'S WORLD

CHAPTER 2: CHILDHOOD ILLNESS IN THE LESS DEVELOPED COUNTRIES OF THE WORLD

CHAPTER 3: OPPORTUNITY FOR IMPROVING HEALTH SERVICES

CHAPTER 5: WHERE NEXT FOR CHILDREN?

INTRODUCTION

This book is about children and their families in the developing world shown through illustrations, cartoons, graphs and line drawings. The book is for the many people who have little time to keep abreast of the enormous and increasing literature on health care.

Fig. 1 How do we try to teach?

Raise questions,
identify problems
and search for answers?

. . . or teach to memorise
and regurgitate our Bla?

For us, the telling illustration is of first importance. In this sense we are interested in the 'picturate' not just the 'literate'. Over the years we have gathered this selection of pictures and diagrams because we have found in our teaching at London University that drawings and pictures will raise questions, identify problems and stay in people's memories long after they forget the printed word. The cathedrals of Europe in the Middle Ages and the temples of India are full of pictures and images, and in a contemporary sense we are trying to follow that tradition of inspiration and teaching. Most illustrations are straightforward, others require discussion and are controversial. Many represent data from the field of 'social epidemiology', trying to find answers to such questions as Who gets ill and why? Where are the resources spent? Who is more likely to die? Illustrations are particularly important if we are to gain a better understanding of the social and epidemiological background to health, the multifactorial causation of disease and the opportunities we now have for preventing ill health rather than spending the larger part of available resources on its treatment.

UNICEF has called for a 'Child Survival Revolution'. This book is in line with that call. It does not evade the severe economic limitations of the present time. It emphasises that if the right steps are taken now, the resources necessary for increased survival and better growth and health during the rest of this century could be available.

The views expressed in this book are those of the authors and in no way seek to represent the views of UNICEF or the Institute of Child Health.

CHAPTER ONE
Our children's world

Fig. 2   Children are powerless

CHILDREN CANNOT SPEAK FOR THEMSELVES

They depend on us to speak for them.
They are powerless.
They suffer most when resources are maldistributed.
They need us to bring their very special needs to the notice
of the powerful.

Fig. 3 When does death occur? When are coffins needed?

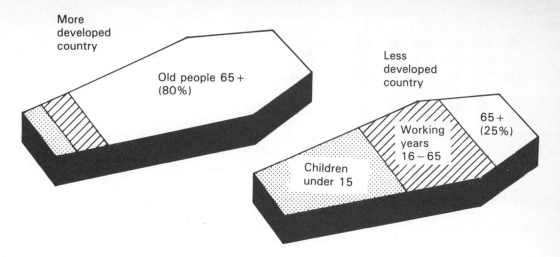

More
developed
country

Old people 65 +
(80%)

Less
developed
country

65 +
(25%)

Working
years
16 – 65

Children
under 15

Deaths by age group as % of all deaths

In the North, 80% of those born live into retirement.
In the South, only a quarter of the population live into
their retirement age. Half of all deaths may be those of
children.

Fig. 4 Distribution of resources

The developing world has . .

75% of the world's people

30% of the world's
food grains

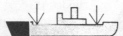

18% of the world
export earnings

17% of the world's GNP

15% of
world energy
consumption

5% of world
science and
technology

6% of the
world health
expenditure

11% of world
education
spending

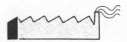

8% of world industry

Fig. 5

As a result, most of those living in less developed countries:
- go hungry
- remain poor
- suffer from preventable diseases
- lack education
- are unemployed
- lack fuel
- do not benefit from science and technology

For most people there is still significance in the old Chinese greeting:

   Have you eaten?

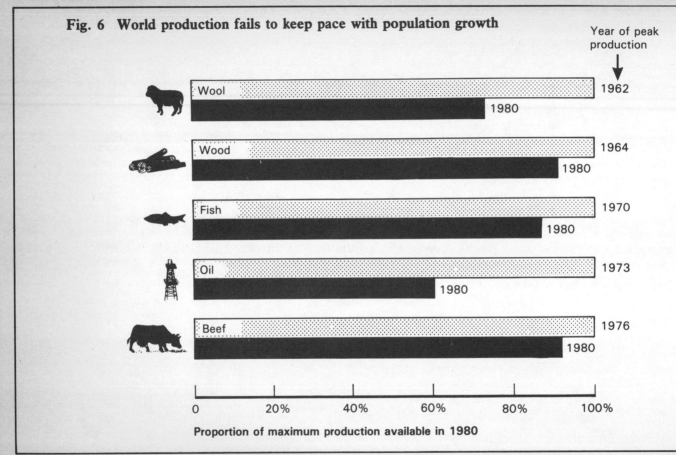

Fig. 6 World production fails to keep pace with population growth

Year of peak production

Wool — 1962 / 1980

Wood — 1964 / 1980

Fish — 1970 / 1980

Oil — 1973 / 1980

Beef — 1976 / 1980

0   20%   40%   60%   80%   100%

Proportion of maximum production available in 1980

If divided evenly, the quantities of wool, wood, fish, oil and beef are diminishing for each one of us.
However, it is those in the South who suffer more from any decrease.

Fig. 7 Conference 'North-South'

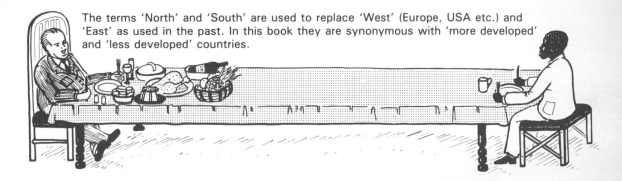

The terms 'North' and 'South' are used to replace 'West' (Europe, USA etc.) and 'East' as used in the past. In this book they are synonymous with 'more developed' and 'less developed' countries.

Fig. 8 Distribution of cereals

For every three bags of grain used in
the North, one is available for a
population of the same size in the South

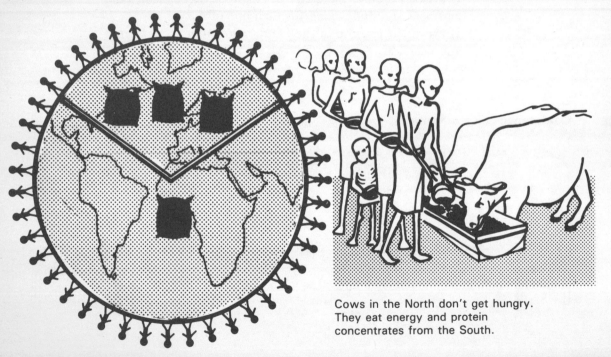

Cows in the North don't get hungry.
They eat energy and protein
concentrates from the South.

Three-quarters of the world's people are short of food, a quarter eat too much.

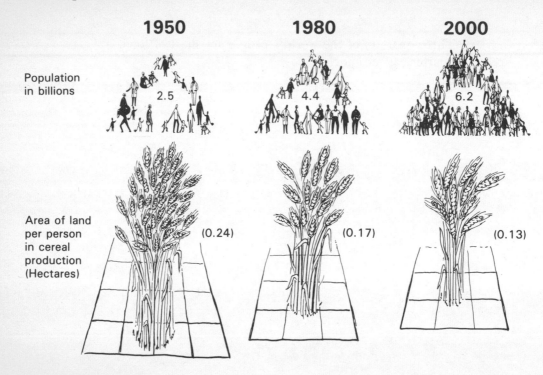

Fig. 9 **World population and land available for cereal production for each person in:**

1950   1980   2000

Population in billions

2.5   4.4   6.2

Area of land per person in cereal production (Hectares)

(0.24)   (0.17)   (0.13)

Each of us has one-third, soon we shall have one-sixth of a football pitch.

Fig. 10 Man creates deserts

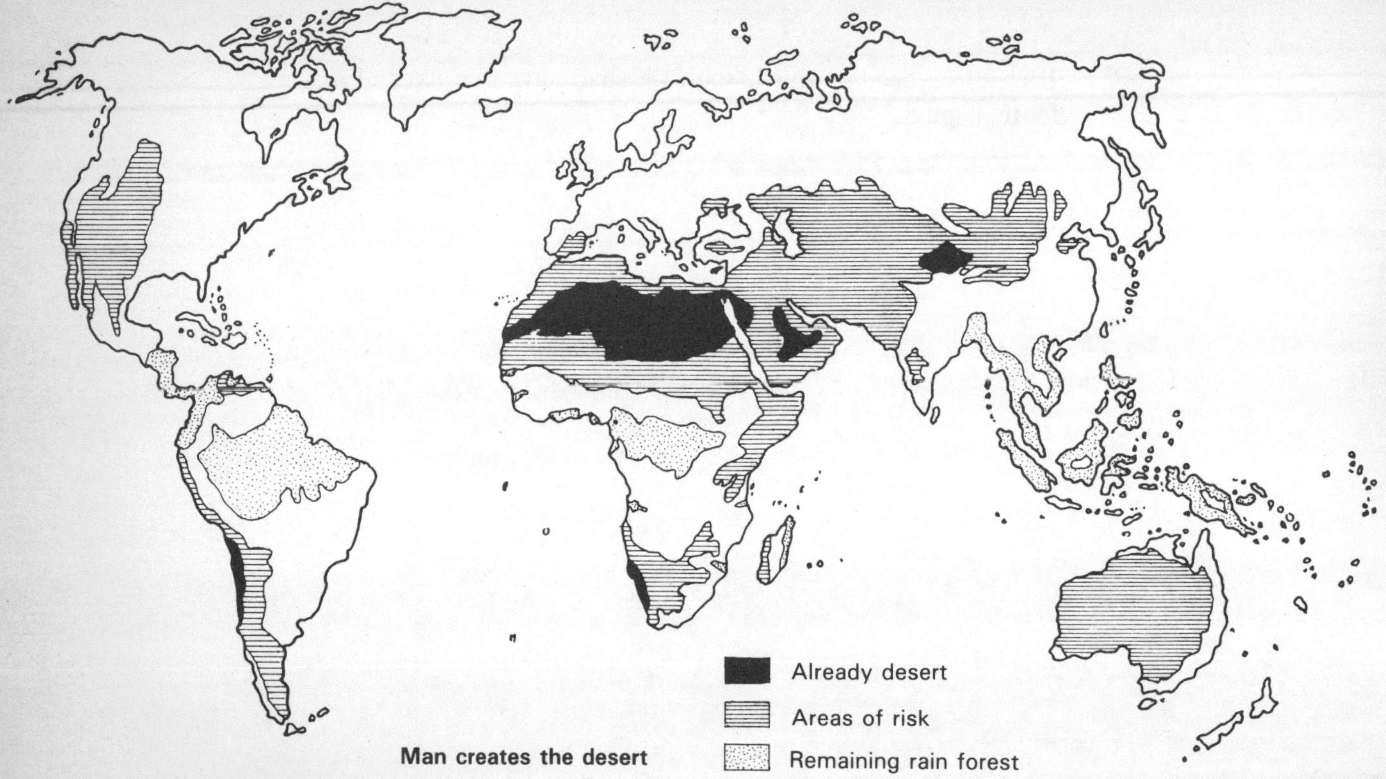

Man creates the desert

- ■ Already desert
- ▤ Areas of risk
- ▦ Remaining rain forest

Each year the 3 billion acres of world croplands lose
23 billion tons of top soil – 7% of the total is lost every
10 years. This turns good land into more deserts.

Fig. 11 Economic factors and health

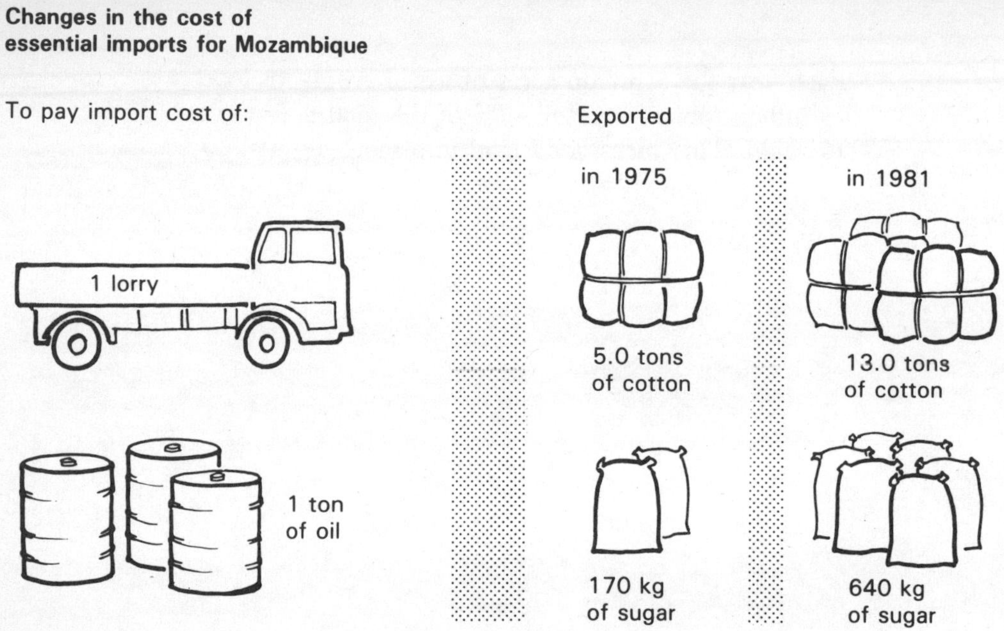

**Changes in the cost of
essential imports for Mozambique**

To pay import cost of:

1 lorry

1 ton
of oil

Exported

in 1975

5.0 tons
of cotton

170 kg
of sugar

in 1981

13.0 tons
of cotton

640 kg
of sugar

ECONOMIC FACTORS AND HEALTH

Increase in the cost of essential imports dramatically affects the health of a nation.

In Mozambique between 1975 and 1981:

- a lorry cost 2½ times more in cotton grown to pay for it.
- a ton of oil cost 3½ times more in sugar grown to pay for that.

How can countries develop or even maintain health services when the price of imports becomes so inflated?

Unfair practices between North and South – far removed from what is usually taught in a medical school – cannot be separated from the quest for better health.

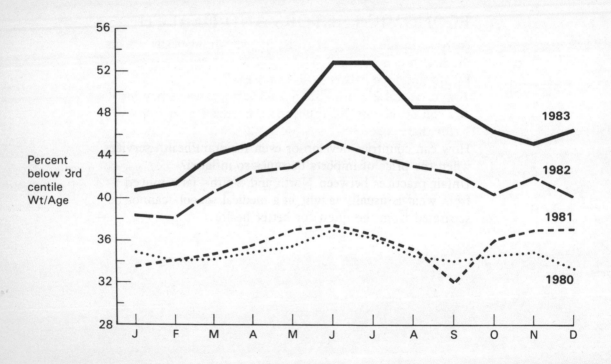

Fig. 12 Undernutrition in pre-school children (7 – 42 mths) on the increase (Ghana)

UNDERNUTRITION ON THE INCREASE

Between 1981 and 1983 the proportion of underweight
children in Ghana increased.
This may be a world-wide trend. How soon can it be
reversed?

'All the flowers of the future are in the seed'

David: The future of the human race is in its children but in decision-making they are voiceless and powerless.

Each year 12–18 million children under five die in our world. Between 95 and 98% of these deaths occur in less developed countries. Those who survive so often grow up under a blanket of undernutrition and disease. They are wanted and loved by their family but may lack food, clothing, shelter, a stimulating environment and adequate schooling.

In some countries more children will be born than can be fed by even improved agricultural production. But a lowering of birth rates, and all else the child will need, can only come through a more just distribution of resources.

Every living thing is struggling for a full life. For human beings too early death and the premature need for a coffin is a sign of failure in our civilisation.

Hermione: What is quite clear is that we all have to die, and while some of us believe in an after-life, death is final for our life here on earth.

With this diagram we emphasise the great differences that exist between those in the North and the majority of people in the South who live in the villages or shanty towns. All those who read and understand this book will be in the group who are likely to live beyond the age of 65. They will be able to complete a full working life, and are likely to die sometime in their retirement.

Not so for children born into the villages and shanty towns of less developed countries. Half of them will require coffins before the age of 15, and three-quarters of them will not reach a retirement age of 65.

David: If we are to seek an answer, in three words, to this difference, I would suggest *redistribution of resources*. This, in economic terms, is what this book is about. China and other countries with different political views have led the way and shown that, even if resources are limited, redistribution can improve the lot of the poor.

Hermione: Three-quarters of the world's population receive less than a quarter of the world's resources. In less developed countries the emphasis is correctly on education. There are

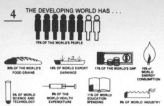

five times as many children in the South but only 11% of the world's educational expenditure is spent on them. Three-quarters of the world's population only receive 6% of the world's health expenditure. For every 100 dollars spent for each person on health care in Europe or North America, rather less than 2 dollars are spent in the less developed countries of our world.

David: Are the resources keeping up with population growth?

Hermione: No. I am afraid that if we look at a number of major resources, we find that, if there was equitable distribution, the quantities available for each one of us have reduced over the last few years. Production has increased and can increase more but the question is always whether the production will keep up with population growth. In Fig. 6 on page 6, seen here again in the margin, we see that by 1980 per capita production of wool, wood, fish, oil and beef was reduced in comparison with peak years of production in the 60s and 70s. Those in the North have hardly noticed this change. Clearly, if there is a shortage it is not those in the North but the poor in the South who go short.

David, as a paediatrician, which do you think is the most serious resource shortage for children?

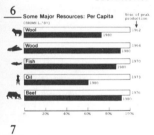

David: I would emphasise the shortage of wood. Two-thirds of our world's population cook on wood or charcoal, and for many it is becoming as expensive in money or time to put the fuel under the pot as to put the food into the pot. The result is that families tend to cook less frequently; because small children need three to four meals a day, it is they who suffer most. The decline in wood per capita is associated with a deforestation which is reducing firewood and lumber supplies. As well as driving up the cost of cooking fuel in the third world villages, the cost of housing everywhere is also increasing.

In this diagram we mention two foods, fish and beef, but for most people in the world these are not important in their diet. They live largely on cereals. What is happening about these?

8

One person in the north consumes enough grain for three people in the south

Cows in the north don't go hungry

Hermione: You are right. Food is the most essential of all resources, and among the foods, cereals are most important. Today, we in the North eat three bags of grain for each bag eaten by a similar size population in the South. You may well say that the plains of Canada, Russia and the USA produce much of the grain in our world. This is true, but unfortunately we feed much of this to chickens, pigs and cattle, so that we can have our steaks, hamburgers and fried chicken. If just 20% of the cereal fed to animals was made available for human consumption, that would make up for any deficit of grain in our world.

9

WORLD POPULATION AND LAND AVAILABLE FOR CEREAL PRODUCTION for each person in:

1950   1980   2000

POPULATION IN BILLIONS   2·5   4·4   6·2

AREA OF LAND PER PERSON IN CEREAL PRODUCTION (Hectares)   (0.24)   (0.17)   (0.13)

David: Fortunately, there is no reason to believe that the population will outgrow the ability to provide food on a world basis. The amount of cereal that can be grown on each hectare can be increased in most countries several times. However, there is the danger of intensive use of the soil, and particularly of soil erosion. Between 1938 and 1970 there was a six-fold increase in cattle in Niger. The Sahel historically has periods of low rainfall so the present problems are not unusual but are made more serious by an explosion in the cattle population and overgrazing. As a result the Sahara is growing by 1.5 million hectares a year.

FAO estimates that 11 million hectares of tropical forest are disappearing every year. The rate at which soil erosion is occurring is very serious. Another commodity which will be in short supply is water; between now and the end of the century the demand for water will increase 300%, mostly in countries where water is already in short supply. Also at the present time, intensive farming depends on the use of fossil fuels, and for each calorie of food many calories of fossil fuel have to be used up. The decrease in land available to each one of us and our increased use of fertilisers is shown in Fig. 13.

There is also a political imbalance. In 1982 the USA controlled 55% of world grain

10

MAN CREATES THE DESERT

■ Already desert
■ Areas of risk
□ Remaining rainforest

Fig. 13   World fertiliser use and grain area per person, 1950-83

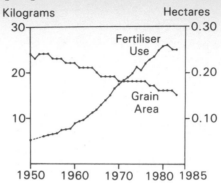

exports. By comparison Saudi Arabia controlled only 32% of world oil exports. Present changes in the North have had appalling effects on the ability of the South to pay for imports. In the North there is the phenomenon of 'jobless growth' while a third or a half of populations in the South are under-employed. Gandhi's principle of 'production by the masses' cannot compete with mass production. The integration of agriculture with local manufacture has been successful in parts of China. However, this requires a strong political commitment to overcome the vested interests that support current rural inequalities. Few dare to ask the question 'is undernutrition on the increase?'

12   *Hermione:*

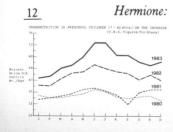

I have worked in Ghana and know very well how much the people have suffered there. These figures from all over Ghana show that in the early 80s there has been a down-ward trend in nutrition with an increase in malnutrition. In India between 1957 and 1978 there was no improvement in the heights and weights of children; these were slightly worse in 1978. Gopalan, a leading Indian nutritionist, is one of the relatively few in developing countries who are willing to state that this undernutrition affects both the physical and mental development of children. We also have records of children becoming lighter in Malawi over twenty years.

Fig. 14 More children in less developed countries

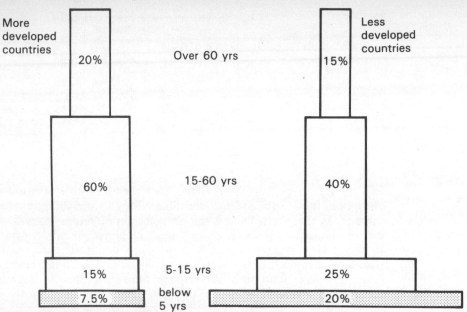

More developed countries

20% — Over 60 yrs

60% — 15-60 yrs

15% — 5-15 yrs

7.5% — below 5 yrs

Less developed countries

15%

40%

25%

20%

Simplified population pyramids with approximate figures

Children make up
- less than a quarter of the population in more developed countries.
- a half in less developed countries.

Fig. 15 Dependence on wage earners

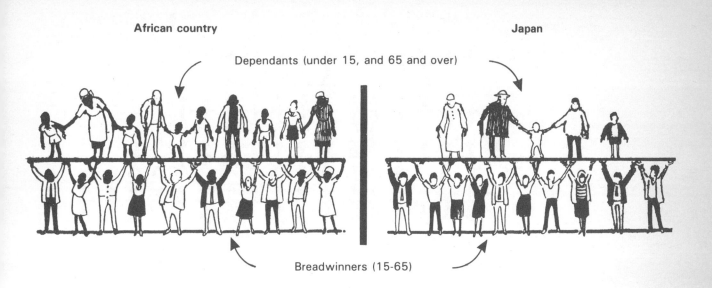

African country

Japan

Dependants (under 15, and 65 and over)

Breadwinners (15-65)

Ten workers support:
- in Africa ten others
- in Japan five others

who are too young or too old to work.

Fig. 16 The number of children in our world is increasing

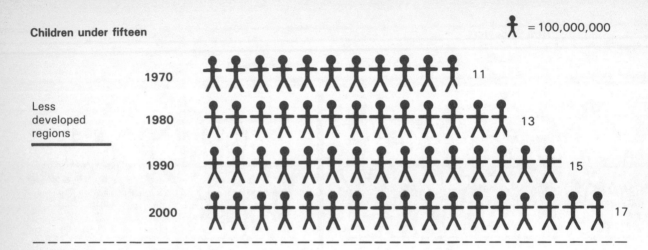

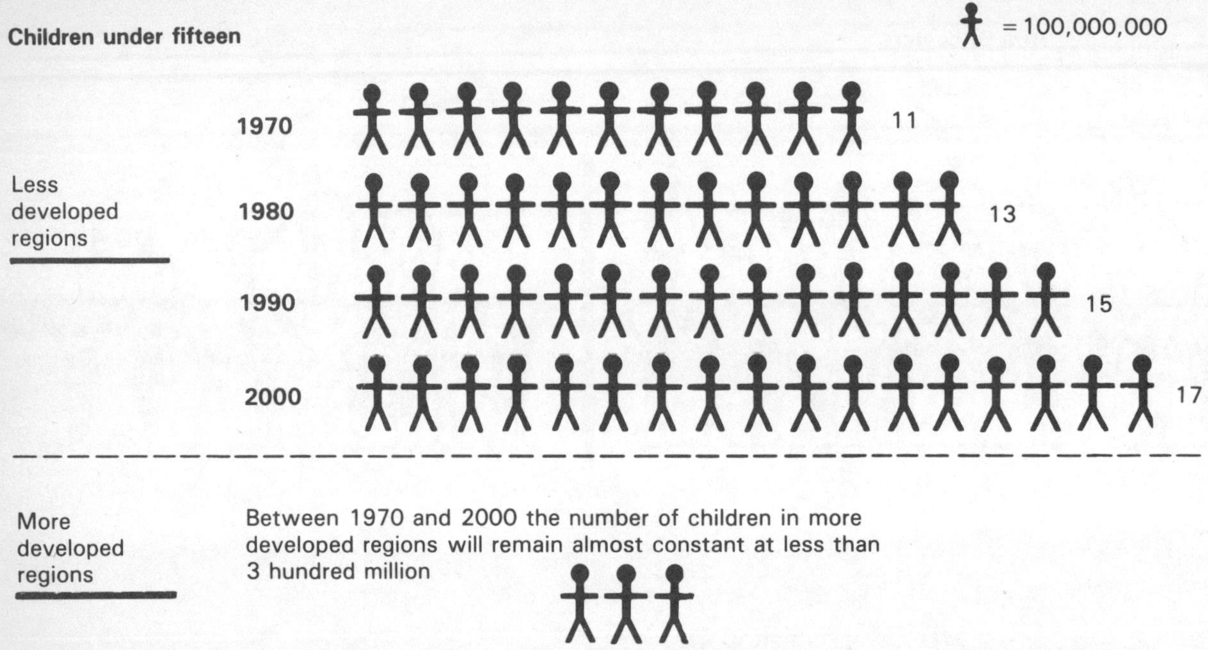

Children under fifteen   � = 100,000,000

Less developed regions

1970	11
1980	13
1990	15
2000	17

More developed regions

Between 1970 and 2000 the number of children in more developed regions will remain almost constant at less than 3 hundred million

THE NUMBER OF CHILDREN IN OUR WORLD IS INCREASING

At 280 million, the number of children in the more developed regions is now constant.

Another 200 million children are added each decade to the total in the less developed regions.

Fig. 17 Our responsibility over the next twenty years

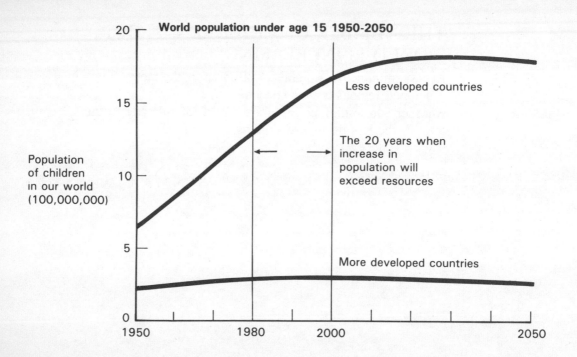

World population under age 15 1950-2050

Population
of children
in our world
(100,000,000)

Less developed countries

The 20 years when
increase in
population will
exceed resources

More developed countries

OUR RESPONSIBILITY – THE NEXT TWENTY YEARS

A rapid increase in the number of children coincides with declining resources.

Fig. 18 The shanty towns will be home to even more children

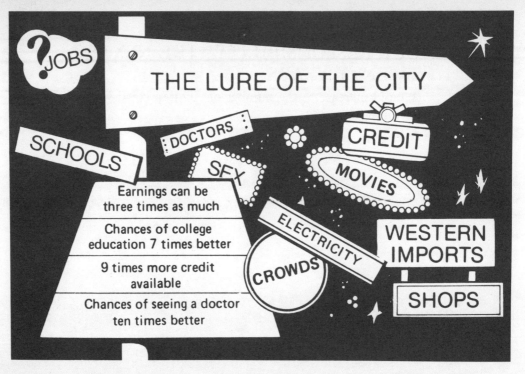

Not only will there be more children but more of them will
be growing up in the shanty towns of the cities of our world.

Fig. 19 The move to the cities

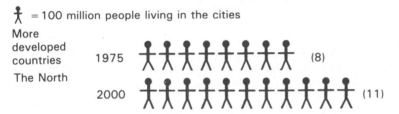

= 100 million people living in the cities

More developed countries

The North

1975 (8)

2000 (11)

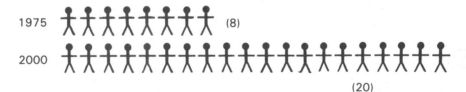

Less developed countries

The South

1975 (8)

2000 (20)

During the last quarter of this century:
- in the North the increase in population in the cities will be from 8 to 11 hundred million.
- in the South from 8 to 20 hundred million.

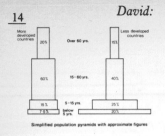

14

Simplified population pyramids with approximate figures

David: These simplified population pyramids demonstrate the great difference in population structure between more developed and less developed countries. The less developed countries have twice as many children as the more developed. Due to mortality in childhood, the number of children below five years old is particularly great, almost three times the number in the more developed countries.

Do you think that children are a resource, an asset, to these countries?

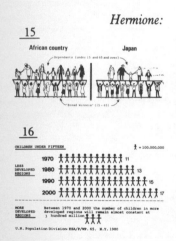

15

16

U.N. Population Division- ESA/P/WP. 65. N.Y. 1980

Hermione: It depends from what position you look. If you are a parent in a more developed country, you would expect children to stay at school at least until the age of fifteen, and they will be dependent and create considerable expense for their parents. However, if you are amongst the poor and under-privileged in most countries, you will look upon children as a financial asset. As we shall be showing, by their labour they may return all that their parents have invested in them by an early age. If, however, we consider that children under fifteen are not an important part of the workforce but should be at school, then we must look on them as dependants. The diagram shows the 'dependence' in an African country where each worker has to support at least one dependant, whereas in Japan there is only one dependant to every two workers. In many countries of the North there are many old people, but their mixed economy is better able to support their dependent population. In the North the number of children is now stable at under 300 million. In the South the number of children is already more than four times as great and is increasing by 200 million each decade.

David: Those who care for children between now and early next century carry a great responsibility. The sort of world our children and grandchildren live in next century will depend on what can be done at a time when the number of children in our world is still rapidly increasing.

Hermione: So many more children and yet declining resources will call for *organisation and managerial* skills to try to ensure that what is available is shared out and used to the best purpose.

David: In the UK we experienced the move to the city over a hundred years ago. What has led the less developed countries to follow this pattern and why can we expect such a flood to the cities during the rest of this century?

Hermione: I think Fig. 18 on page 28, seen here again in the margin, puts the tremendous advantages to those who move into the cities, particularly in their material way of life. One reason this situation has arisen is that the cities contain the powerful political élite of the country. They persuade Government to spend resources in the cities rather than rural areas. Money is spent where there are higher concentrations of people who benefit from a water supply, education and many other resources. When the population is scattered, as in a rural community, these services are usually more expensive to provide.

18

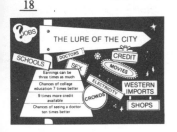

David: The prosperity of cities such as Cairo, Bombay or Jakarta depends on cheap labour drawn from the rural poor. 'Rural poverty' is exported to become 'urban poverty'. How do you think this move to the cities will affect the life of the children?

Hermione: In almost all countries, children living in the towns have a lower mortality rate. *This is largely related to better education of the mother and socio-economic advantages.* One important advantage for children is a steady supply of food. Apparently sewage disposal, water supply and health facilities cannot be shown to play much part. The expensive urban infrastructures do not cause a large reduction in child mortality. Children living in an urban area frequently have a more stimulating environment than those in rural areas. However, there are special problems for children. For example, with the violence and traffic of many cities, parents will lock up their children in the room when they both leave to go out to work. This can have a disastrous effect on the children.

A new situation has developed in South America where there is said to be something of the order of 50 million 'street children'. These are children who are out of touch with their families and are living rough on the streets, gaining a living by street selling or through petty crime. This is a new phenomenon that we have hardly considered. It is spreading to other countries in the world and is a sign of the break-up of families.

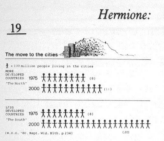

19

The move to the cities

⚱ = 100 million people living in the cities

MORE
DEVELOPED
COUNTRIES   1975 ⚱⚱⚱⚱⚱⚱⚱⚱ (8)
'The North'
             2000 ⚱⚱⚱⚱⚱⚱⚱⚱⚱⚱⚱ (11)

LESS
DEVELOPED
COUNTRIES   1975 ⚱⚱⚱⚱⚱⚱⚱⚱ (8)
'The South'
             2000 ⚱⚱⚱⚱⚱⚱⚱⚱⚱⚱⚱⚱⚱⚱⚱⚱⚱⚱⚱⚱ (20)

(W.H.O. '80. Rept. Wld. Hlth. p.234)

David: Is it only the material advantages which have produced this flow of people to the cities?

Hermione: As well as the material advantages of the cities, there is pressure from rural areas arising from population increase and inequitable distribution of land. This inequitable distribution of land is particularly serious in many of the countries of Latin America, the Philippines and now Nigeria where international 'agri' business forces small farmers off the land. This leads to a positive pressure forcing people, particularly the landless, into the cities. The wealth of cities has been gained from the rural areas. The urban élite purchase material goods, channelling the wealth to the North where those goods are made.

Fig. 20 Why the poor need children

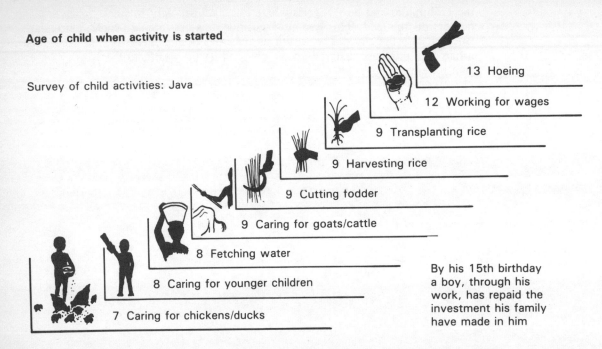

Age of child when activity is started

Survey of child activities: Java

13 Hoeing

12 Working for wages

9 Transplanting rice

9 Harvesting rice

9 Cutting fodder

9 Caring for goats/cattle

8 Fetching water

8 Caring for younger children

7 Caring for chickens/ducks

By his 15th birthday a boy, through his work, has repaid the investment his family have made in him

Why the poor need children. In the UK, a child costs his parents $100,000 by his fifteenth birthday.

Fig. 21 Parents need children

Proportion of parents desiring children for economic support

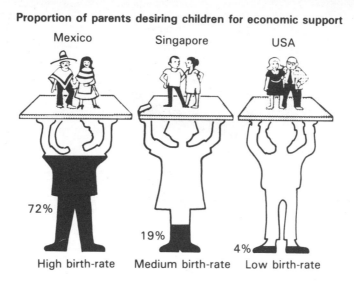

In poor countries parents see children as an economic support, particularly for their old age.

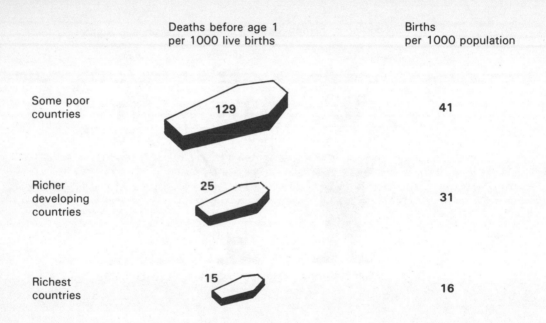

Fig. 22 Which comes first: fewer births or fewer deaths?

	Deaths before age 1 per 1000 live births	Births per 1000 population
Some poor countries	129	41
Richer developing countries	25	31
Richest countries	15	16

In those countries which have succeeded in reducing the number of deaths in children, there is a decline in the birth-rate within one generation. Once parents have confidence that their children will survive, the need to have many children declines. In the past, it took one or two generations for the birth-rate to fall in a country after the fall of the child death-rate. Now it takes less than a generation. A fall in child deaths has always come before a fall in birth-rates.

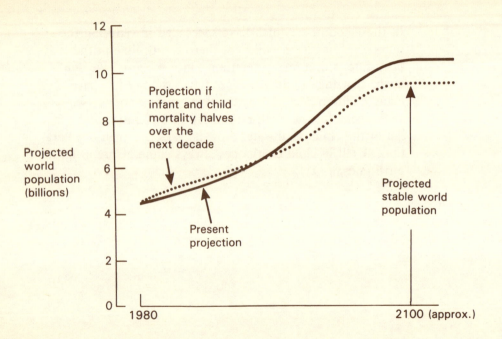

Fig. 23 Impact on population growth of a reduction in child deaths

Projected world population (billions)

Projection if infant and child mortality halves over the next decade

Present projection

Projected stable world population

1980

2100 (approx.)

IF MORE CHILDREN SURVIVE NOW, THE WORLD POPULATION WILL BE LESS

Halving the mortality of infants and small children will lead to an *immediate increase* in population but in the long term a *significant reduction*.

Fig. 24 Three children: enough?

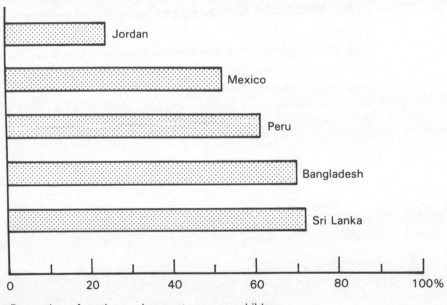

Desired family size among mothers with 3 children:
the response given by mothers who already have 3 living children.

Jordan

Mexico

Peru

Bangladesh

Sri Lanka

0   20   40   60   80   100%

Proportion of mothers who want no more children

Studies show that in some countries where large families
were previously desired, two-thirds of the parents now
want three children.
Do they have the knowledge and family-planning facilities
to achieve this?

Hermione: When you were working in Imesi-Ile, West Africa, were the children a financial asset to the family?

David: Yes, very much so. I well remember small girls that we were observing in our study of children growing up who were out selling cola nuts in the market before their fifth birthday. For these families and many others, children are a great asset. This is one reason why the population pyramid is so different for such areas. Another is the memory of the high child death-rate. However, elders in the village of Imesi-Ile soon appreciated that their farms could not absorb all these children; they hoped they would find work in the cities.

A study undertaken by an economist in Java brought this out well as he showed how children of different ages can contribute to the family. By the age of fifteen a boy through his labour had refunded to his family all the investment that they had made in him. Across the world it is true to say that for the poor family, the obvious way in which they can possibly increase their capital resources is through children and the labour that these children undertake.

In West Africa I remember that once a child could walk it would like to mimic its mother carrying a bowl of water on its head back from the stream or well.

Hermione: I saw some figures recently which suggest that a first child in Britain will cost the parents $100,000 up to the age of 16; this high figure is due in part to the mother losing income through not working while her child is small. You do not have many years now before you will retire. Do you expect your children to look after you?

20

Age of child when activity is started

SURVEY OF CHILD ACTIVITIES : JAVA

13 HOEING
12 WORKING FOR WAGES
9 TRANSPLANTING RICE
9 HARVESTING RICE
9 CUTTING FODDER
9 CARING FOR GOATS / CATTLE
8 FETCHING WATER
8 CARING FOR YOUNGER CHILDREN
7 CARING FOR CHICKENS / DUCKS

By his 15th birthday a boy, through his work has repaid the investment his family have made in him.

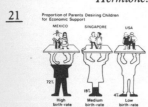

21

Proportion of Parents Desiring Children for Economic Support

MEXICO   SINGAPORE   USA

72%   18%   4%
High   Medium   Low
birth-rate   birth-rate   birth-rate

Source: East-West Population Institute

David: I shall officially retire within the next five years. Not that I intend to stop working then: I hope I shall find plenty to do. Fortunately I will have a good pension, and I do not see my children having a responsibility to look after me. However, I have a number of friends who have retired at the age of 65, and are now looking after their parents who are in their nineties. We are fortunate. Most people in our world do look to their children to give them economic support in their old age.

Do you think it is true to say that in all countries where the death-rate has come down there has also been a fall in birth-rate?

Hermione: Yes. I think this is true of all countries. The only difference seems to be that in some countries the birth-rate took longer to fall than in others. An example is Malta. This is a Roman Catholic country and effective family-planning methods are officially discouraged. However, there was a rapid fall in family size about thirty years after the child mortality had fallen. In Europe we took the best part of eighty years to achieve a zero population growth.

Recent figures from demographers suggest that if the mortality among children could be halved over the next decade then there would be a significant reduction in the size of the final population in our world. As we shall see, China may achieve the same in twenty years.

David, you came from a large family, didn't you?

22

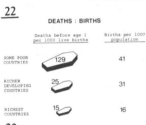

DEATHS : BIRTHS

	Deaths before age 1 per 1000 live births	Births per 1000 population
SOME POOR COUNTRIES	129	41
RICHER DEVELOPING COUNTRIES	25	31
RICHEST COUNTRIES	15	16

23

Impact on population growth of a reduction in child deaths

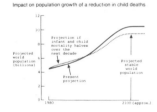

David: Yes, I am the youngest of seven and my mother was one of twelve. Large families like this were common in Europe early in this century, so different from most of Europe now where few families have more than three children, many have two, only one, or no children at all. Many women who were born before the last war tended to start their families late and four out of ten went on to have a third or fourth child, as did our Queen. Now we are not having enough children to replace the population; for this we would need to maintain an average family size of 2.1 children per family. Our average family size was at that level in 1971, but over the next twelve years it declined further and in 1983 it reached 1.76 children per family. Many would argue that in the UK we already have too large a population and so a family size below the replacement level may be a good step. How do you think parents come to a decision to have a smaller family?

Hermione: Whether or not a husband and wife will decide to plan the number and spacing of their children is closely related to their own sense of control over their own lives and circumstances. Malnutrition, illiteracy, ill-health and oppression can leave people with so little sense of control over their own lives and circumstances that they are alienated from the very idea of 'planning'. To expect adults who cannot control or plan any other major aspect of their lives to suddenly start planning just their families is not to understand what powerlessness means. If there is progress in health and education, a hope for political participation, a sense that decisions can be taken, then people can feel that circumstances may change, and their lives will improve. The idea of family spacing may well be welcomed as another opportunity to take more control over one's own life.

24

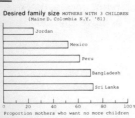

Desired family size MOTHERS WITH 3 CHILDREN
(Maine D. Colombia N.Y. '81)

Proportion mothers who want no more children

David: We are already seeing a change, illustrated by Sri Lanka and Bangladesh, where three-quarters of mothers with three young children do not want any more.

Fig. 25 Mother's schooling, child growth and mortality

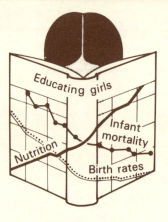

The education of girls is closely associated with a falling infant mortality and birth rate and improved nutrition.

'Train a man and you train an individual: train a woman and you build a nation.'
(Bishop Nzimbe, Machakos, Kenya, May 1985)

Fig. 26 Literacy in women and men, 1982

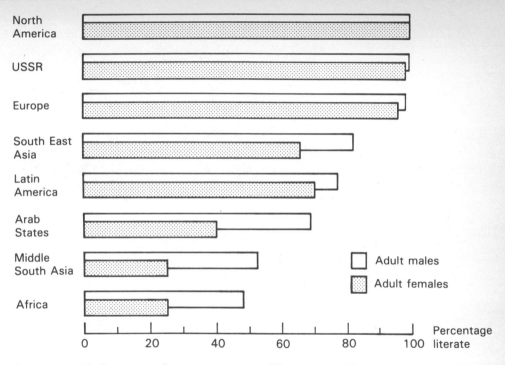

In our world four out of ten women are illiterate; and in some African and Arab countries eight out of ten. The health and well-being of the family is highly dependent on the literacy of the mother.

Fig. 27 Schools cannot keep pace with population growth

No room!

SCHOOL

THE TEACHER TRAINING COLLEGES

In the developing world one new teacher is needed every minute

The growth of populations adds school-age children faster than education services can grow.

Fig. 28 Children without schools (6-11 years of age)

1970: 113 million
They could encircle the
world **three** times

1985: 165 million
They could encircle the
world **four** times

Due to the growth in population, for every three children
who could not find places in schools in the 70s, there are
likely to be four or more without schooling in the 80s.
Building schools cannot keep pace with population growth.

Fig. 29

Do those of us who have the knowledge examine its relevance to those we try to help? We must be particularly sensitive to the difficulty of giving help to those who earn the food they eat from work undertaken on that day.

Fig. 30 The expert and the farmers

"Because you've done it successfully your way for generations, it doesn't mean it works."

David: Education of girls is, I know, something you are particularly interested in.

Hermione: Yes. Even 'free' education is expensive when parents are too poor to easily afford books, clothes, shoes and transport. Mothers want girls to help with household tasks and provide care for small children. Girls' school education is often not considered to be so necessary, and parents are sometimes unwilling to spend money on girls when they will spend it on boys. So the investment which could improve life tomorrow is withdrawn to help cope with life today.

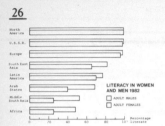

26

LITERACY IN WOMEN
AND MEN 1982
☐ ADULT MALES
☐ ADULT FEMALES

Despite low levels in the past, education for girls is a change which is well under way. The proportion of 6 to 11-year-old girls who are enrolled in school in the poorest half of the world, for example, has jumped from 34% to 80% since 1960. Each year 150 million people around the world learn to read. But only one in three of these new literates will become a regular reader. The rest will drop back into illiteracy or at best become virtually non-readers. Of the 825 million illiterates in the world, 801 million are in the less developed countries. In less developed countries, only one book becomes available each year for every two potential readers; in the more developed countries, we have ten for each reader. The same problem is mirrored within the health professions. Too many doctors, nurses and others fail to read and keep up with new developments and approaches. Health professionals have not been sufficiently motivated to undertake regular reading, nor do they have access to libraries or journals or low-cost books which would help them keep up with advances in health care. Even in the capital cities it is reported, for example, that the University of Nairobi was last able to order books five years ago, the University of Dar-es-Salaam seven years ago and Makerere thirteen years ago.

129

Health workers need and love books

but hate today's prices

David: Just how important is women's education in improving health?

Hermione: In total, over twenty-four separate studies in fifteen different nations have established that the level of the mother's education – even within the same economic class – is a key determinant of her children's health. In Pakistan and Indonesia, for example, the infant mortality rate among children whose mothers have had four years' schooling was found to be 50% lower than among the children of women who were illiterate. In eleven countries studied by the Latin American Demographic Centre (CELADE), the influence of the mother's education on the child's chances of survival was found to be stronger even than the level of household income. One particular study in Kenya has even gone so far as to say that 86% of the decline in infant mortality in that country over the last twenty years can be 'explained' by the rise in female education.

David: Recent studies have clearly established that the more educated the mother, the greater are the chances that her child will survive till five. A decrease in child mortality is more strongly and consistently related to the level of maternal education than any other easily measurable factor. Schooling seems to enhance a woman's ability to care for her children. Studies show that this is not just because she is better off. She is less fatalistic, more knowledgeable about health, hygiene and particularly nutrition. She is better equipped to make use of new ideas and institutions. Her status and power within the family are improved and she may be willing to abandon customs such as providing food for male adults at the expense of children.

Hermione: For almost all children, the most important primary health care worker is the mother. It is the mother's level of education and access to information which will decide whether or not she will go herself for a tetanus shot in pregnancy; whether a trained person will be present at the birth; whether she knows about the advantages of breast-feeding; whether her child will be weaned on appropriate foods at the right time; whether the best available foods will be cooked in the best possible way; whether water will be boiled and hands washed; whether bouts of diarrhoea will be treated by administering fluids and foods; whether a child will be weighed and vaccinated; and whether there will be an adequate interval between births. Too often these resources are not available, but female literacy increases both the demand for them and the chance of their being used when they become available. Achieving higher levels of literacy can be a particular problem in Moslem societies because of the status of women.

David: However, I am always surprised how perceptive illiterate or semi-literate people are if we will only listen to them. You will remember how a student of ours found the mothers had a good understanding of growth and expected beads around the waist to

THE EDUCATION OF GIRLS IS CLOSELY ASSOCIATED WITH A FALLING INFANT MORTALITY AND BIRTH RATE AND IMPROVED NUTRITION

25

be regularly increased. I can think of many similar findings which would illustrate the wisdom of illiterate people. There is a very useful booklet about this called *Whose Knowledge Counts?*

Hermione: There are studies which show patients' preference for care for different problems (Fig.31).

Fig. 31 Parents' preferences for sources of health care

The preference of parents in the Punjab for the source of advice and treatment for some childhood diseases

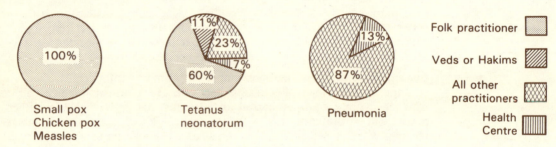

Small pox
Chicken pox
Measles

Tetanus
neonatorum

Pneumonia

Folk practitioner

Veds or Hakims

All other practitioners

Health Centre

These suggest that even a largely illiterate population makes a good choice and consults Western medicine only for conditions it can help. Mothers are the most important primary health care workers, and many of them are very good at it. Other health workers need to learn from them.

There has been a great increase in teacher training across the world, but the output of new teachers cannot keep pace with the demands of the new schools and an ever-increasing population. New teachers are required at the rate of one a minute. Whereas Austria has forty-three primary school teachers for every 1000 school-age children in the population, Zaire has twenty-nine and Bangladesh thirteen. The difference is even worse for secondary school teachers.

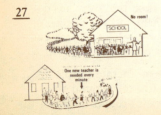

27

Fig. 32 Women, men and food production

Food
Almost all the training and technology for improving agriculture is given to men . . .

50 per cent of the agricultural production and all of the food processing is the responsibility of women.

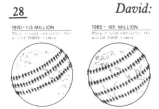

28

1970 - 113 MILLION
They could encircle the world THREE times

1985 - 165 MILLION
They could encircle the world FOUR times

David: The problem of children who will never reach school is dramatically demonstrated in the idea that if all the children who could not get to school in 1970 held hands, they would go round the world three times. By 1985, they would go round the world four times. I think this question of providing sufficient primary schooling highlights the many problems that exist as populations increase too fast to allow development to keep up.

Hermione: In the first part of this book, we are considering some of the problems of health-care systems and how they have gone wrong. Our colleagues in education in less developed countries perhaps have more serious problems than even we in health. Schools have reached almost every village in the world. If we examine the objectives of schools, we find that for the parent, the teacher and the child, the first objective of the school is to get the brighter pupils into secondary school. As a result these brighter students are likely to leave the village, and this is even more likely if they go on to higher education. Thus we see that the school system is a filter which encourages the majority of the brighter, hard working children with more drive to leave the village and rural circumstances of their family, and migrate to the city. As the economy of many less developed countries depends on their agriculture, this can be disastrous.

David: Unfortunately, the education too is frequently inappropriate. For example, education in agriculture has been influenced by farming in temperate zones and only recently have agriculturalists examined what is appropriate in a tropical climate for small farmers. The apparently disorganised muddle of mixed cropping on African farmers' fields scarcely appeared a place to learn anything. Yet many of what were once thought to be the irrational and wasteful practices of traditional African farming are now found to be prudent and sound. Mixed cropping has been shown to have many advantages including:

- different rooting systems exploit different levels in the soil profile for moisture and nutrients;
- one crop may provide a favourable micro-climate for another;
- nitrogen-fixing plants fertilise non-nitrogen fixing plants;
- crops which are scattered among others are less vulnerable to pest attack than single stands;
- labour requirements are less, especially in reducing weeds;
- labour peaks are spread out;
- more moisture is retained in the soil;
- returns are higher per unit of land;
- successive sowing of crop mixtures supplies a mixed diet over an extended harvesting period;
- risk of crop failure is less;
- where labour is scarce the returns on labour are increased at the time of the year when labour is limited.

29

Who is
ignorant ?

Few here have made such a case against the irrelevant education that we have exported to Africa as Dumont; he said: 'In Dakar we now have 920 Senegalese who have Masters degrees but no jobs. At the beginning you needed a primary school certificate for the right to sell bread. In the 50s you needed a junior high school education. Now you need a high school diploma. Perhaps some day you will need a Masters degree just to sell bread.'

Hermione: Another writer, Chambers, has shown why we fail to appreciate the problems of rural poverty. He has described six major biases which make it so difficult for us to get near enough to really comunicate with and understand the problems of the rural and urban poor. There is the bias of easy accessibility. We, the outsiders, tend to visit only known areas, along tarmac roads, and to talk and observe in villages near the roadside. There is project bias; we visit projects rather than non-project areas. There is person bias; we talk to the élite, the men, the users of new ideas rather than to people of low status, the women, the non-users, the drop-outs. Only rarely is enquiry made about those who have died. The fourth bias is the dry season. Most visits by outsiders to an area are done when weather conditions are easier for travel, rarely in the rainy period. The fifth bias is that of propriety and politeness shown by local people. The sixth is the professional bias which inevitably draws professionals to other professionals rather than those who are not professionals.

Some good ideas on practical ways of overcoming these biases are also described: one key factor is to start recognising that these biases exist. 'Rapid rural appraisal' is a simple, effective way of gathering pertinent information.

David: I agree that Chambers' book *Rural Development* is essential reading for those who are going to be involved in developing countries' real problems. Above all, we need to listen to ordinary people and learn how they have learnt to cope.

Hermione: The problems are obviously immense. If UNICEF, as we all hope, is successful in creating a child health revolution and halves the number of child deaths over the next decade, then the problems of schooling will temporarily be even greater as more of the children survive into the school-age group.

David: We have been critical of the inappropriateness of some education, yet we repeat once more that the education of girls – the mothers of the future – is the most important factor in reducing child mortality.

25

57

Fig. 33 Decline in deaths under age one in China

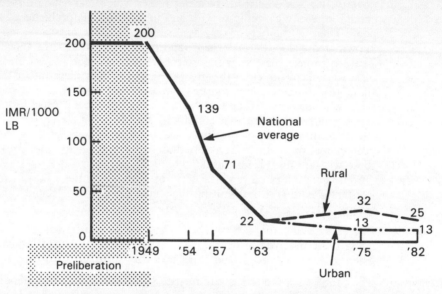

After 1949 with the end of the Japanese invasion and a strong central government, resources were redistributed in China. Within fifteen years mortality in children under one fell from around 200 per thousand to 20.

Fig. 34 China's population 1940-1982

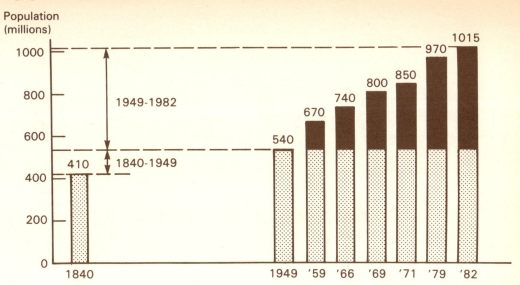

GROWTH OF POPULATION IN CHINA

The population in China grew more in the ten years after 1949 than in the previous 100 years. The majority of people in China are, or soon will be, in the fertile years of life. China, an overcrowded country, is threatened with a further great increase in its population.

Fig. 35 Why China's people have decided on the one child family

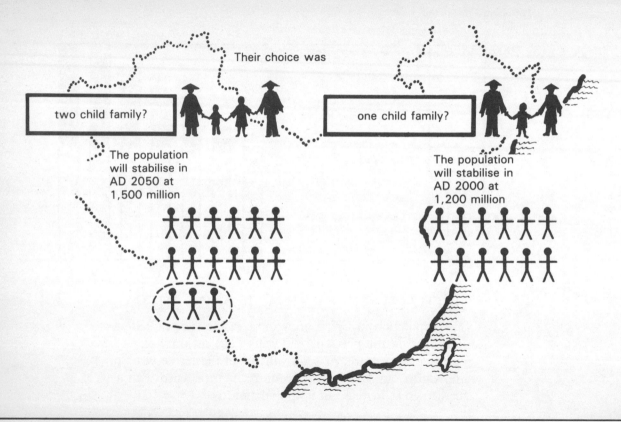

The sacrifice being made by Chinese parents for the future of their country.

Fig. 36 Our changing world: A problem for the future

Longer average life expectancy

Fewer babies
Birth rate
1950 – 36/1000
2050 – 18/1000

Average
age
of
death

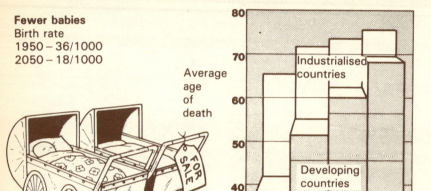

Industrialised
countries

Developing
countries

1950 1975 2000 2025

More old people
By age 80
in industrialised
countries, the
Women to Men
Ratio is 2 : 1

When one problem is solved, another will appear.

Hermione: You have visited China. What did you find there?

David: China contains rather more than one fifth of the people on our planet. What they have achieved since 1949 should be an example to other countries. They have shown how redistribution of resources, particularly agricultural land, can, within a few years, create a revolution in child survival. After the end of Japanese occupation and liberation in 1949, the infant mortality rate fell in only fifteen years to below 30 from around 200. Now a further fifteen years on, mortality rates in the cities are similar to those in the countries of Europe.

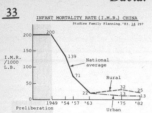

Hermione: This must have had a dramatic effect on population growth.

David: In the 50s the average family size was six to seven children. Within ten years, the population increased by as much as it had during the previous hundred years. During the Cultural Revolution, less was done to limit families. After this period the danger was appreciated and by the late 70s the average family size was down to 2.6 children.

Hermione: Did you find China a crowded country?

David: China is crowded. Peering down at the valleys of the Yangtze and Yellow Rivers from a jet, one can make out the dark pattern of the villages separated by limited areas of paddy fields. In this fertile area live the majority of the population. In China 80% of the population (90% of children) live in rural areas. The cities too are crowded. The streets are so full of pedestrians they spill off the pavement. The major means of mass transport is the bicycle. Beijing, with a population of 9 million, is reputed to have over 3 million bicycles. The articulated buses each hold well over 100 people in the rush hour. I was told that a possible hazard of travelling on Shanghai buses is a crush injury

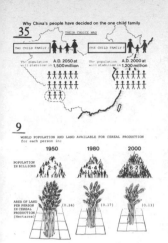

35 Why China's people have decided on the one child family

THEIR CHOICE WAS

TWO CHILD FAMILY — A.D. 2050 the population will stabilize in 1,500 million

ONE CHILD FAMILY — A.D. 2000 the population will stabilize in 1,200 million

9 WORLD POPULATION AND LAND AVAILABLE FOR CEREAL PRODUCTION for each person in:

1950 · 1980 · 2000

POPULATION IN BILLIONS — 2.5 · 4.4 · 6.2

AREA OF LAND PER PERSON IN CEREAL PRODUCTION (Hectares) — (0.24) · (0.17) · (0.13)

of the chest! Fortunately, there is no private transport in the form of cars, which would cause a city like Shanghai to grind to a halt. The 1981 census worried the leaders with the realisation that their population already exceeded a billion. They worked to create a climate of opinion which would accept the one-child family. This has required both education and incentives. In the rural areas, each production team (120 people) calculates what the land available can produce and how many mouths this can feed. China has only 0.1 hectares of arable land per head, less than the world average (see Fig.9 on page 10). Through intense discussion the people came to realise the limitations of land resources and the danger of further population growth. Many privileges are awarded to those couples who have pledged themselves to a one-child family, including a 10% increase in salary, a greater proportion of land to farm, guaranteed education for the child and a pension for the parents in their old age. All these and other benefits vary from commune to commune and they will be lost if the pledge is broken and a second child is born. Scrupulously careful records are to be found in each 'lane' or work brigade. A record is kept of each woman's menstruation and of the family planning method being used by all married women.

Hermione: What methods of family planning are used?

David: By 1983 70% of fertile couples were using some modern method. As shown in the figure the IUD is particularly popular.

Abortion has been used but attempts are being made to reduce it. In one county I visited, the abortion rate, which was similar to that in Britain, was considered a matter of anxiety. On investigation it was found to be due in many cases to the unrecognised loss of an intrauterine device in the first year after giving birth. During this first year post partum, an additional method of family planning is now recommended in the county, and the number of abortions has since declined.

Hermione: This chapter has looked at some of the problems that are facing particularly the children of the less developed world. These problems are crying out for an urgent solution and are a great challenge to us. However, we must not think that when these have been overcome, there will not be others, and one of these is going to be the large

Fig. 37 Contraceptive methods used in China

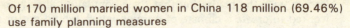

Of 170 million married women in China 118 million (69.46%) use family planning measures

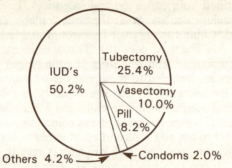

IUD's 50.2%

Tubectomy 25.4%

Vasectomy 10.0%

Pill 8.2%

Others 4.2%

Condoms 2.0%

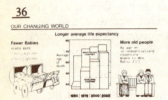

36

OUR CHANGING WORLD

number of old people, particularly women in industrialised societies; I wonder what sort of life it will be for old people in twenty-five years hence when I am due to retire.

David: There are likely to be other serious problems. Even as we are completing this book the full impact which the new infection AIDS may have in less developed countries is becoming apparent.

CHAPTER TWO
Childhood illness in the less developed countries of the world

Fig. 38 Who gets sick?

Questions to ask when resources are limited.

Fig. 39 Causes of death in less and more developed countries

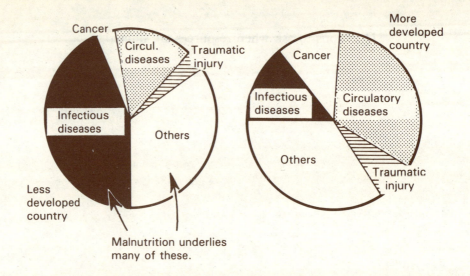

In less developed countries, infection and malnutrition in childhood are the common causes of death.
In the more developed world, cancer and circulatory disease are the common causes of death but are mostly in old people.

Fig. 40 Too much illness early in life

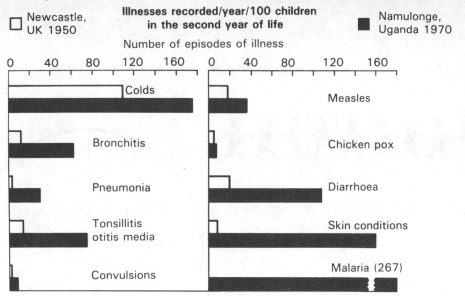

In less developed countries, illness is concentrated in the early years of life.

In this diagram, the Ugandan child in the second year of life has five to ten times as many illnesses, both of a greater variety and more dangerous, compared with the child in England.

Fig. 41 World frequency of chronic disability

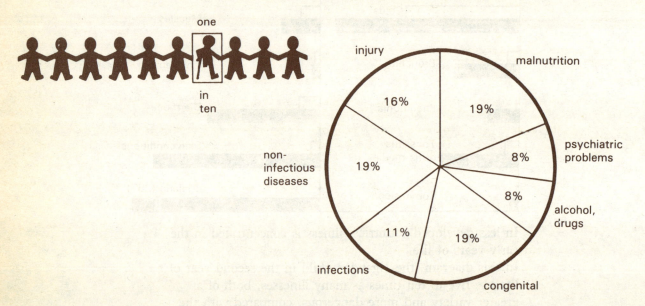

Proportion (%) of total of 514 millions disabled

one

in
ten

injury

malnutrition

16%   19%

non-
infectious
diseases

19%   8%   psychiatric
problems

8%   alcohol,
drugs

11%   19%

infections   congenital

FREQUENCY OF DISABILITY

Frequent and severe illness leads to much chronic disability as well as a high mortality. Much of this follows illness in childhood and is preventable.

David:

I know, Hermione, that you particularly like the first illustration in this chapter. It comes from David Werner's book *Where There is no Doctor*, which to me has been the most important book to have come out in the last twenty years. This book has done so much to de-mystify medicine and help people realise that they can so often cope with disease themselves.

Hermione:

You and I, David, are amongst the minority – we are the 'outsiders'. We are relatively well off, literate, and urban-based. We carry no parasites, expect long life and eat more than we need. We, like the reader of this book, can read books and buy newspapers. There are people like us living in every country of the world, belonging to all nationalities and holding jobs in every profession and discipline. We are a class.

Why do so few of us do so little about this? A few have chosen to reject the privileges of this class and respond to the conviction that we must get nearer to the starving child suffering from measles. We can only hope that this drawing and many others in this book will help more people to try to answer these questions and will take you the reader a little closer to the problems that face so many in our world.

The drawing actually refers to both this and the next chapter. In this chapter we are looking at 'who' gets sick, 'with what', 'where', 'when' and 'why'. In the next chapter we will be looking at existing health services in developing countries. Perhaps we could refer back to Fig.3 on page 3 of the two coffins. Too few people in our world realise the differences between mortality in the North and South. In the North and amongst the élite in the South, well over three-quarters of all deaths occur after the age of 65. Amongst the vast majority of people in the South, and if it were not for China we could say the vast majority of people in our world, three-quarters of deaths occur before the age of 65, as they did 150 years ago in Europe. In this chapter we will be looking at some of the reasons for this difference in mortality.

WHEN DEATH OCCURS?

DEATHS BY AGE GROUP AS % OF ALL DEATHS (Taylor '82)

CAUSES OF DEATH IN DEVELOPING AND INDUSTRIALISED COUNTRIES (Taylor '82)

David: I would like to start off by emphasising that half of the population who die in childhood do not die from exotic causes, requiring sophisticated cures: 5 million die from dehydration caused by diarrhoea; more than 3 million die from pneumonia; 2 million die from measles; 1½ million die from whooping cough; another million die from tetanus. And for every child who dies, many more live on in hunger and ill health.

Hermione: This book paints the background to the large number of easily preventable deaths in children. 'Any Government which now decides to make a serious commitment to saving the lives and protecting the health and growth of its children can now move towards that goal. And any Government, institution or individual in the industrialized world wishing to assist in that process also now has a clear opportunity to do so.' (*State of the World's Children* '84. p. 3.)

David: In the less developed countries, infectious diseases cause almost half of the deaths; in the more developed countries they cause about one eighth of the deaths. The difference is more striking if we examine the different age-groups in which infections cause death. In the more developed countries, most deaths from infectious diseases are in old people after retirement and rarely in children, as in the less developed countries. The other striking change is the greater proportion of deaths from circulatory disease and cancer in the more developed countries. This is because of the greater age of the population and because both of these types of condition may be brought on by the way of life in the North.

Hermione: The high incidence of infections in the second year of life in Namalonge, Uganda, is striking in comparison with that in Newcastle.

David:

Yes. These are perhaps not the best two places to compare, but they are the only figures I know where the incidence of disease was carefully recorded by the same group of doctors using the same criteria in categorising diseases. Why there is so much more respiratory disease in Uganda is difficult to know. Newcastle was a smoky town in 1950 and Namalonge had good clean air, except within the huts. Perhaps nutrition plays some part, also the children in Uganda may live closer together and receive a larger infecting dose. However, I think there may well be some immunological factors we do not yet appreciate. One interesting possibility is that substances such as aflotoxin which are present in large quantities in many foods in less developed countries may depress cellular immunity as well as growth. The difference in the diarrhoea is more easy to explain, with the lack of water for washing which we now realise is so important in reducing its incidence. The skin conditions can also be relatively easily explained by the large number of insect bites the children receive, which lead to scratching. Without water to wash there is much cross-infection, with many infected spots and sores, particularly on the legs.

I am afraid doctors put emphasis on preventing death from these acute conditions and overlook the disabilities, many of which may persist for long periods, even a lifetime.

Hermione:

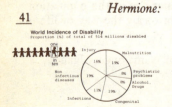

Yes. These figures from WHO suggesting that one in ten of the people in less developed countries have some disability are striking. These are the findings of those from outside the community. Certainly most of these would not consider themselves disabled. Those who are malnourished and many of those with psychiatric problems will not accept that they have a disability. This is clearly an immense problem which is still left almost entirely to the family and community to cope with. Disabilities are not only a problem for the individual but also for the family. Before long we must expect to train those in the community who can give the family support and guidance. They will help the family to rehabilitate the individual with a disability. With their assistance the previously disabled will become effective members of the family and society. We at the Tropical Child Health Unit certainly look on this as a priority.

Fig. 42 Life after birth

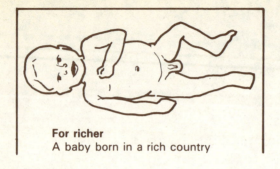

For richer
A baby born in a rich country

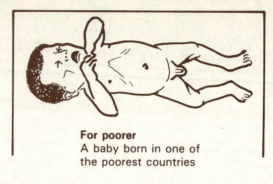

For poorer
A baby born in one of
the poorest countries

Chances of dying before age one	1 in 100	1 in 5
Life expectancy	70 years	50 years
Chance of seeing a health worker	all	1 in 10
Probable years at school	11 years	2 years

WHAT CAN THEY HOPE FOR AFTER BIRTH?

Children born in rich and poor countries have very different prospects.

Fig. 43 Wages and infant deaths

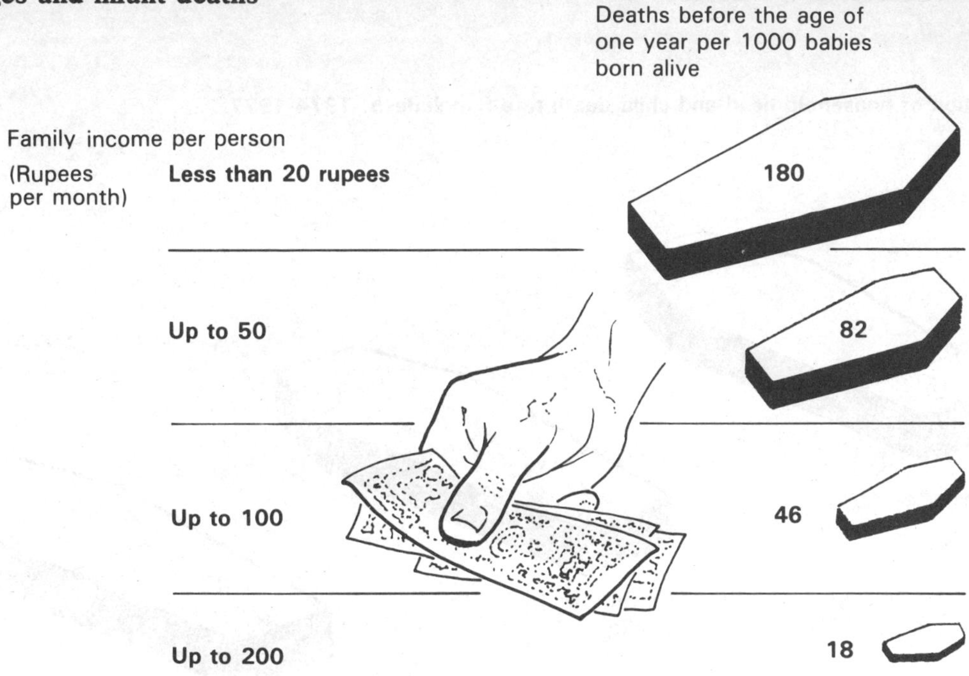

Deaths before the age of
one year per 1000 babies
born alive

Family income per person

(Rupees
per month)

Less than 20 rupees

180

Up to 50

82

Up to 100

46

Up to 200

18

High mortality is related to extreme poverty. The number
in extreme poverty will increase as the shanty towns in our
world steadily increase.

Fig. 44 More children of the landless die

Occupation of household head and child death rate Bangladesh, 1974-1977

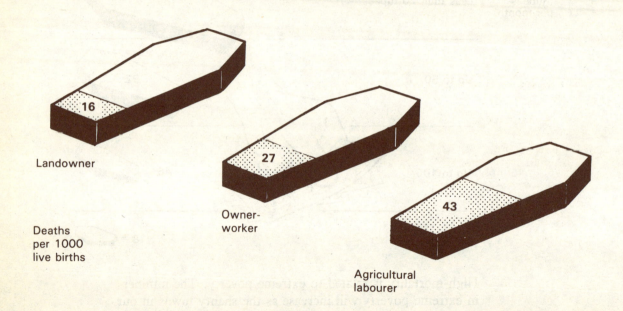

16
Landowner

27
Owner-
worker

43
Agricultural
labourer

Deaths
per 1000
live births

Redistribution of land is the best way to:
- increase food production
- reduce poverty
- lower mortality.

Fig. 45 The mother's working day

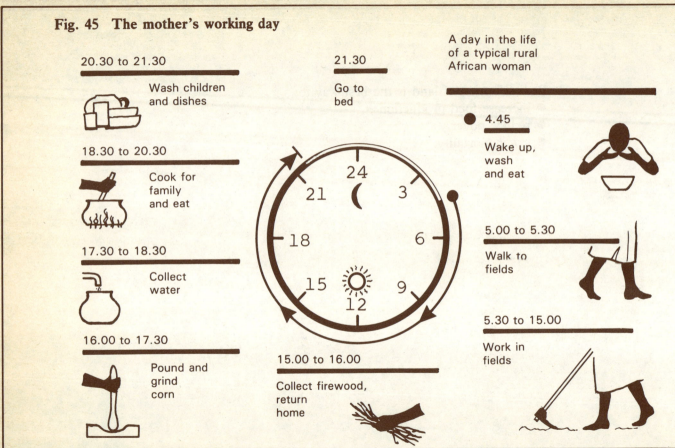

20.30 to 21.30

Wash children and dishes

18.30 to 20.30

Cook for family and eat

17.30 to 18.30

Collect water

16.00 to 17.30

Pound and grind corn

15.00 to 16.00

Collect firewood, return home

21.30

Go to bed

A day in the life of a typical rural African woman

4.45

Wake up, wash and eat

5.00 to 5.30

Walk to fields

5.30 to 15.00

Work in fields

Among the rural poor the mother is working from early morning until after dark. She has little time that she can make available for better child care.

Fig. 46   The cycle of undernutrition

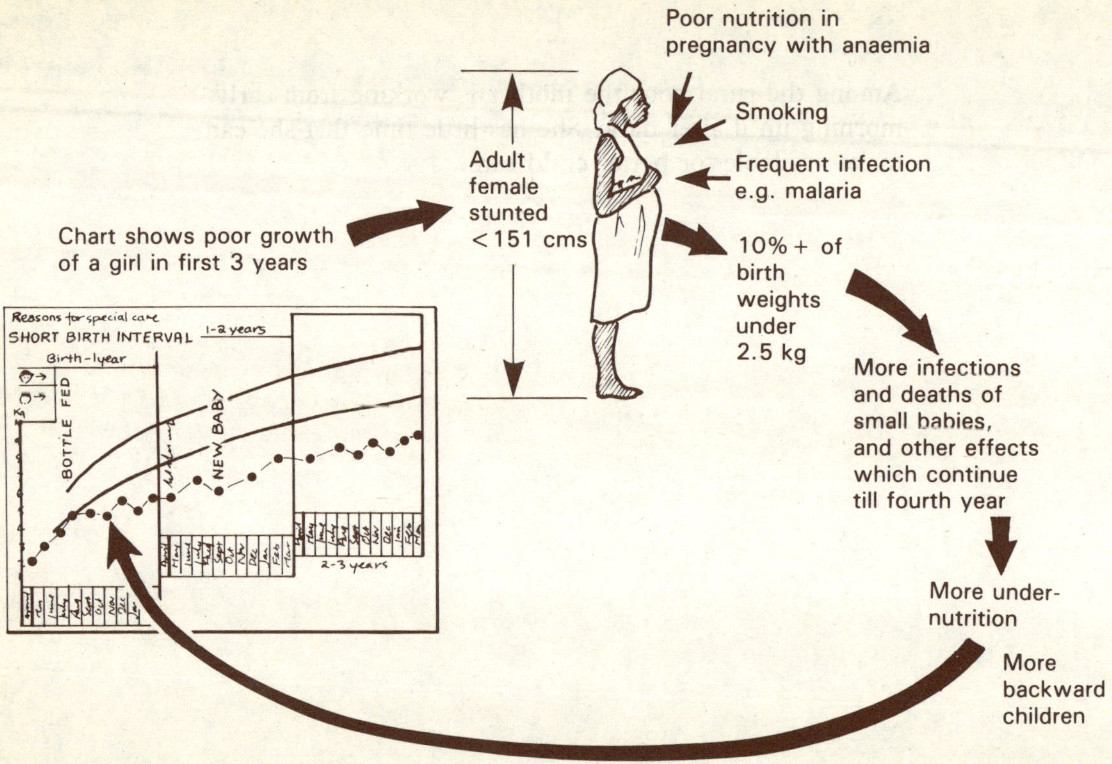

Poor nutrition in pregnancy with anaemia

Smoking

Frequent infection e.g. malaria

Adult female stunted <151 cms

Chart shows poor growth of a girl in first 3 years

10% + of birth weights under 2.5 kg

More infections and deaths of small babies, and other effects which continue till fourth year

More under-nutrition

More backward children

Reasons for special care
SHORT BIRTH INTERVAL

Birth - 1 year   1-2 years

BOTTLE FED

NEW BABY

2-3 years

THE CYCLE OF UNDERNUTRITION

The weight chart shows that the child grew poorly.
A stunted child becomes a small mother.
A small mother gives birth to a small baby.
Small babies grow less well.
Girls who grow less well become small mothers.
We have to identify the places where we can break this cycle.

Fig. 47 Female life expectancy and total fertility rates

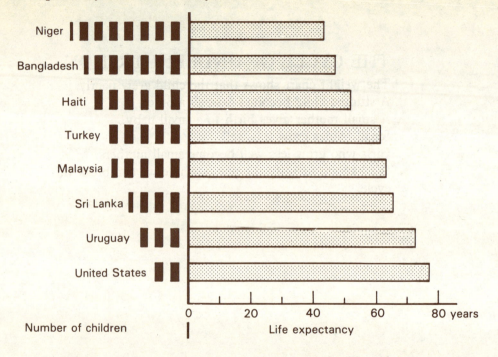

Those countries where mothers have small families of two or three children are also the countries where women live longer.

Fig. 48

Fig. 49

Too young: Children born to women under the age of 20 are approximately twice as likely to die in infancy as children born to women in their mid-20s.

Too many: The risks to the health of both mother and infant increase steeply after the third child.

Age of mother   No. of infant deaths (per 1000 live births)

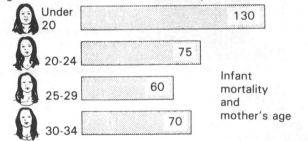

Infant mortality and mother's age

From a survey in Argentina

No. of children   No. of infant deaths (per 1000 births)

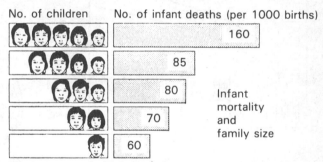

Infant mortality and family size

From a survey in El Salvador

Fig. 50 **The cycle of deprivation**
Early growth and final height

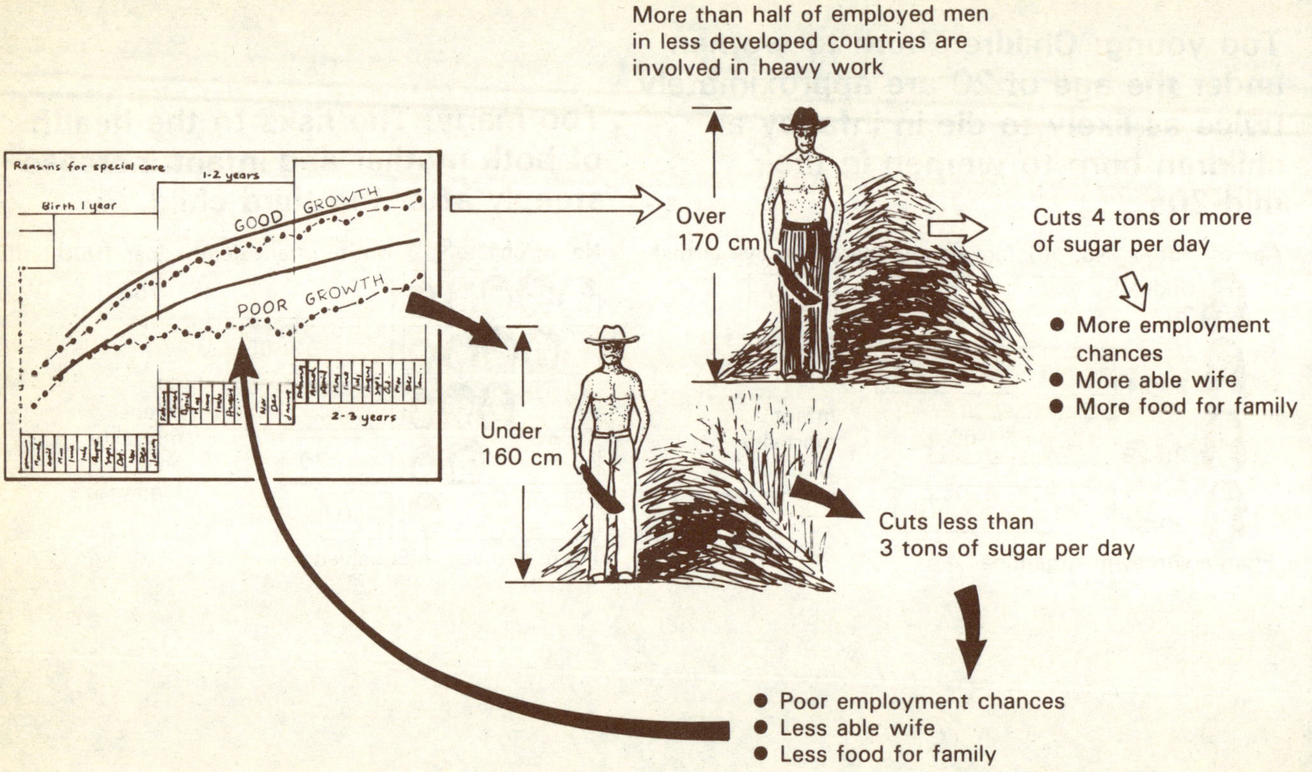

More than half of employed men
in less developed countries are
involved in heavy work

Reasons for special care

Birth 1 year

1-2 years

GOOD GROWTH

POOR GROWTH

2-3 years

Over
170 cm

Under
160 cm

Cuts 4 tons or more
of sugar per day

● More employment
  chances
● More able wife
● More food for family

Cuts less than
3 tons of sugar per day

● Poor employment chances
● Less able wife
● Less food for family

When the stunted child grows into a short man, his family too may suffer.

Fig. 51 Use of land: to feed few or many?

10 acres (5 football pitches) = 4 hectares
will support:

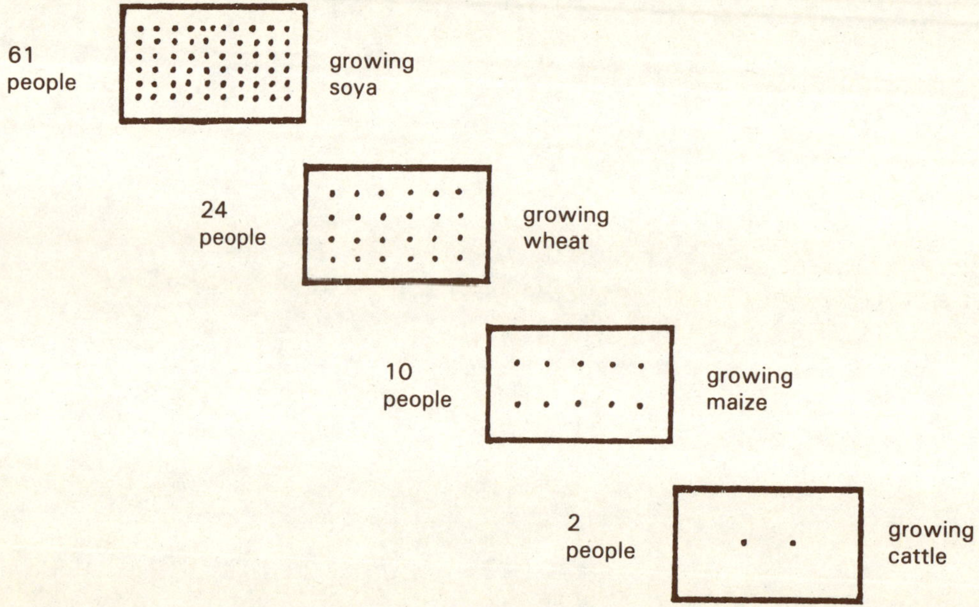

61
people

growing
soya

24
people

growing
wheat

10
people

growing
maize

2
people

growing
cattle

The world can support a much larger population but this
will depend on the use made of the land.

2 Childhood Illness in the Less Developed Countries of the World

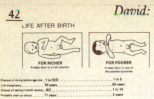

42

LIFE AFTER BIRTH

FOR RICHER
A baby born in a rich country

FOR POORER
A baby born in one of the poorest countries

Chances of dying before age one . . 1 in 100 _____ 1 in 5
Life expectancy _____ 70 years _____ 50 years
Chance of seeing a health worker . All _____ 1 in 10
Probable years at school _____ 11 years _____ 2 years

David: The difference in the outlook for children depending on where they are born is well known, but the figures are striking. I find the figure produced by UNICEF in 1980, that in some countries only one in ten children will ever be seen by a health worker, difficult to believe.

Hermione: I agree it is difficult to accept that countries exist where nine out of ten children in some rural areas may never see a health worker. However, this is a reflection of the poor coverage by health services in many countries.

David: The figures from New Delhi I find impressive. It is hard to accept that there could be such differences in mortality in one city.

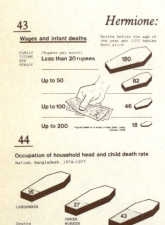

43

Wages and infant deaths

Deaths before the age of one year per 1000 babies born alive

FAMILY INCOME PER PERSON (Rupees per month)

Less than 20 rupees — 180

Up to 50 — 82

Up to 100 — 46

Up to 200 — 18

Figures based on a study in New Delhi, India. (Ghosh, 1976)

44

Occupation of household head and child death rate
Matlab, Bangladesh, 1974–1977

LANDOWNER — 16

OWNER WORKER — 27

AGRICULTURAL LABOURER — 43

Deaths per 1000 live births

Hermione: Yes, it is. The figures show that variation in mortality is nothing to do with genetics or climate, as in the one city ten times as much money to spend per individual is associated with a mortality ten times lower. Much has been written in the past on the importance of land distribution, and this again is well demonstrated in Bangladesh where the mortality shows such a large difference between those who are land owners and those who have to rely on employment as agricultural labourers. After money or land, the level of education of the mother seems to be the most important factor that reduces infant mortality.

The maldistribution of land between families reflects an even more serious maldistribution between men and women. In most cultures women work far longer hours than men but only receive a fraction of the income. They make up 50% of the world population and constitute one third of the world's workforce. They put in nearly two-thirds of the world's total working hours (Fig. 52) and produce half of the developing world's food. They receive only one tenth of the world's income and own less than one hundredth of the world's real estate.

45

David: We health workers have all sorts of advice to give to the mother on how she might improve the health of her children. However, when we see how full her day is we realise how difficult it is for her to do any more than she does for her children.

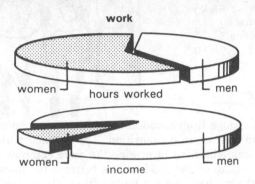

Fig. 52   Women's work and income

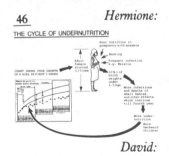

46

Hermione: However, quite simple steps may be available. For example, a mechanical corn grinder can in two or three minutes grind corn to better flour than mothers can grind it in one to two hours by hand. Bringing electricity to a village can do so much to help the women. The cost of grinding corn each day can be as little as 2–5 US cents. The light from one bulb can extend the mother's activities, and perhaps allow her some recreation. Similarly, piping water to the home can make a great difference to the time the mother has and the amount of water she can use.

David: Unfortunately, few governments appreciate the need to invest in women, particularly young girls, to break this cycle of malnutrition. The eventual size of a woman in terms of height and weight depends on how she grew in childhood. The difference in size of the women (or men) we meet in a developing country depends on their growth, particularly in the first three years of life.

Fig. 53 Average weights for women

Average weights
of women in:
USA   58 kg
Central
America 50 kg
India   45 kg

A change from a traditional subsistence economy to a cash economy frequently leads to an increase in malnutrition. The parents, particularly the mother, may need help through education in making the more complex decisions necessary in a cash economy. The health of the child will be better if the money available to the family can be spent by the mother, and not by the father. If, as usually happens, the father has first access to money in a cash crop situation, the new income will not be put into better food, and malnutrition may increase (Fig.54).

Fig. 54

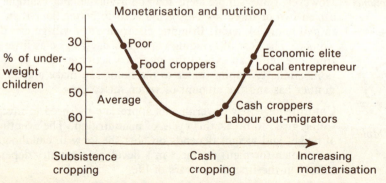

Monetarisation and nutrition

Hermione: Education of the mother is most important and depends on a direct impact. Mortality does vary with the education of the father but his education is of much less importance when other factors are considered and probably depends largely on the greater income which the more educated father can bring into the home. Programmes to improve the mothers' education will be more cost-beneficial in lowering child mortality than educating future fathers.

David: We also need to educate communities that girls below the age of eighteen should not, for many reasons, become pregnant. In many countries such as Nepal, Senegal and Pakistan, the average age of marriage is only sixteen while in Bangladesh it is only thirteen years. Studies in Spain showed the age group twenty-two to twenty-seven to have the lowest incidence of mental handicap, 0.77/1,000 births. After the age of thirty-five, incidence of mental handicap may increase almost ten-fold to 7.4/1,000 births.

48

TOO YOUNG Children born to women under the age of 20 are approximately twice as likely to die in infancy as children born to women in their mid-20s.

Age of mother	No of infant deaths (per 1000 live births)
UNDER 20	130
20–24	75
25–29	60
30–34	70

Infant mortality and mothers age

From a survey in Argentina   People, Vol.11, 4

Hermione: We also need to spread the information that larger families have a higher mortality. The practical way to try to achieve small families is by later marriage and then emphasising to mothers and fathers the advantages to them and their future family of having three years between the births of each child.

49

TOO MANY The risks to the health of both mother and infant increase steeply after the third child.

No of children	No of infant deaths (per 1000 births)
	160
	85
	80
	70
	60

Infant mortality and family size

From a survey in El Salvador   People, Vol.11, 4

David: When we look at the reproductive cycle of women who are undernourished and deprived, we realise the great problem that presents to achieve change among the poor in many countries. There are a number of places where this cycle of malnutrition can be broken. As a paediatrician I would emphasise support to the mother so that her children can achieve good growth in the first three years.

Hermione: The best chance of breaking the cycles of 'malnutrition' and 'deprivation' is through improving children's nutrition in their early years. We need to find techniques through which we can identify the undernourished and deprived in any particular community. They need help to find a way by which they can break out of this cycle. Resources to break the cycle of undernutrition in the mother and deprivation in the whole family are particularly needed.

The Indian poet Appadura understood the dilemma mothers face.

> Decide mother
> who goes without.
> Is it Rama, the strongest
> Or Baca, the weakest
> Who may not need it much longer
> Or perhaps Sita?
> Who may be expendable?
> Decide mother
> Kill a part of yourself
> As you resolve the dilemma. . .

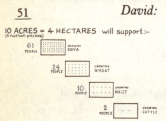

51

10 ACRES = 4 HECTARES will support:-
(5 football pitches)

61 PEOPLE — GROWING SOYA

24 PEOPLE — GROWING WHEAT

10 PEOPLE — GROWING MAIZE

2 PEOPLE — GROWING CATTLE

David: In India, it is the social system which needs to be changed. In Latin America, the landowner frequently has the best land which may be used for running cattle or raising export crops while the landless are forced to work higher and higher in the hills with more difficult soil and more problems from erosion.

Unfortunately, the production of meat leads to inappropriate land usage. Across the world it is now well recognised that the small farmer, particularly if he owns his own land, is more productive than the large farmer. One reason for this is that the large farmer is likely to be producing food for export, and particularly producing animals. We have known for many years that one of the prime needs in developing countries is the redistribution of land. I think when we see how many people different crops can support, we realise how inappropriate it is to have, for example, large cattle-raising areas in so many developing countries, especially the countries of South America.

Hermione: By the way, I understand guinea pigs are on the increase. With one male and ten females, in principle a farmer could have 3,000 within one year! They can produce meat more efficiently than cattle, sheep, pigs or goats. Recent breeding has increased their average size, from just over 700 gm to 1.8 kg. This is an excellent example of innovation which could help some of the countries with such pressure on their food supply to have a more varied diet. Unfortunately, guinea pigs are not yet prestigious like cattle and only recently has research started on their use.

Land distribution is particularly important in those countries in which a high proportion of the people work on the land. In some countries over three-quarters of the people work on the land whereas in Europe or North America only about 2% of the population are agricultural workers. In Brazil, a country of small farmers, there would be no more hunger if small farmers owned more of the land. They have only 21% of the land but grow 73% of the food. Bishop Arns of Sao Paulo diocese suggests that national priorities should be determined by the basic needs of the majority. Redistribution of land is a basic need.

Just as with the mother, the growth of the father as a boy in the first three years of life will determine his size and physique as an adult. The tall man has better employment advantages which will improve the chances of his children growing up healthy and strong.

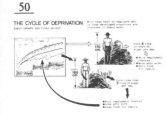

50

THE CYCLE OF DEPRIVATION
EARLY GROWTH AND FINAL WEIGHT

Fig. 55   Proportion of workforce employed on the land: in some countries, three-quarters of the people are farmers

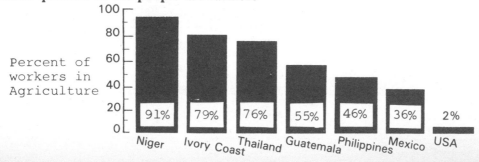

97

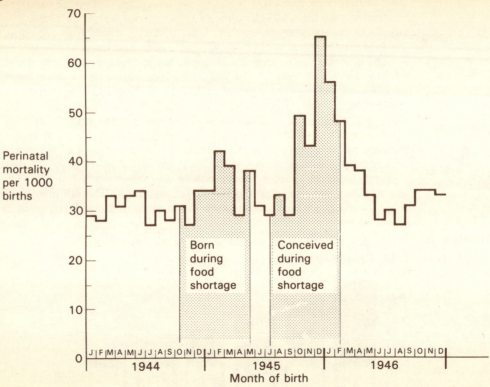

Fig. 56 Perinatal mortality of babies born or conceived through the Dutch Hunger Winter of 1944-45

HEALTH AROUND CONCEPTION

More attention is now being paid to the health of the mother before and after conception. Conception during a period of severe deprivation may be followed by increased chance of mortality in the child after birth.

Fig. 57 Dangerous days for the foetus

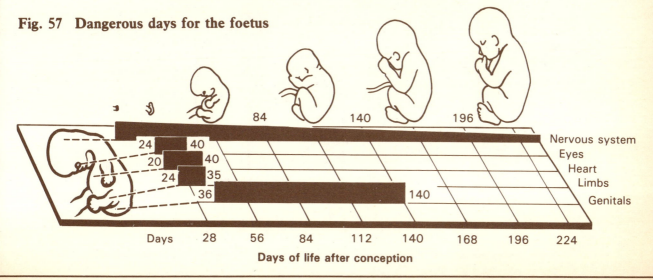

Fig. 58 Weight gain in pregnancy

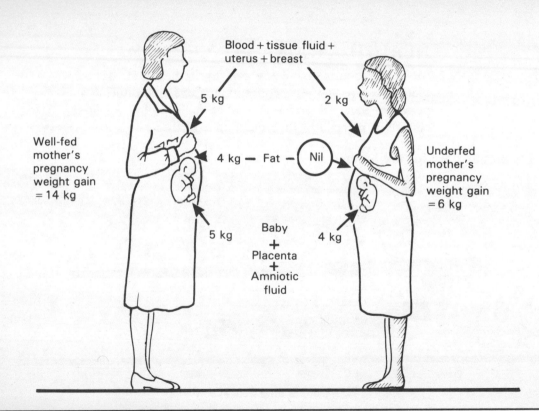

Blood + tissue fluid +
uterus + breast

5 kg

2 kg

Well-fed
mother's
pregnancy
weight gain
= 14 kg

4 kg — Fat — Nil

Underfed
mother's
pregnancy
weight gain
= 6 kg

5 kg

4 kg

Baby
+
Placenta
+
Amniotic
fluid

Because so many women have too little food and too much work, they often fail to gain sufficient weight during pregnancy. The result is the physical depletion of the mother, a greater risk of low birth-weight babies and fewer reserves for successful breastfeeding.

Fig. 59 Normal pregnancy and pregnancy in poverty

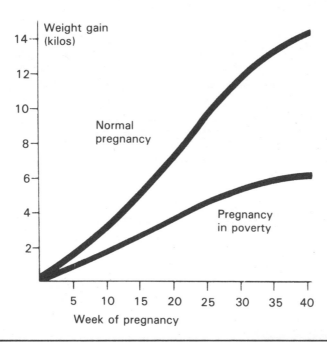

Weight gain (kilos)

Normal pregnancy

Pregnancy in poverty

Week of pregnancy

Fig. 60 Seasonal effects on pregnancy and lactation

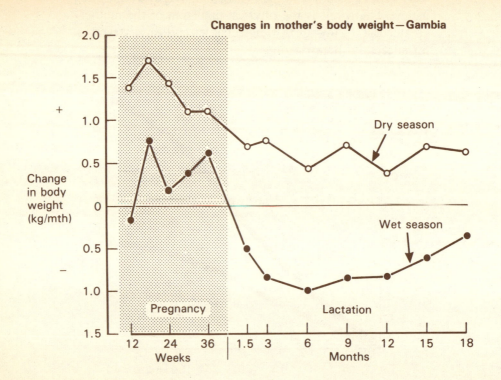

Changes in mother's body weight—Gambia

MOTHERS' WEIGHT

Poor food supply and heavy energy expenditure from farming may lead to the mother losing weight, particularly when breastfeeding.

Fig. 61 Mothers' burden of children and agriculture

Fig. 62 Birthweight and mortality

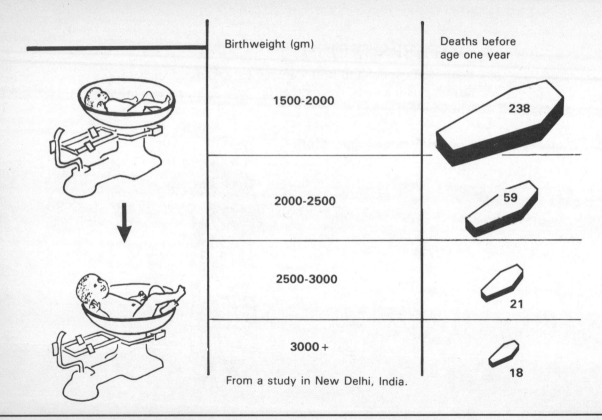

Birthweight (gm)

Deaths before age one year

1500-2000 — 238

2000-2500 — 59

2500-3000 — 21

3000+ — 18

From a study in New Delhi, India.

Smaller infants die more often and if they survive are more likely to grow up short and undernourished.
A major cause of low birth weight is short, undernourished mothers.

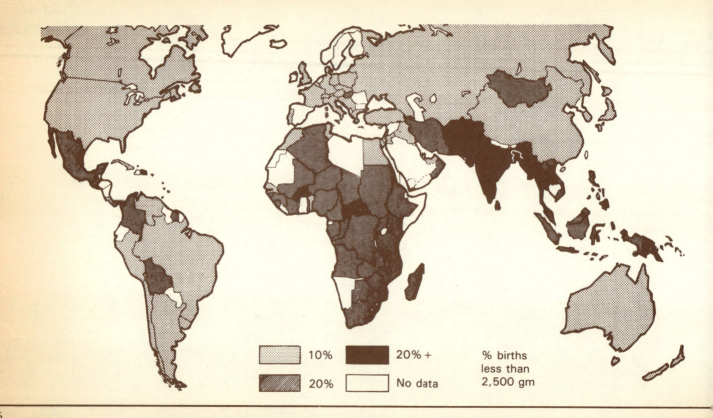

Fig. 63   Incidence of low birthweight, by country

10%   20% +   % births
less than
20%   No data   2,500 gm

Under 10% in all developed countries may be over 20% in less developed ones.

Hermione: The study of the effects of the Dutch Hunger Winter is particularly dramatic.

David: In developing countries, infections and poor nutrition are likely to play their part in the mortality around birth. A fresh examination of the starvation experienced by Dutch women in 1944 showed that the food shortage had some immediate effect on babies *born during* that period but had a far more striking effect in increasing the number of deaths amongst children *conceived during* the period of extreme undernutrition.

Infections such as maternal rubella (German Measles) and drugs such as thalidomide have taught us that the foetus during the first forty days is particularly susceptible to damage. Damage leads to permanent deformity as a congenital defect. In the past we have thought that the ill-effects on the foetus of poor nutrition was concentrated during the last three months of pregnancy. This study perhaps emphasises that there may also be problems for babies who are conceived during periods of food shortage. Perhaps their immunity is not so good when they are born. In the past most obstetrical interest has been in the last three months of pregnancy as this is the period when pregnancy is likely to have an adverse effect on the normal health of some mothers. This is the period when toxaemia and other problems may arise, and these may lead to stillbirth. Now we are also interested in the possible effects on the *child*, and these are of course particularly important in the first three months of pregnancy. Undernutrition or any form of poison in this period affects the multiplication of the cells of the foetus and may lead to congenital abnormalities.

You must have a particular interest in the changes during pregnancy, Hermione, as you have recently given birth to your second child.

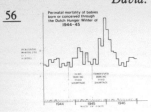

56 Perinatal mortality of babies born or conceived through the Dutch Hunger Winter of 1944-45

57 DANGEROUS DAYS FOR THE FOETUS

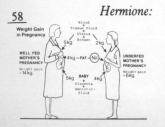

58 Weight Gain in Pregnancy

Hermione: There are dramatic differences in my personal experience of pregnancy and giving birth compared with less fortunate mothers in the less developed world, although we still have much room for improvement in Europe. The French politicians, in 1970, were made aware that death and handicap originating in the perinatal period cost the nation 30% more than road accidents. The French Health Ministry decided to set up a national programme nationwide to prevent these deaths and handicaps. Seven cost-effective measures were introduced. The 1970 Perinatal Mortality Rate was 26/1,000

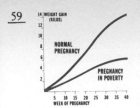

59

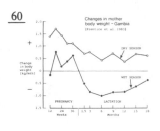

60

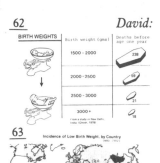

62

63

David:

and this was reduced to 18/1,000 in ten years. It is not clear whether these improvements were due to better medical care or improved living standards.

We women in the North gain much more weight during pregnancy, the difficulty is that neither we nor our obstetricians can tell us what is the right amount of weight to put on! Certainly, most of us end pregnancy with a good reserve of fat which we can then use to create breast milk for the child during the one or two years that our infant is breastfed. Not that all pregnant women in the UK have a satisfactory diet. A study showed that the less fortunate mothers living in Hackney, a socio-economically deprived area of London, ate only twelve items of food a day. They had a lower intake of calories, minerals and vitamins than Hampstead mothers who had a much more varied diet, eating thirty-two items of food a day. This difference in diet was reflected in birth weights. Among the Hackney mothers, 50% had infants below 3,000 gm and 12% were under 2,500 gm. Amongst the Hampstead mothers, only 17% were below 3,000 gm and none below 2,500 gm. The mothers in Hackney who gave birth to infants below 2,500 gm had eaten on average 40% less than the 'recommended' calorie intake for pregnant women. We now accept that nutrition of the mother during her own childhood and her pregnancy will affect her infant's weight at birth.

This is probably so. Some studies suggest good nutrition during the last three months of a mother's pregnancy will increase the birth weight of her child; other studies have brought out less clear-cut results. Certainly I would advise all fathers in the less developed world to see that their wives undertake less heavy manual work and are well fed during pregnancy, and in many cultures there is a tradition which supports this view.

The figures that we have from New Delhi suggest a dramatic difference in survival rates, depending on the weight of the children. Whereas we in Europe expect most infants weighing between 1.5 and 2 kg at birth to survive, we see that in India at least a quarter of these will die. However, for infants born in New Delhi weighing more than 3 kg at birth, mortality over the first year is almost identical with that in Europe and North America. This is another example of the effect of the cycle of malnutrition.

Fig. 64

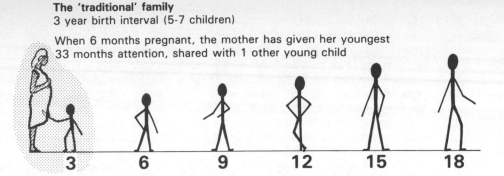

The 'traditional' family
3 year birth interval (5-7 children)

When 6 months pregnant, the mother has given her youngest
33 months attention, shared with 1 other young child

The 'modern' family
1½ year birth interval (12+ children)

When 6 months pregnant, the mother has given her youngest only
15 months attention and this had to be shared with 3 other young children

Mothers concentrate on their youngest

SPACING BETWEEN BIRTHS

Families in traditional societies had children well spaced so that they received optimum care. Every gardener knows that plants placed close together do not grow well.

Fig. 65 Spacing carrots

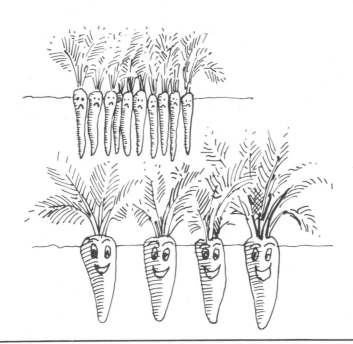

Fig. 66 Spacing births reduces deaths

Bangladesh: World Fertility Survey

Spacing between births	Infant deaths/ 1000 births	Toddler deaths/ 1000 alive	Child deaths/ 1000 alive
	0-1st birthday	1st-2nd birthday	2nd-4th birthday
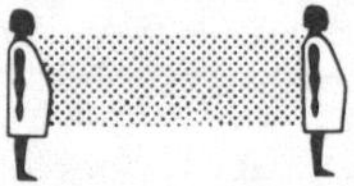 Less than 2 years	185	42	81
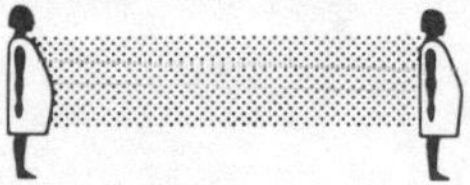 2-4 years	89	28	62
Over 4 years	58	10	27

All twenty-nine other countries studied showed similar trends

SPACING BIRTHS REDUCES DEATHS

The extra care provided by the mother in well-spaced families is associated with a much reduced mortality in the children.

Fig. 67 Spacing births gives taller and heavier children

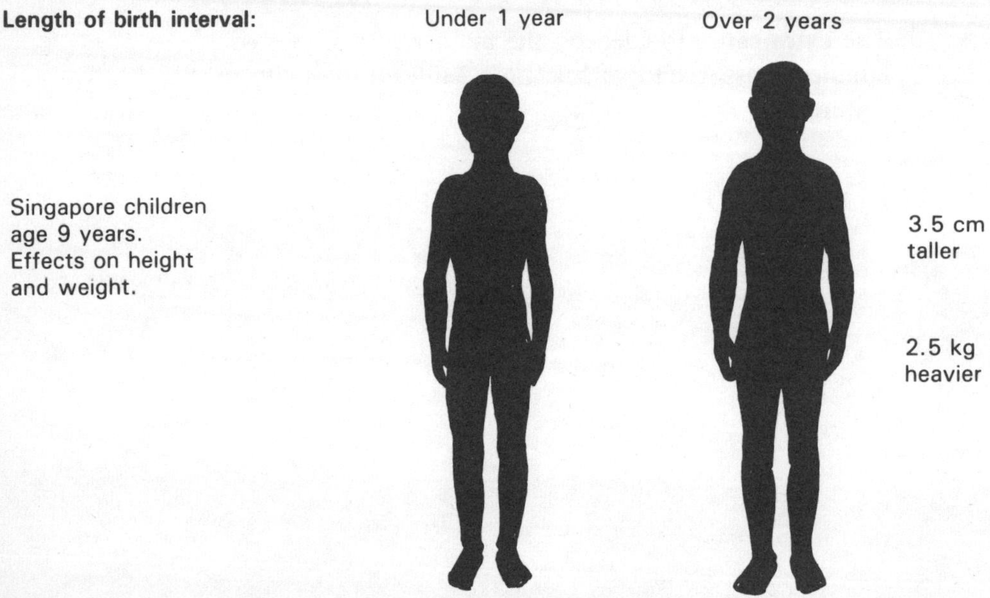

Length of birth interval: Under 1 year   Over 2 years

Singapore children
age 9 years.
Effects on height
and weight.

3.5 cm
taller

2.5 kg
heavier

Parents need to know that children born at a longer birth
interval will be taller and heavier.

Fig. 68 Spacing of births and intelligence

Short
birth interval

64%

Teachers' assessment
of nine-year-olds

Long
birth interval

41%

10%

5%

■ % Brighter than average
□ % Less bright than average

Teachers who did not know the spacing of the children in
their class selected those with short spacing as below
average, those with long spacing as above average in
intelligence.

David: Gardeners know that plants should be well spaced, and this knowledge is also accepted by traditional societies. In practice, the possibility of children being born close together has arisen with the introduction of breast milk substitutes. In the past, when the only chance of a baby surviving was adequate breastfeeding, there was less chance of babies being born at a short birth interval. Do you think mothers understand the need to space births?

65

Hermione: Most women do not need scientific surveys to tell them that too many births close together is dangerous for their own and their children's health. In a recent study in Zimbabwe, the mothers said spacing was done mainly for the health and care of the children. They believe that children born close together 'burn' each other and kill each other by passing diseases easily and many children in such circumstances will die. Out of 21,000 women interviewed by WHO in several developing countries, nine out of ten knew that the health of both mother and child was better if there were fewer births and longer intervals in between. If all births were at least two years apart, the infant mortality rates would be reduced by 10% and the mortality from one to four years by 16%. The recent World Fertility Survey has also reported that the proportion of women with three living children who do not want more is 70% in Sri Lanka, 65% in Bangladesh, 60% in Thailand and Peru, and 50% in Costa Rica, Mexico and the Dominican Republic.

64

THE TRADITIONAL FAMILY
3 year birth interval (1-7 children)

THE MODERN FAMILY
1½ year birth interval (12+ children)

In traditional families, the mother breastfeeds her infant frequently (once or twice an hour) and as a result there are likely to be at least two years of breastfeeding and a birth interval of three years. Over twenty years she is unlikely to have more than seven children. The mother who breastfeeds only every 2 or 3 hours or who uses breast milk substitutes, and who does not have access to contraception, is likely to have thirteen children in twenty years. Each of these children will only have had about a year as the youngest child, and will have had to compete with perhaps two other children under five for the mother's attention. The child born at a longer birth interval will have had two and a half years of the mother's attention and only one other child under five competing for her attention.

David: Hermione, you have just had the experience of caring for your second child through his first nine months. What are your feelings on the birth interval?

Hermione: I know very well the time that even two children demand from the mother, and clearly three or four children below the age of five create an even greater demand, so that the mother cannot concentrate on the youngest, most in need of her attention. We now appreciate the problems that mothers face in less developed countries rather better than in the past, but we still do not appreciate the immense problems when babies are born close together. However, I think, David, you have figures from the medical side to show how this can affect the survival, growth and intelligence of children.

David: Yes. We have some fairly recent figures, particularly from the large world fertility survey. The figures from Bangladesh are impressive and we see that between birth and the fourth year, the mortality is three times greater when infants are born less than two years apart as compared with those born over four years apart. Many in traditional societies wish to have large families for good reasons. As mentioned already, they need them for the work they will do, for the prestige of many sons, and to look after the parents in their old age. In our efforts to reduce the speed of population growth, we should start by encouraging a good spacing between births and inform parents that in this way they will have stronger and more intelligent children who are more likely to survive.

Two ethnic groups were compared in Guinea Bissau, one with a long birth interval and one with a short. In the group with a short birth interval there was much more crowding of young children, particularly sleeping close together at night. There was much infection and a higher mortality in this group and in spite of more births in the

66

SPACING BIRTHS: REDUCES DEATHS
Bangladesh: World Fertility Survey. Rutstein '82

Spacing between birth	Infant Deaths /1000 births	Toddler Deaths /1000 alive	Child Deaths /1000 alive
	0 - 1st. birthday	1st.- 2nd. birthday	2nd.- 4th. birthday
Less than 2 years	185	42	81
2 - 4 years	89	28	62
Over 4 years	58	10	27

All twentynine other countries studied showed similar trends

21

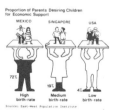

Proportion of Parents Desiring Children for Economic Support

MEXICO	SINGAPORE	USA
72%	19%	41%
High birth-rate	Medium birth-rate	Low birth-rate

Source: East-West Population Institute

117

20

Age of child when activity is started

SURVEY OF CHILD ACTIVITIES : JAVA

(Fig : a Developing World, Sept '77)

13 HOEING
12 WORKING FOR WAGES
9 TRANSPLANTING RICE
9 HARVESTING RICE
9 CUTTING FODDER
9 CARING FOR GOATS / CATTLE
8 FETCHING WATER
8 CARING FOR YOUNGER CHILDREN
7 CARING FOR CHICKENS / DUCKS

By his 15th birthday
a boy, through his
work has repaid the
investment his family
have made in him.

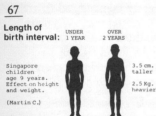

67

Length of
birth interval: UNDER   OVER
                   1 YEAR   2 YEARS

Singapore
children
age 9 years.
Effect on height
and weight.

(Martin C.)

3.5 cm.
taller

2.5 Kg.
heavier

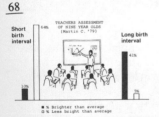

68

Short
birth
interval

TEACHERS ASSESSMENT
OF NINE YEAR OLDS
(Martin C. '79)

Long birth
interval

64%

41%

10%

5%

■ % Brighter than average
□ % Less bright than average

families, the proportion of these people in the community had not increased during thirty years compared with the group with a longer birth interval, less crowding and lower mortality.

There are many studies which show that where children are born at a longer birth interval, they are heavier and taller. The study I have chosen is from Singapore, as children there are not now likely to suffer from undernutrition. However, the Singapore Chinese child born at a longer birth interval is both taller and heavier. Perhaps even more dramatic is the findings when school teachers were questioned about nine-year-olds in the class. The teachers were asked to classify these children into those brighter than average, the average, and the less bright than average. The figures were striking for those children born after a short birth interval. Few of these were considered brighter than usual, and two-thirds were considered less bright than average. Amongst the longer birth interval, almost half the children were considered amongst the bright, and few amongst the less bright. To me this is a most significant finding, and the study needs repeating in other societies. The research worker undertook a detailed statistical study and showed that the birth interval accounted for the majority of the difference; wealth, and other factors were much less important. It is good evidence for persuading parents that if they want their children to do well in school, then they should allow an interval of three to four years between each birth.

Hermione: Unfortunately, relatively few parents in the North appreciate the importance of a birth interval of at least two to three years for the better physical growth and intelligence of their children. Nor is the importance of a long birth interval taught in high school . . .

David: . . . or even in many medical schools.

Fig. 69 Abortion worldwide

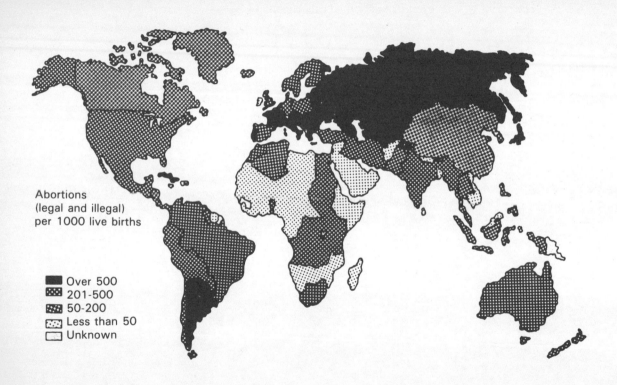

Abortions
(legal and illegal)
per 1000 live births

- ■ Over 500
- ▨ 201-500
- ▨ 50-200
- ▧ Less than 50
- ☐ Unknown

Some countries have one procured abortion for every birth.

Fig. 70

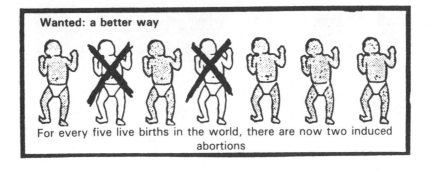

Fig. 71 Government policy to family planning

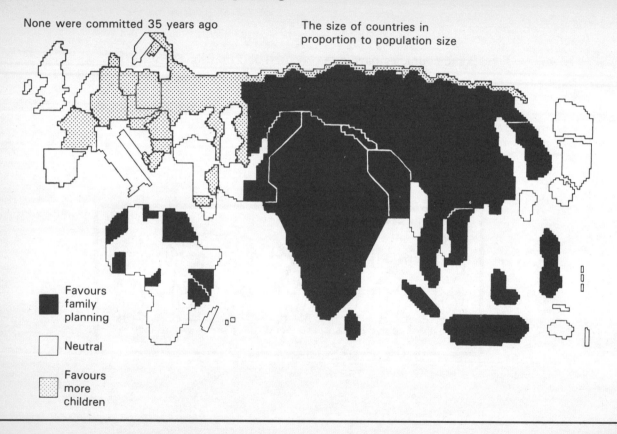

None were committed 35 years ago

The size of countries in proportion to population size

Favours family planning

Neutral

Favours more children

2 Childhood Illness in the Less Developed Countries of the World

69

Abortions
(legal and
illegal)
per 1,000
live births

- Over 500
- 201 – 500
- 50 – 200
- Less than 50
- Unknown

Hermione: I know you have strong views on the problem of abortion.

David: Yes. I think this is a tragedy, almost as great a tragedy for a woman as the loss of a living child. There are a number of parts of the world where the number of abortions equals the number of births, and this is a great cause of distress among women. These abortions indicate a failure to make family planning services easily available so that women can space their children adequately or can limit the family to the size that they and their husbands desire.

71

Governments Policy to Family Planning

The ease of countries in
proportion to population size

FAVOURS
FAMILY
PLANNING

NEUTRAL

FAVOURS
MORE
CHILDREN

N. & S. America neutral
(except Argentina which favours more children)
People. Vol.9, 4,p6

Hermione: I would not like people to think that we are critical of what has been achieved by those concerned with family planning. To me it is impressive what has been achieved. Only thirty-five years ago, there was not a nation in the world which was committed – even on paper – to the provision of family planning services. Today, 118 nations have adopted national family planning strategies. The knowledge and the means to space child births has spread throughout the world with amazing speed. This is a tribute to the work of thousands of governmental and non-governmental organisations of all kinds who have helped to bring the change about. These developments are particularly important in India and China which together contain one third of the world's population. Both India and China have a larger population than all the Americas, or Europe or Africa. In practice, many women do not have either the means or the freedom to exercise a preference for family planning methods. Where do you see the greatest problems for countries?

David: By the year 2100, the population of Asia will at least double and will present many problems, although if some more countries can follow China's example, the overcrowding will be reduced. Perhaps the greatest problems arise in Africa where the population will increase five fold.

Fig. 72 The global village 2000 AD

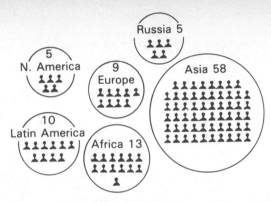

The distribution of every 100 of the world's population

Fig. 73

Results of a 3% population growth rate on a village of 10 houses
The population will double every 20 years

Village of 10 houses
(when Grannie was a child)

**80 houses
after 60 years**
(now)

**320 houses
after 100 years**
(when we are grandparents)

A 3% growth each year means a population doubling every twenty years. It trebles in a generation of thirty years and increases thirty-two times in a century.
This illustration shows what happens to a ten-house village in a hundred years.

Fig. 74 Many countries are doubling their population too quickly

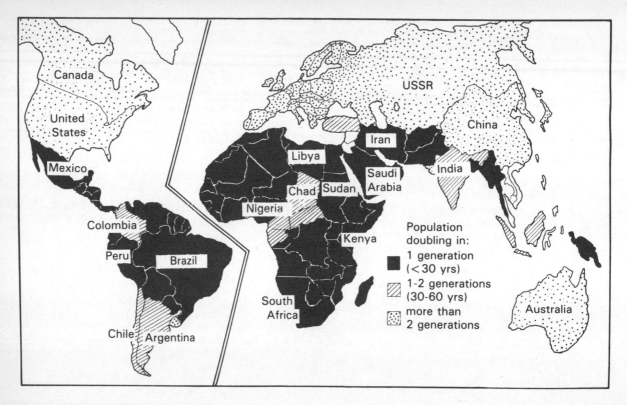

POPULATION DOUBLING TIME

Many countries are doubling their population in less than thirty years, some in less than twenty years. Even with oil or other resources in a country, an appropriate environment for children cannot be provided with this level of population growth. Slowing down in growth can decrease the size of the final population on our planet.

Fig. 75 Medium and low projection for population growth

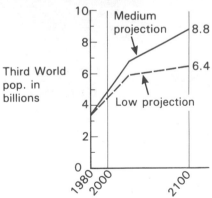

Population in less developed countries (billions)

Medium projection 8.8

Low projection 6.4

Third World pop. in billions

Fig. 76 Population growth till 2100 AD

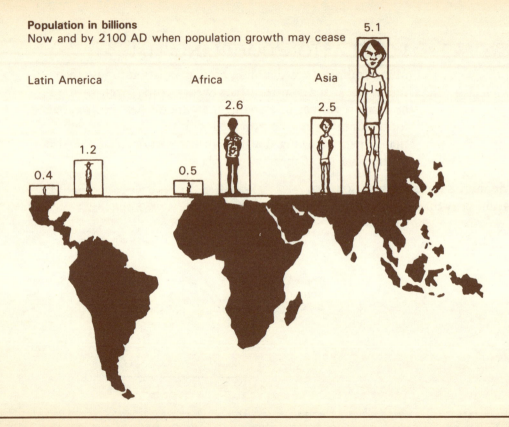

Population in billions
Now and by 2100 AD when population growth may cease

Crowded Asia will double its population.
South America may increase three times.
Africa may increase five times – but Africa's per capita food
production *declined 11%* from 1970 to 1980. At the present
time Africa's population doubles every twenty-two years.

Fig. 77   Africa in great trouble

Fig. 78 Population density per square kilometre

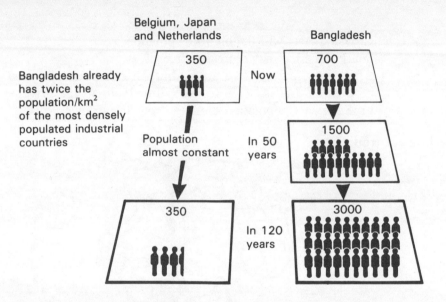

Belgium, Japan
and Netherlands

Bangladesh

Bangladesh already
has twice the
population/km^2
of the most densely
populated industrial
countries

350

Now

700

Population
almost constant

In 50
years

1500

350

In 120
years

3000

All will have eight times the population of 'over-populated'
industrial countries.

Fig. 79 The number of people in our world

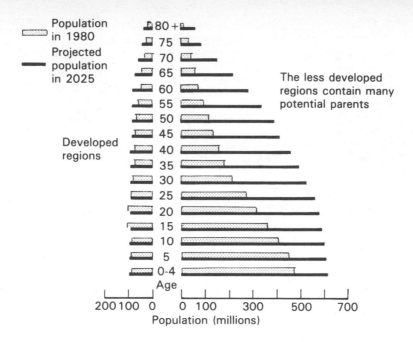

Population in 1980

Projected population in 2025

Developed regions

The less developed regions contain many potential parents

Age

Population (millions)

Populations continue to increase long after the birth rate falls.

Fig. 80 Development: Where the effort goes

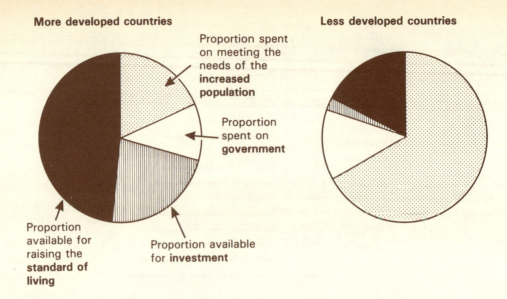

More developed countries

Proportion spent on meeting the needs of the **increased population**

Proportion spent on **government**

Proportion available for raising the **standard of living**

Proportion available for **investment**

Less developed countries

Because most resources are absorbed to meet the needs of increased population, planners have little to invest and only a small amount to raise the standard of living in less developed countries.

Fig. 81 In India 13 million people are added each year

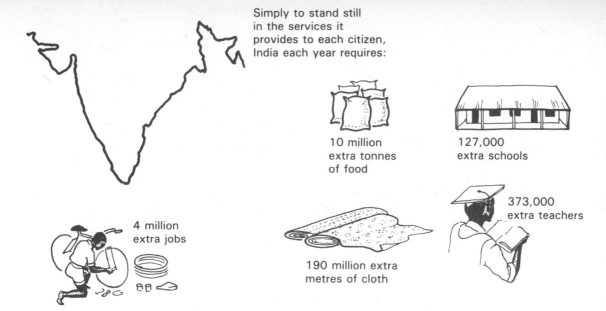

Simply to stand still
in the services it
provides to each citizen,
India each year requires:

10 million
extra tonnes
of food

127,000
extra schools

373,000
extra teachers

4 million
extra jobs

190 million extra
metres of cloth

PROBLEMS FOR THE INDIAN PLANNER

To maintain the *present level* of education India needs
127,000 new schools *every year*.

Fig. 82 Demographic transition

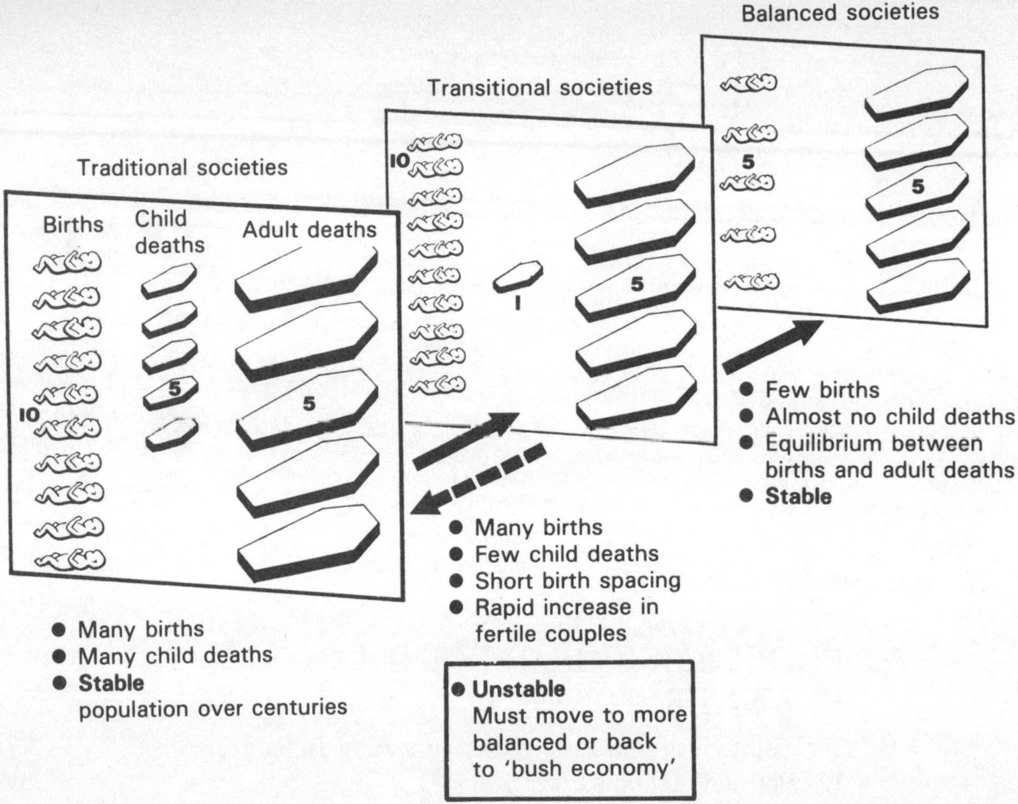

Balanced societies

Transitional societies

Traditional societies

Births   Child deaths   Adult deaths

10

5

5

10

I

5

5

5

- Many births
- Many child deaths
- **Stable**
  population over centuries

- Many births
- Few child deaths
- Short birth spacing
- Rapid increase in fertile couples

- **Unstable**
  Must move to more balanced or back to 'bush economy'

- Few births
- Almost no child deaths
- Equilibrium between births and adult deaths
- **Stable**

THE UNSTABLE TRANSITIONAL SOCIETY

Many countries are in what the demographers call a transitional state. They must move towards a stable state. The longer this is delayed, the greater the danger they may move back to a 'bush economy' where their high birth rate will be equalised by a high child death rate, as in the past.

Hermione: From your experience in developing countries, do you think that people appreciate the significance of population growth?

David: Yes. I think some of the older people have some understanding. I remember standing on a hill with a villager in South America. Looking across a valley he told me that when he was a child it was forest all the way across, and now we could see that all the land was taken up by farms. However, I think few people can grasp how populations grow in a logarithmic way. The drawings which show how a hamlet of ten houses will increase if there is a 3% growth over 100 years attempt to get this point across. It is even more difficult to grasp that even when decisions are taken by a country to limit its population, there is still a continued period of growth. The large number of young people in these countries are all potential parents. They will produce children and increase the population even if they are persuaded to limit their families to two children only. It took mankind a million years to reach a population of a billion, the second billion required 120 years, the third billion thirty-two years, and the fourth billion fifteen years. To me it is frightening to see how many countries still have a population that is doubling in twenty years, and in one generation of thirty years they will have three times the population. A leader in the Sudan recently claimed his country could absorb 2 million people and is encouraging mothers to have more than five children by the giving of medals. In recent years the Iraqi Government has encouraged families to have many children in a bid to replace its war losses. Unfortunately, the emphasis has been on the number of children rather than their quality in terms of health and intelligence. Children born after a short birth interval (less than two years) are likely to be smaller and will do less well at school than those born at a larger birth interval (over two years).

Just as many developing countries are beginning to accept population restraint, some countries such as France are trying to restrict abortion for fear of a decline in population!

We must not place all the blame on the leaders. Chinyelu Onwurah, writing on the Woman's Page of the *Guardian* (14 January 1985), comments on the plight of women in the child-orientated Nigerian society. Women are under tremendous pressure to have

73 Results of a 3% population growth rate on a village of 10 houses. The population will double every 30 years

74 MANY COUNTRIES ARE DOUBLING THEIR POPULATION TOO QUICKLY

39 CAUSES OF DEATH IN DEVELOPING AND INDUSTRIALISED COUNTRIES (Taylor '82)

children, particularly boys. A doctor who prescribes the Pill to women knows they face beatings and disgrace if they are discovered. In Catholic areas, the Pill is considered immoral, and such attitudes are supported by local women's magazines. Those in government in developing countries need to become aware how much of any new resources is taken up in trying to meet the needs of an increased population.

Hermione:

76 Population in billions
Now and in 2000 A.D. when population growth may stabilise

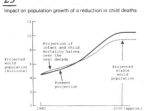

23 Impact on population growth of a reduction in child deaths

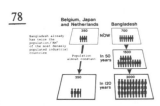

78

Demographers predict that in 120 years' time the world's population may have almost stabilised. Even now a determined effort could lead to many countries drastically limiting their population and China has set an excellent example. Demographers believe that determined effort could lead to 25% less in the world's population when it stabilises (see Fig.75 on page 129). Contrary to what many people think, one of the most urgent steps is to cut infant and child mortality in those countries where it remains high; this should surely be a priority. Unfortunately most governments are in the pockets of local business communities and have little incentive to change policies and spending to support the child survival and development revolution described in the final chapter. There is still a tremendous unmet desire for family planning. WHO estimates there are 300 million couples who do not want more children but have no access to family planning methods. Primary Health Care should be an ideal medium for spreading this form of care so essential in creating a stable society.

David: There are two separate problems: the first is the eventual size of population; but more important is the *rate* of growth and the effect this has on a country. One national leader who understands this is President Nyerere. In the Arusha Declaration which tried to plot the future development of Tanzania he stated:

'It is very good to increase our population, because our country is large and there is plenty of unused land. But it is necessary to remember that these 350,000 extra people every year will be babies in arms, not workers. They will have to be fed, clothed, given medical attention, schooling, and many other services for very many years before they will be able to contribute to the economy of the country through their work. This is right and proper and is in accordance with the teachings of the Arusha Declaration. But it is obvious that just as the number of our children is increasing, so the burden on the adults – the workers – is also increasing. Giving birth is something in which mankind and animals are equal, but rearing the young, and specially educating them for many years, is something which is a unique gift and responsibility of men. It is for this reason that it is important for human beings to put emphasis on caring for children and the ability to look after them properly, rather than thinking only about the numbers of children and the ability to give birth. For it often happens that men's ability to give birth is greater than their ability to bring up the children in a proper manner.'

Hermione: President Nyerere's statement is well brought out by this diagram. In the less developed countries, almost three-quarters of new resources as they become available are absorbed by an increase in population. The proportion which can be used to raise the standard of living is high in the industrialised or more developed countries, and there is also a large amount which can be put to investment for the future. A rapid increase of population makes any development of a country such as India very difficult.

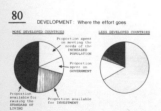

80

DEVELOPMENT: Where the effort goes

MORE DEVELOPED COUNTRIES   LESS DEVELOPED COUNTRIES

Proportion spent on meeting the needs of the INCREASED POPULATION

Proportion spent on GOVERNMENT

Proportion available for raising the STANDARD OF LIVING

Proportion available for INVESTMENT

81

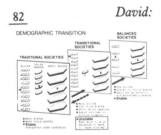

IN INDIA 13 MILLION PEOPLE ARE ADDED EACH YEAR

SIMPLY TO STAND STILL
IN THE SERVICES IT
PROVIDES TO EACH CITIZEN,
INDIA EACH YEAR REQUIRES:

10 million extra tonnes of food

127,000 extra schools

4 million extra jobs

190 million extra metres of cloth

373,000 extra teachers

(Bull. UNESCO. Reg. Asia Off. 22 June '81)

David: I think the problems of population growth are well illustrated in India. India each year adds a population of 13 million, equal to the total population of Australia. As well as more food, more jobs, more cloth and more teachers, India requires 127,000 extra schools every year. How can governments face up to the problem of giving their children even primary education over the next twenty years?

Hermione: If India builds 127,000 schools each year between January and December, then the level of education in December will be as good as it was in January. All these extra schools will have done nothing to raise the standard of education. These are required just for the new population.

82

DEMOGRAPHIC TRANSITION

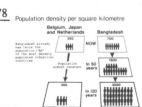

David: The concept of the unstable transitional society is to me important. This is a term developed by demographers. Societies must move forwards to become stable. If they fail to do this then there is a real threat of their returning to a 'bush economy'. Nigeria is now the home of 91 million people. With present projections they may end up with 527 million, more than the existing population of all Africa. Similarly, Iran is growing at 3.2% per year and Syria at 3.7% per year. Their oil reserves will be exhausted long before their future enormous population stabilises.

78

Population density per square kilometre

141

Hermione: Unfortunately, even when a country's leaders are convinced of the political need for a policy of limiting the growth of population, they still need first to convince their people. After limitation of family size is accepted, growth will continue for at least another half century, if all children already born have only two children. It is this delay in achieving a stable population which has led China to attempt a one-child family policy.

CHAPTER THREE
Opportunity for improving health services

Fig. 83 The primary health care cycle

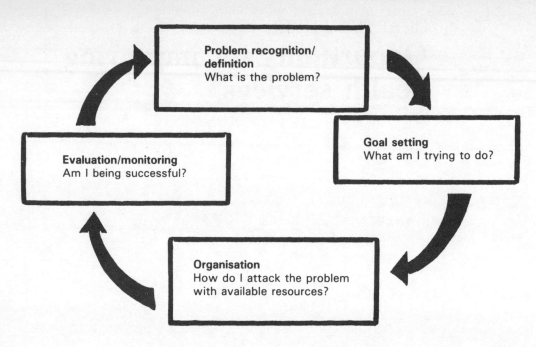

How well do the health services match the local disease pattern?

Hermione: Chapter Two has shown us the main pattern of disease facing children in developing countries now. One problem facing the health services is that frequently they have not devoted the majority of their attention to the most important diseases striking the largest number of children in the country. The very first challenge of the effectiveness of any health service is to find out how well it matches the pattern of ill-health in its own local community.

David: Yes, I agree with this. Too often in the past, health services have grown up in response to a new piece of equipment, or drug, rather than in trying to meet the needs of the majority in a particular community. The diagram (Fig.83) on page 144 is useful for showing how, once the main problems are correctly identified, the appropriate health care can be provided in three steps of goal-setting, organisation and monitoring/evaluation.

Fig. 84 Imbalance in present investment in health
Concept: Cost increases with specialisation

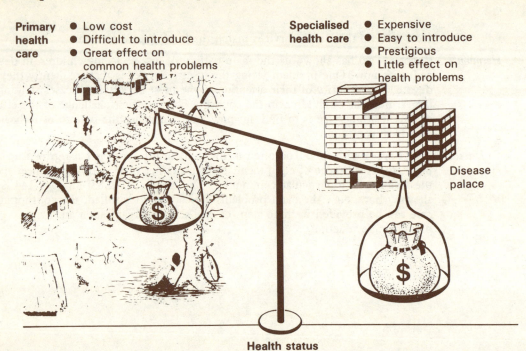

Primary
health
care
- Low cost
- Difficult to introduce
- Great effect on
  common health problems

Specialised
health care
- Expensive
- Easy to introduce
- Prestigious
- Little effect on
  health problems

Disease
palace

Health status

Specialised health care is simple to import, but is expensive and has a limited effect.

Primary health care is difficult to create, but appropriate for meeting health problems.

Fig. 85 The health care dilemma in Ghana

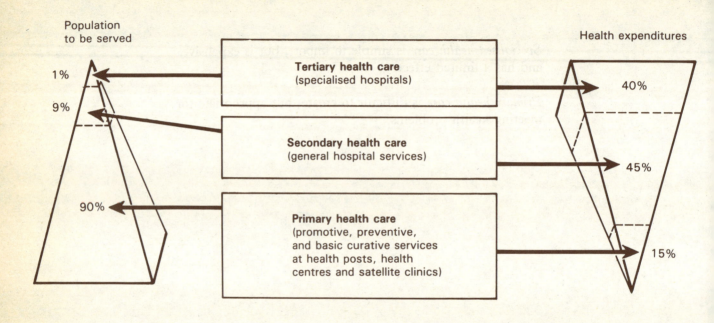

Population to be served

Health expenditures

1%

9%

90%

Tertiary health care (specialised hospitals)

Secondary health care (general hospital services)

Primary health care (promotive, preventive, and basic curative services at health posts, health centres and satellite clinics)

40%

45%

15%

85% of health expenditure goes to hospitals for 10% of the people.
15% goes to primary care for 90% of the people.

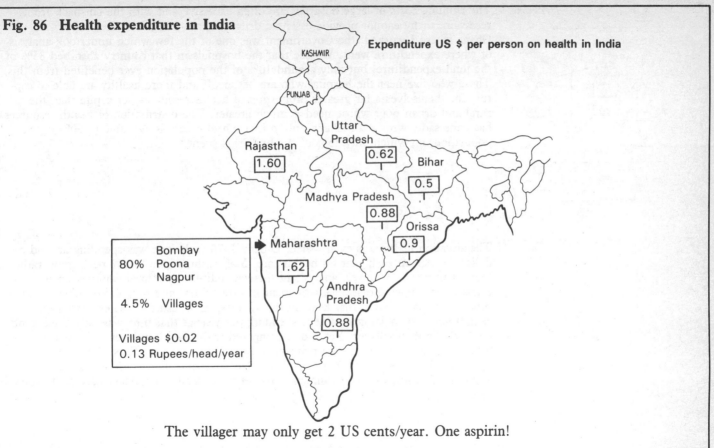

Fig. 86 Health expenditure in India

Expenditure US $ per person on health in India

KASHMIR

PUNJAB

Rajasthan
1.60

Uttar
Pradesh
0.62

Bihar
0.5

Madhya Pradesh
0.88

Orissa
0.9

Maharashtra
1.62

Andhra
Pradesh
0.88

80% Bombay
      Poona
      Nagpur

4.5% Villages

Villages $0.02
0.13 Rupees/head/year

The villager may only get 2 US cents/year. One aspirin!

3 Opportunity for Improving Health Services

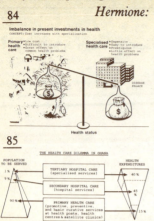

Hermione: The running costs of large hospitals are often excessive and with the cut-back from recession, many cannot provide essential drugs or have a regular water supply. In Ghana where I worked, the Government was one of the few which undertook analysis of where expenditure went. We see that the hospitals in that country absorbed 85% of the total expenditure, but only around 10% of the population ever benefited from this. Those who live near the hospital who are better off and more healthy are able to capture for themselves a far greater proportion of health resources per capita than the rural and urban poor whose need is much greater. The distribution of health resources has gone sadly wrong. In Ghana only primary health care is available to 90% of the population, on which only 15% of the budget is spent.

David: The situation in India is even worse. During 1976 each state was spending around one dollar per person each year on health care. Maharashtra spent $1.62 per capita, rather more than most. However, analysis of this expenditure by a local commission in Maharashtra showed that 80% was spent in three cities, and only 4.5% among the five times bigger population that lived in the villages. As a result it was estimated that central and provincial government spending per year at that time was only 2 US cents per year for each villager. Yet India, compared with many countries, has done so much to develop health care through primary health centres in every 'block' of 100,000 people in the country. We hope in future that governments and groups concerned with appropriate health care will campaign in every country for a similar analysis of expenditure.

Hermione: Health economists tell us that reversing this expenditure is extremely difficult. Perhaps the first step governments could take would be to impose strict limits on existing expenditure on curative care. Next they need to invest all new monies in preventive care and in limited treatment of proved value, at primary level. We need to emphasise repeatedly the problems of heavy capital investment, which ties up future resources due to high recurrent costs.

Unfortunately, many present governments, and colonial powers and donor governments in the past, have not appreciated the relative importance of recurrent compared with capital costs. For example, the large modern hospital probably takes at least a quarter of its initial cost each year for running, particularly for wages, which makes up

Fig. 87 Breakdown of lifetime cost of cold chain equipment over 10 year period

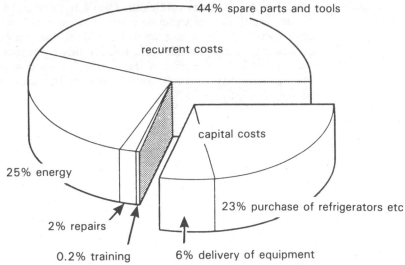

60–70% of most recurrent health budgets. These recurrent costs tend to increase year by year.

However, if wages are not taken into account, capital costs are still a relatively small part of the total cost. Costs of cold chain equipment (*e.g.* refrigerators to keep vaccines cold) have recently been analysed and this is used as an example. Over a ten-year period, the capital cost was less than a quarter of the total cost. The largest single cost was spare parts and tools. These calculations did not include the most important recurrent cost – the wages of those using the cold chain equipment. Any government or voluntary agency working in the less developed world should think twice before accepting any capital equipment or building until adequate allowance has been made for recurrent costs. Over the next ten years, the maintenance and servicing of any piece of equipment is likely to exceed the initial cost by as much as four times.

David: When I visit a Ministry of Health, I am often presented with a description of the primary health care programme which may be excellent. However, I am usually greeted with a stony silence when I ask about the comparative budgets for hospital services and primary health care. Usually this is because those making the presentations do not know the costs of their 'paper' plans if implemented on a national scale.

Introducing primary health care is so very difficult compared with providing specialised health care.

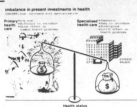

Hermione: We can find a hill anywhere in the developing world, clear the bush and build a large hospital. No problem, we are filling a void. However, when we go into a village or district community and try to help the local people build up a primary health care programme, we find ourselves in real difficulty. We are facing existing traditional health care systems, or those who are using western medicine for personal gain. Even more serious, we soon find we are involved with local political and social groups and their vested interests.

Fig. 88 National resources for health

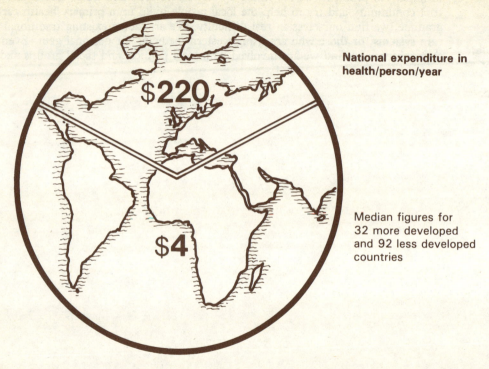

National expenditure in health/person/year

Median figures for
32 more developed
and 92 less developed
countries

In the South $4 is spent for each person each year. This is
only 2% of the amount spent in the North.

Fig. 89 The price of health

Providing primary
health care –
including water
and sanitation,
trained workers
communicable
disease control
and basic drugs –
would cost an
extra $50 billion
a year for the
next 20 years
That is $12.50 per
person per year.

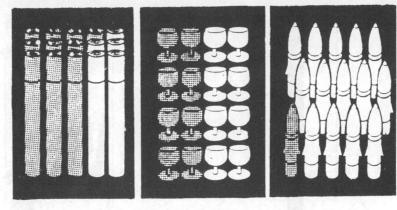

$\frac{2}{3}$ of world spending on cigarettes

$\frac{1}{2}$ of world spending on alcohol

$\frac{1}{15}$ of world military spending

ESSENTIALS FOR ALL?

The cost of providing this is small compared with other
expenditure.

Fig. 90 What does a soldier cost? (millions $ US '80)

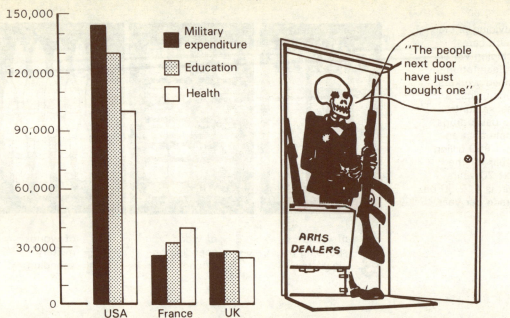

FEAR DIVERTS RESOURCES

Rich and some poor countries may spend as much on
armaments as on health or education.

Fear is the driving force behind this expenditure.

Fig. 91 The choice is ours

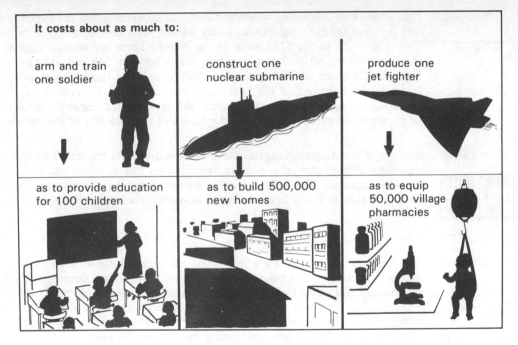

It costs about as much to:

arm and train
one soldier

construct one
nuclear submarine

produce one
jet fighter

as to provide education
for 100 children

as to build 500,000
new homes

as to equip
50,000 village
pharmacies

ARMAMENTS ARE NOT ESSENTIAL

Let us try to cut down on armaments and build up the
essentials.

David: I am going to be so bold as to suggest that existing health services in the South have a limited effect on the health of the population.

88

National Expenditure in
Health/Person/Year

Median figures for
32 more developed
and 92 less developed
countries.

Health Sector Policy Paper
World Bank 1980

Hermione: This is not very surprising when you come to appreciate that the expenditure on health care per year for each individual is only $4 per year, that is, 8 US cents each week. This is only 2% of the $220 spent in the North. These are median figures, and amongst the better-off countries the expenditure varies between $40 and $550 per head. Amongst the poor countries, a third spend less than $2 and two-thirds less than $8 (US $ in 1980). Particularly when we find out how badly distributed this expenditure is in developing countries, we come to appreciate that health services at present are unlikely to play a large part in effectively improving the health of the majority of the people.

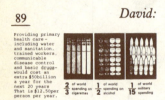

89

Providing primary
health care –
including water
and sanitation,
trained workers,
communicable
disease control
and basic drugs –
would cost an
extra $50billion
a year for the
next 20 years.
That is $12.50per
person per year.

$\frac{2}{3}$ of world
spending on
cigarettes

$\frac{1}{2}$ of world
spending on
alcohol

$\frac{1}{15}$ of world
military
spending

David: And yet as the diagram suggests there are resources. At present the expenditures on cigarettes, alcohol and arms prevent spending on health. More and more people in all countries question whether these items are worth having at that cost. Unfortunately, the image that so many have of 'health services' is a large hospital.

91

IT COSTS ABOUT AS MUCH TO:

Hermione: Our children are born into a world where the expenditure on forces of destruction – that is, armaments – is a major expenditure even in the less developed countries. Every government will claim that they wish to spend more on children but resources are not available. Can we claim we are short of resources when so much is spent on armaments? When the cost of building one modern fighter is more than a country such as Tanzania spends for health care during the course of a year?

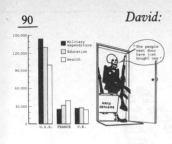

David: Those countries that consider themselves leaders in our world spend twice as much on armaments as on health and education. Of the world resources spent on research and development, more than 50% is spent on armaments. To justify this expenditure, the Pentagon, for example, employs a larger public relations group than any industrial firm. Even among poor developing countries, armaments represent a priority in spending.

In all countries, the major motivation for spending on armaments arises through fear of neighbours or in some countries through a fear among the élite that the masses may demand a more just redistribution of resources. Prevention will only come by removal of this fear through political change.

Hermione: Rich countries who have the largest armies are also those who have arms industries. To reduce the enormous overheads of developing new weapons for killing, they are also involved in selling arms and therefore encouraging smaller countries, particularly those in the less developed areas of the world, to buy and increase their armaments.

David: It frightens me that as we look around the world and see how countries who for some reason have developed new wealth spend this on armaments and before long become involved in fighting their neighbours, or suppressing their population.

Hermione: Expenditure on conventional arms is serious; how much more is the expenditure on the potential for total destruction of life for hundreds of years through nuclear weapons? In 1809 Thomas Jefferson of the US wrote:

'The care of human life and happiness, and not their destruction, is the first and only legitimate object of good government.'

Fig. 92 Limited money: which choice?

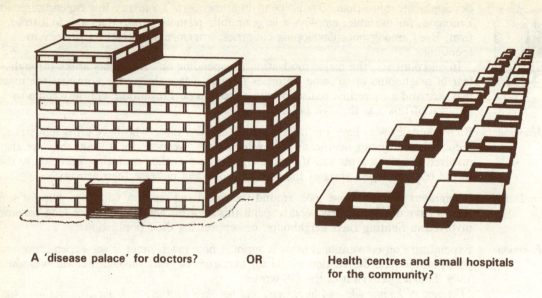

A 'disease palace' for doctors? OR Health centres and small hospitals for the community?

Large hospitals are favoured by doctors, politicians and the patients who can gain access to them. They have little effect on the health of most people in less developed countries.

Fig. 93   Health expenditure in Tanzania

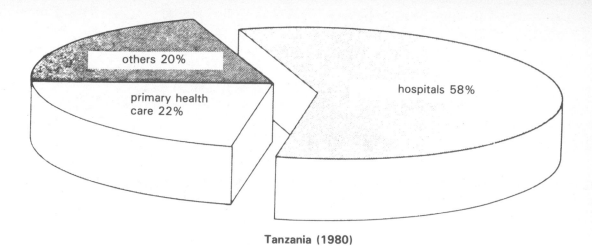

others 20%

primary health
care 22%

hospitals 58%

Tanzania (1980)

Even in such countries as Tanzania where primary health care has been accepted as a national priority, great difficulties arise in diverting money to such care. Expenditure in hospitals remains high and has continued to increase rapidly.

Fig. 94 Do hospitals or health centres provide better care?

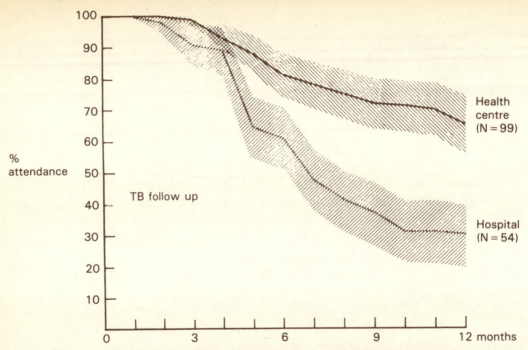

Patients who continue to attend are more likely to be satisfied with the treatment they receive. Attendance at a health centre for TB treatment was better than at a hospital.

Fig. 95 The vicious circle of drug over-use

Those practising medicine for private gain must accept much responsibility for this.

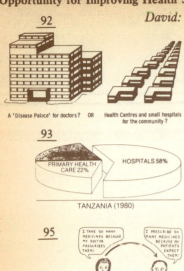

David: For many years now I have been saying that the relatively enormous investment in large 'disease palaces' has been one of the great tragedies of health care in the developing countries. The hospital is only a part of a good health care system. There is growing evidence of how inefficient large complexes can be. These large hospitals are favoured by doctors and politicians but are little help to the mass of the people. *They have put the whole direction of medicine into a 'curative', 'doctor-oriented' form, which continues to absorb almost all the health resources of the country.* If only investment had been made in health centres and small hospitals, we would now be almost certainly a lot further on in providing health care for the people of these countries.

Tanzania is one country where health expenditure has been carefully planned. Nyerere in the late 60s said, '. . . *We must not again be tempted by offers of big new hospitals with all the costs involved until at least every one of our citizens has a basic medical service readily available to him. . .*' In twenty years, Tanzania has doubled the number of dispensaries and seen a ten-fold increase in health centres. Expansion of rural services in Tanzania has been rapid. However, hospitals have also increased in cost; twenty years after independence they absorb 58% of expenditure. This increase in hospital expenditure has far exceeded that for primary care which still receives less than a quarter of total expenditure.

Hermione: If in countries such as Tanzania, where the leaders have made a determined effort to bring health care to the people, the increase in primary health care is limited, we must realise that the chance for more appropriate spending in other countries is not good.

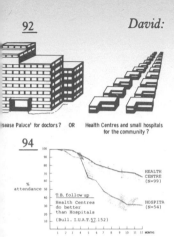

92

'sease Palace' for doctors? OR Health Centres and small hospitals for the community?

94

% attendance

T.B. follow up
Health Centres
do better
than Hospitals
(Bull. I.U.A.T. 57.152)

HEALTH
CENTRE
(N=99)

HOSPITA
(N=54)

David: I think some of the fault at least must be borne by the medical profession who are so powerful in every country. The powerful medical élite work in the hospitals and they try to persuade governments to spend more money on these institutions. Unfortunately we have relatively few good studies in which the health care provided by health centre services has been compared with that provided in hospitals. Because of their greater facilities, the assumption has always been made that hospitals provide better care than health centres. However, this may not be true for all conditions and as this diagram shows, more patients may attend regularly for follow-up and on-going treatment of their tuberculosis at health centres than at hospitals.

Less busy peripheral units can provide services earlier in a disease. They are more likely to offer a truly comprehensive service of 'Under Fives Clinic' where preventive and curative services go hand-in-hand for all children who attend. It does seem that under certain circumstances patients are more likely to attend health centres than hospitals. While men being more mobile can reach the hospital, women and children are more likely to make use of local clinics.

Hermione: This is perhaps not very surprising as the distance to the health centre is likely to be smaller. Those working in the health centre may be well known to the patients who are then more likely to attend regularly.

One of the attractions of the hospitals is the greater availability of medicines.

David: I recently visited Kenya where they have a new policy for the distribution of drugs. A kit containing some 38 generic drugs is sent from Nairobi sealed up to each dispensary; one kit is sent for every 3,000 new patients seen. The health centres as a result are well stocked and the morale of the staff is much higher, with the people attending the health centres more and the hospitals less. Through large scale purchases, the cost of items has been reduced and the new system, with many times more medicines available, costs US $0.24 per capita compared with a previous cost of US $0.26 each year.

Fig. 96 Medical Schools and the Ministry of Health

Faculty of Medicine

Ministry of Health

Their expectations for doctors are not the same.

The University trains doctors towards 'international standards'.
The Ministry of health needs doctors to service rural health programmes.

Fig. 97 Teaching in disease palaces or in the community?

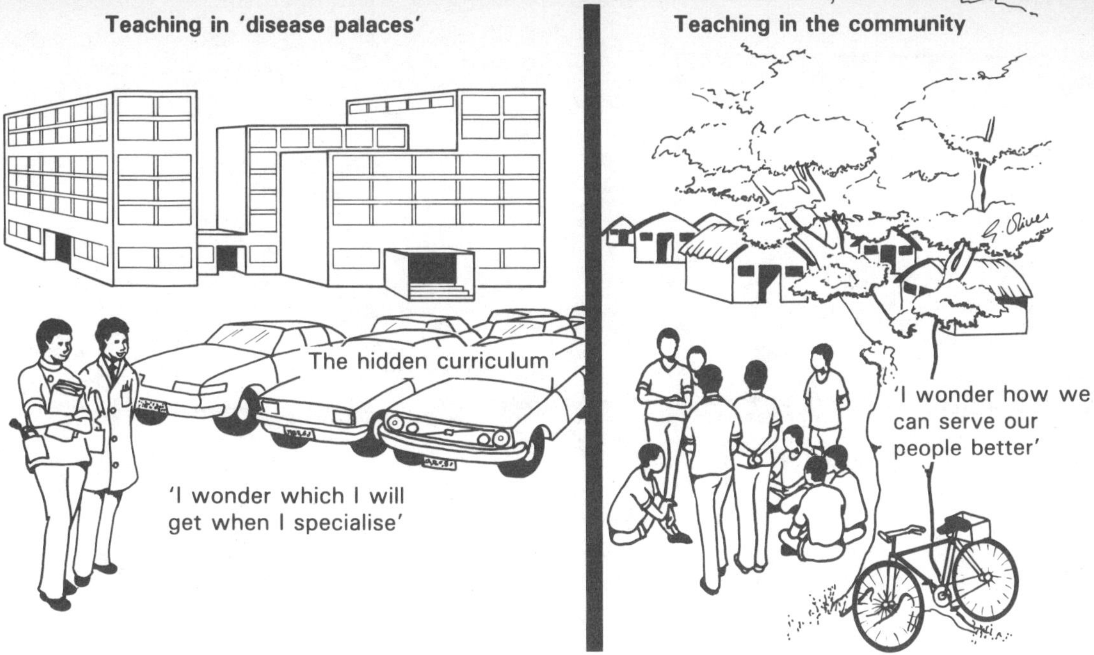

Teaching in 'disease palaces'

Teaching in the community

The hidden curriculum

'I wonder which I will get when I specialise'

'I wonder how we can serve our people better'

WHERE DO WE TEACH OUR DOCTORS OF THE FUTURE?

Students follow the example and lifestyle of teachers.

Fig. 98 Inappropriate training

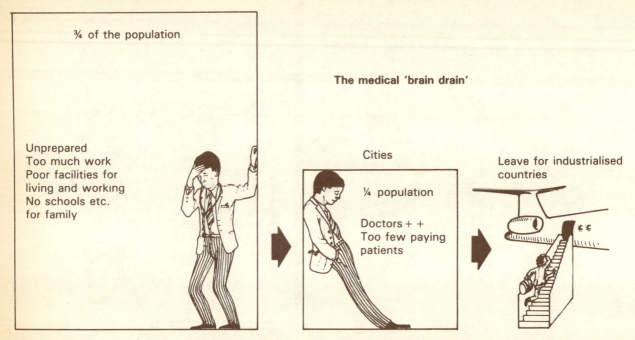

Rural areas

¾ of the population

The medical 'brain drain'

Unprepared
Too much work
Poor facilities for
living and working
No schools etc.
for family

Cities

¼ population

Doctors + +
Too few paying
patients

Leave for industrialised
countries

Inappropriate training leads to poor performance, dissatisfaction and unhappiness.

Fig. 99 Good health care includes home visits

This doctor does not make home visits.
He cannot understand his patients' problems.

This doctor does make home visits.
He knows he's giving better care.

The education of doctors as well as other health workers
will include home visits.

David: I hope you realise the responsibility we have as university teachers: we have done so little to prepare doctors appropriately for the country in which they serve. University teachers have trained doctors so that they may not be happy either in the rural areas, nor the cities, nor if they migrate to the industrialised countries. Through the way we live, we have created an expectation for material goods which doctors, without private practice involvement, cannot achieve. The cities of less developed regions are already over-doctored and the doctor may be unhappy and ill-prepared to do a useful job wherever he works. In Kenya, 60% of the doctors live in Nairobi. Four small countries in Africa which have the best child health services do not have a medical school! Perhaps existing medical schools act as sponges, absorbing people and resources.

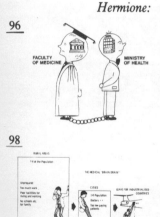

96

98

Hermione: Unfortunately, too, the Faculty of Medicine in most universities trains doctors who will be able to present papers in international forums and make uncommon diagnoses and treat the rare conditions. The medical school and Ministry of Health are too often looking in opposite directions. Usually the university wishes to train doctors who would be acceptable to work in Europe, while the Ministry needs health workers for rural programmes in their own country. Because the attitude and training of doctors from these universities have been so inappropriate to the needs of Third World countries, many have migrated to Europe and the USA. Those that remained stayed largely in the cities. The brain drain has been an asset to more developed countries but a great loss to the less developed. There are over 20,000 doctors trained overseas practising in the UK. This is equivalent to seven years' output from UK medical schools! However, sometimes the university lobbies for preventive programmes of health care which the Ministry does not adopt. So few countries have taken steps to try to bring together the needs of the Ministry and the work of the university. Some have had success by involving those from the Ministry in teaching while asking academics to join them in planning.

Planned programmes of change are needed to enable medical schools to review and change their function and activities if they are to produce 'Health For All' and not 'Health For Some'.

David: You and I, Hermione, are amongst the profession that carries much of the responsibility for this state of affairs. The health profession particularly has put so much emphasis on teaching in the large hospital, and so little in getting out into the community. *The recruitment and training of doctors has been based on the needs of countries in the North and not on the needs of the doctors' own country.*

Hermione: With my more sociological background and my interest in teaching, I know that medical students taught in 'large hospitals' are often exposed to a 'hidden curriculum'. They will wish to follow the lifestyle of their teachers, some of whom run large cars and earn generous sums in private practice. Their teachers may achieve a large private practice income from the prestige they gain through appointment as consultants to a teaching hospital. They stimulate the students' interest in unusual referred cases, not in the management of the 'easy' common condition. Students too often are taught to rely on laboratories and X-rays, and feel frustrated when they do not have these facilities. Unfortunately, we do not yet have enough teachers or adequate knowledge on how to teach medical students within the rural or shanty town community. As long as teachers can have a much better lifestyle and earn much more money in the cities through private practice, appropriate teaching in rural or shanty town communities seems unlikely. However, in many countries such teachers are appearing: teachers whose primary aim is service to their community.

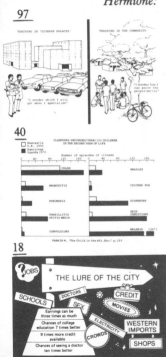

97

TEACHING IN 'DISEASE PALACES'   TEACHING IN THE COMMUNITY

"I wonder which I will get when I specialise"   "I wonder how I can serve the people better"

40

ILLNESSES-RECORDED/YEAR/100 CHILDREN IN THE SECOND YEAR OF LIFE

□ Newcastle U.K. 1950
■ Bamulonge Uganda 1970

Number of episodes of illness

COLDS   MEASLES

BRONCHITIS   CHICKEN POX

PNEUMONIA   DIARRHOEA

TONSILLITIS OTITIS MEDIA   SKIN CONDITIONS

CONVULSIONS   MALARIA (267)

PARKIN M. 'The Child in the Afr. Env.' p.193

18

THE LURE OF THE CITY

?JOBS
SCHOOLS   DOCTORS   CREDIT
SEX   MOVIES
Earnings can be three times as much
ELECTRICITY
Chances of college education 7 times better   WESTERN IMPORTS
9 times more credit available
CROWDS
Chances of seeing a doctor ten times better   SHOPS

The Gonoshasthaya Kendra programme at Savar Bangladesh suggests that training should prepare doctors to carry out the following functions:

1 Diagnosis of health problems and priorities of the area using scientific epidemiological tools.
2 Planning, execution and evaluation of a community health programme in accordance with the community diagram.
3 Accurate and competent treatment of common as well as important clinical problems.
4 Training of the team, including the village health workers.
5 Supervision and leadership of the health team.
6 Function as a change agent in the health system.
7 Understanding the problems of the masses and actively associating with them.

Zafrullah Chowdhury, the originator of the above proposal, has written:

'Primary health care is generally only lacking when other rights are also being denied. Usually it is only lacking where the greed of some goes unchecked and unrecognized (or unacknowledged) as being the cause. Once primary health is accepted as a human right, then the primary health worker [and, we might say, the *public* health worker] becomes, first and foremost, a political figure, involved in the life of the community and its integrity. With a sensitivity to the villagers and the community as a whole, he will be better able to diagnose and prescribe. Basically, though, he will bring about the health that is the birthright of the community by facing the more comprehensive political problems of oppression and injustice, . . . apathy, and misguided goodwill.'

38

David:

Young doctors need leadership and commitment from senior doctors so as to have a community orientation. There will need to be a strong political commitment to serve the underprivileged if we are to turn the tide. Unfortunately, teachers and students seldom get out into the community to see how the people live who they are attempting to serve. My belief is that only when all levels of health worker visit patients in their home can they come to know the real problems of their patients. They must be regularly reminded of the background in which these patients live and work.

99

This doctor does not make home visits. He cannot understand his patients' problems.

This doctor does make home visits. He knows he's giving better care.

Hermione: Unfortunately, in almost every country across the world, the doctors are making fewer visits to the home. One reason for this is due to their high level of pay, they have to justify seeing many patients and this can more easily be achieved in the clinic environment. However, the majority of patients would prefer to be visited in their own home, and doctors are more likely to understand the majority of conditions better if homes are visited. By such visits they will encourage others in the health team who should be spending most of their time in home visits.

Fig. 100 The health minister and his pain

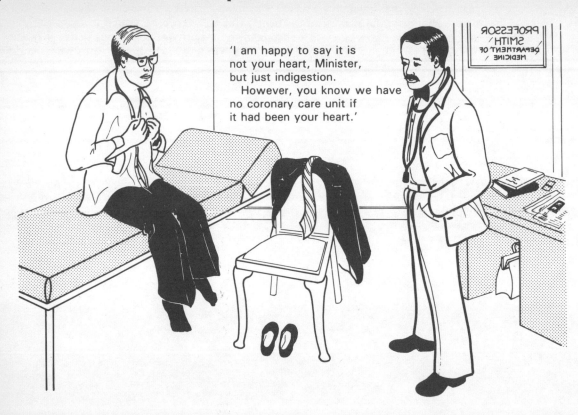

'I am happy to say it is not your heart, Minister, but just indigestion.
   However, you know we have no coronary care unit if it had been your heart.'

THE HEALTH MINISTER AND HIS
FEAR OF A CORONARY

Subtle pressure from a senior consultant may provide that consultant with almost useless technology at the expense of the Minister's Primary Health Care Programme.

Fig. 101 The doctor's lifestyle

The satisfaction achieved will depend on the attitude and expectations his training and his background have produced.

Fig. 102 People want cures

A healthy balance between preventive and curative medicine
must take into consideration what the people want.

The desire is always for the treatment of illness.

Hermione: Why is there such a demand for expensive new equipment and new units to house it?

David: One possible answer is in the old saying, 'The difference between an adult and a child is the size and complexity of the toys they play with'. Research in England has failed to demonstrate epidemiological proof of a significant increase in survival amongst those taken to coronary care units compared with those treated elsewhere. These units have been developed and introduced on a wide scale at enormous expense in spite of the lack of evidence they do any good.

Satyajit Ray, a noted Indian film maker, was sent to Houston Hospital, USA, for a by-pass operation financed by the West Bengal and Central governments at a cost of 700,000 Rupees. This is equal to the total health care budget of a block of 100,000 people over a year in some Indian states. By-pass surgery relieves pain but probably does not significantly extend life.

By setting up such specialised and expensive units in less developed countries, the Ministry of Health and their advisors are tying up finance which could be used to instruct mothers in oral rehydration or to immunise hundreds of thousands of small children. Signing the cheque for such a unit may be signing the death certificate for thousands of children whose lives could have been saved if money were used differently.

Hermione: Ministries of Health have their problems, they rightly see the need for preventive medicine as a priority. However, they may fail to realise that preventive care alone is unacceptable, and must be combined with basic, inexpensive, effective curative care. The Minister of Health will be under many pressures, some from his own political machine, to divert resources from primary health care programmes so as to make more medical technology available, particularly in large hospitals.

100

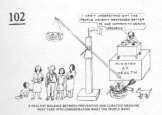

102

178

David: The private medical sector, in terms of expenditure, may be as large as or larger than the government health service. However, it can lead to maldistribution of health care because it is providing resources for those who can pay rather than those in need. The doctor working in private practice has great difficulty in providing health resources to those who need them most. He seldom gathers around him an adequate team who will cope with common problems and allow him to concentrate his skills where they are most needed. The doctor in public service can play a major part in seeing that the less privileged in the community receive the services they so desperately require. Do some doctors serve those who need them least and ignore those who need them most?

Governments need to encourage the local health team to provide a comprehensive care and in this way provide the doctor with a worthwhile and more interesting job than his colleague working in private practice. Those working successfully in remote areas deserve special allowances and priority for further training opportunities. Perhaps the doctor in private practice should be heavily taxed? After all, his country made a heavy investment in his education!

<u>95</u>

THE VICIOUS CIRCLE THAT LEADS
TO THE OVERUSE OF MEDICINE

<u>101</u>

Fig. 103 Continuing education for every doctor

So many doctors close their books when they qualify. They forget that their black bag of knowledge has a hole in it!

Fig. 104 Distance learning concept

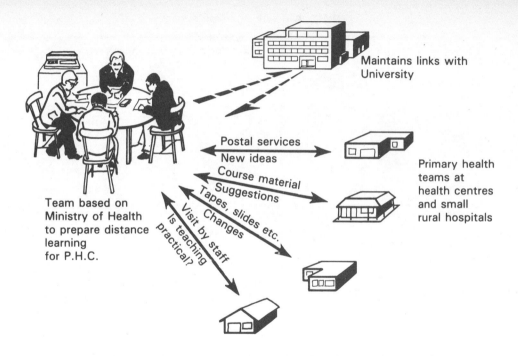

Maintains links with University

Postal services
New ideas
Course material
Suggestions
Tapes, slides etc.
Changes
Visit by staff
Is teaching practical?

Team based on
Ministry of Health
to prepare distance
learning
for P.H.C.

Primary health
teams at
health centres
and small
rural hospitals

The primary health care team is well placed to gain from
this development in educational techniques.

Fig. 105 Who provides primary health care?

Primary child care — which option?

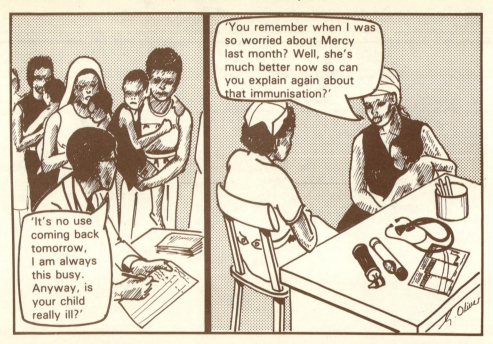

A doctor?   Auxiliary health worker or nurse?

WHO PROVIDES PRIMARY HEALTH CARE?

One or two minutes from a doctor trained for five years to seek out disease.

Five or ten minutes from a local person trained for one to two years in comprehensive child care.

Hermione: It is unfortunate that so few governments have seen the opportunity there is for giving the doctor a worthwhile job. If only the doctor can be encouraged to accept his responsibilities, offered reasonable facilities, kept in one post for a sufficient time, he can attempt with the local community to achieve an appropriate health programme.

David: What do you think of the on-going training of doctors?

Hermione: From what I saw in Ghana, nurses and medical assistants can do a great deal if only they have the on-going training. Unfortunately, even the doctors do not get this, and I think we both know of many countries where the majority of doctors read and study little once they are qualified.

103

David: A great failing of medical and much other education is that those trained do not see themselves as perpetual students. In health care as in every other field, advances are so rapid that within ten years the doctor who does not study will be out of date. Creating a desire to continually add to their knowledge needs to be a priority in improved educational techniques for health workers. *The continuing education of the whole health team will remain the most important investment for any government concerned with improving health care.*

104 DISTANCE TEACHING FOR THE PRIMARY HEALTH TEAM

Hermione: For me, one of the great opportunities that is being missed is in failing to use the skills that have been developed in distance-learning to provide good on-going education for the primary health care teams scattered over developing countries. I believe this could be an inspiration to them. Led by a doctor or senior health worker, they would be involved in teaching each other and learning together. Through distance-learning they could come to see how they and the community which they serve could work together to provide a more appropriate health care system.

David: In most countries, the position and prestige held by doctors is very different from that of nurses. The salary received by senior doctors is many times that received by senior nurses. A better distribution of resources, and (even more important) a better working relationship with mutual respect between these groups, would lead to better health care.

I am always concerned about the poor relationships one so often sees between doctors and nurses: as one who is neither a doctor nor a nurse, what are your observations on this?

Hermione: This is a complex subject and is bound up with how different societies look on men and women. Unfortunately, in most societies the first impressions of children are their mothers or other women being involved in all the domestic chores. This is even more obvious among the 'well off'; as children they experience service from underpaid girl servants in almost every society, and men grow up with the acceptance of women in a subservient situation. In nursing this is made worse in those societies where human excreta is considered defiling, and where there are strong taboos against women touching men.

Because caring occurs in all family situations, and was emphasised by religious groups, the financial rewards for nurses have always been very different from the rewards for doctors. The attitude of men in the health field to women as nurses has been a serious brake on the development of health services. Another factor about which little is expressed and nothing written is the sexual harassment from which women, particularly nurses, suffer. These difficulties become even more apparent as we move into the primary health care field.

David: I agree. In almost every country, it is now appreciated that if primary health care is to be provided at village level, then we must involve women who have had experience of child birth and bringing up young children. It is the pregnant or lactating woman and the young child who particularly require primary health care, and for whom most can be done easily and at low cost. In almost all societies, these are better cared for by respected women who are concerned for their community. In some countries, we have

Fig. 106 Nurses' pay

'Well, you ought to get used to having less pocket money than other girls if you're going to be a nurse.'

seen failure because only men, who have perhaps achieved some secondary education, were trained as the village or part-time health worker. Once they have received this training, some leave for the cities where they can put their skills to increasing their financial returns and obtaining more material benefits.

Hermione: From my contact with health professionals, I have come to realise that the present

105

A DOCTOR?   MEDICAL ASSISTANT? (OR NURSE)

training of a doctor largely in a hospital tends to make him search for disease often without really considering the underlying causes of ill health.

Doctors are trained as experts and they do not do well when they spend most of their time repeating the treatment of common and to them uninteresting diseases. This means treating the same child with the same preventable condition with the same medicine, so the same child can return to the same environment to get the same condition again, and again, and again. Unfortunately, national leaders do not understand that doctors are not necessarily the best people for primary health care. Fidel Castro when asked about the possibility of too many doctors being trained in Cuba replied, 'Why not a physician on every corner, on every boat, in every factory?'
Surely this would be an appalling waste of training and other resources. Such an approach will lead to a great deal of dissatisfaction among doctors. However, if he had substituted 'an appropriate health worker' for 'doctor' he would have got it right!
Well-trained auxiliaries or nurses are usually more appropriate for primary health care. They can be encouraged to consistently apply preventive measures such as immunisation and charting the growth of children. What do you suggest is the doctors' place in seeing patients?

David: I developed a diagram which represented my experience some years ago. Only over a period of time have I come to realise its significance and full meaning, which I suggest is as follows.

Fig. 107   The doctor working with a nurse

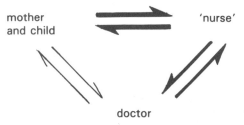

As individuals there are only a limited number of people we can know well enough to understand their problems and interact with them. This will be about 1,000, though for some it may be more. In the forseeable future there will not be enough doctors for all children and their mothers to be 'known' by a doctor. However, we can hope that there may be enough 'nurses', 'auxiliaries', or others to whom the mother feels she can turn and who will know her as an individual. So the strong link – the thickest arrow – needs to be between the patient (mother and child) and the 'nurse'. *The doctors' concern should be to increase the respect of the mother for the nurse and avoid creating a belief that only doctors can offer good health care.*

In the situation we have discussed, a doctor and nurse were working together. The same method can apply to other levels of health worker.

Fig. 108   The senior health worker working with a junior

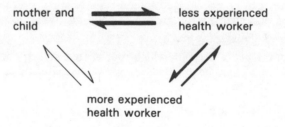

The more experienced health worker has a responsibility to train and support the less experienced. There is also a responsibility to build up the mother's confidence in the less experienced worker. The effective doctor in primary health care will be the one who sees it as his responsibility to *serve* the nurses, auxiliaries and part-time workers who are his front line troops against disease and death. The doctor should create and sustain a team who between them can multiply and extend his knowledge and skills and take them to the community.

Fig. 109   Decline in infectious diseases

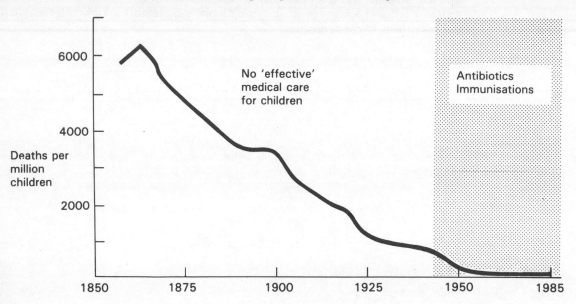

Deaths below 15 years attributed to scarlet fever, diphtheria, whooping cough and measles, England and Wales

No 'effective' medical care for children

Antibiotics Immunisations

Deaths per million children

MORTALITY FELL LONG BEFORE SPECIFIC SERVICES DEVELOPED

Deaths from scarlet fever, diphtheria, whooping cough and measles started to fall a hundred years ago in England and Wales.

Immunisation and antibiotics have been available for less than fifty years.

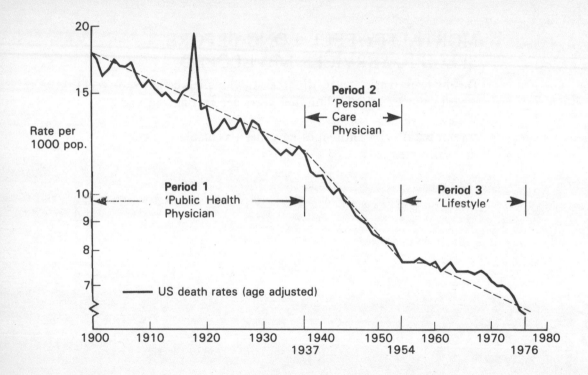

Fig. 110 Three periods of health care

THREE PERIODS OF HEALTH CARE

1 Improved nutrition, living conditions, water supply and waste disposal, achieved by social reformers not doctors.

2 Individual care, vaccines and antibiotics.

3 Health improvement dependent on changes in lifestyle and environment.

Fig. 111 Lifestyle and health care

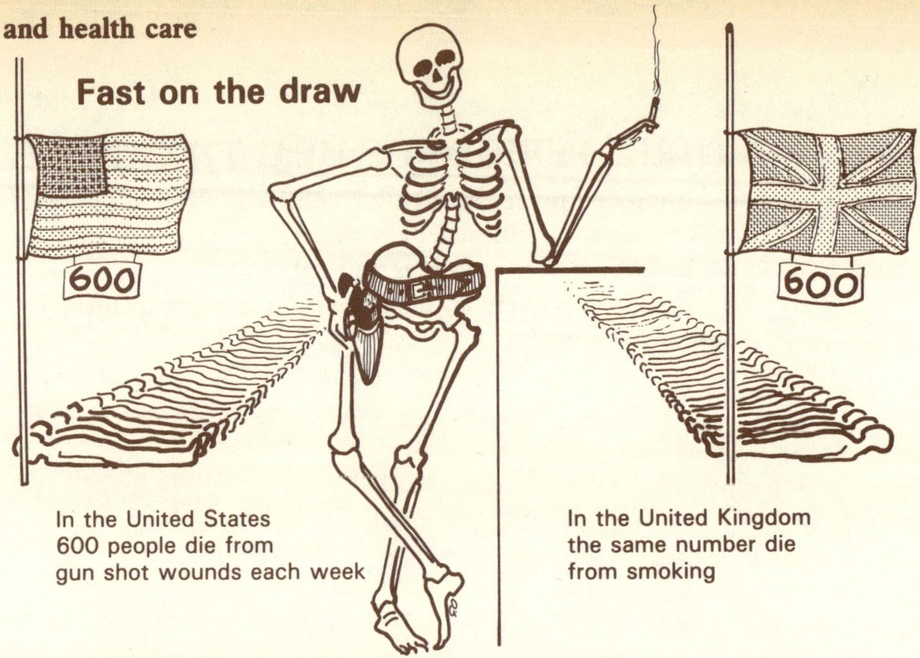

Fast on the draw

600

600

In the United States
600 people die from
gun shot wounds each week

In the United Kingdom
the same number die
from smoking

CHANGES IN LIFESTYLES TO IMPROVE HEALTH CARE WILL INVOLVE:

- In the UK, overcoming the political pressure of the tobacco and alcohol 'multinationals'.
- In the US overcoming these and the 'gun lobby'.

Fig. 112 Where do we start building the health pyramid?

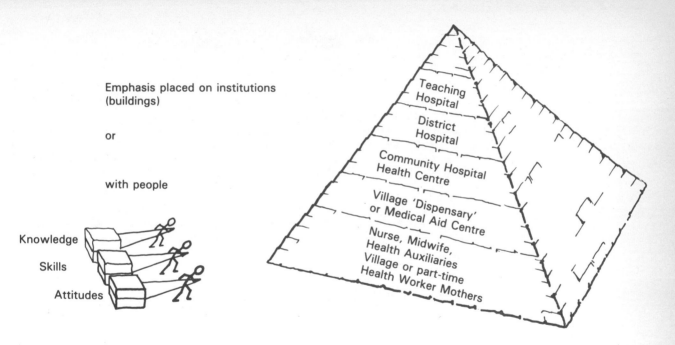

Emphasis placed on institutions (buildings)

or

with people

Knowledge

Skills

Attitudes

Teaching Hospital

District Hospital

Community Hospital Health Centre

Village 'Dispensary' or Medical Aid Centre

Nurse, Midwife, Health Auxiliaries Village or part-time Health Worker Mothers

The Egyptians built from the bottom!!

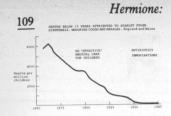

109

DEATHS BELOW 15 YEARS ATTRIBUTED TO SCARLET FEVER,
DIPHTHERIA, WHOOPING COUGH AND MEASLES. England and Wales

Hermione: I know that you find this decline in scarlet fever, diphtheria, whooping cough and measles one of the most dramatic of our illustrations, and one of the most difficult to explain.

David: Yes. I use this frequently for discussion in teaching. If I ask doctors which diseases were serious in the past and have been overcome by our modern antibiotics and immunisation, I am sure that many would include scarlet fever, diphtheria, whooping cough, measles and tuberculosis. Yet when we examine the figures, we find that *most of the reduction in mortality occurred before we had antibiotics and immunisations*. What do you think is the reason for this?

Hermione: It is difficult to explain. First of all, while improved sanitation and housing played some part, these were only available in the UK following the Sanitary Acts and the revolution in housing that followed. These acts were passed around 1900, and yet the decline in deaths started long before this. My own view is that it was probably improved nutrition among children.

David: Although we will be discussing this later and some people may think me eccentric, I particularly emphasise the improved energy (calorie) intake that children achieved through this improvement in nutrition. I would put the emphasis particularly on oils and fats being more widely available and on improved grinding of cereals by replacing stone with steel roller mills. These changes and the increased consumption of sugar all make it relatively easy for the mother in Europe or North America to give her child an adequate calorie intake.

Hermione: A different approach is to try to separate the decline in mortality into stages. The first stage up to 1940, before we had vaccines and antibiotics, represents measures applied to the whole community. For example, improved living conditions, sanitation and food supplies have played a major part in the decline in mortality. There was also a greatly improved standard of living due to a much improved per capita income. Then came a stage when there was a rapid decline in mortality due to the provision of specific personal care through antibiotics and immunisations. This led to a considerable improvement, but this reduction was counteracted by the adverse lifestyles that individuals were living. From the mid-fifties to the present time, health services have played a less important role, except in as far as they influence lifestyle. The mortality now will be more altered by health education and legislation against firearms, accidents, smoking, pollution of the environment and inappropriate diet. Some of these adverse influences such as smoking have been encouraged by sales pressures from multinationals. Only now, when we realise the difference that lifestyle can make, is more emphasis being placed on appropriate legislation by the national governments, often encouraged by the United Nations Organisation.

110

THREE STAGES OF HEALTH CARE

David: An example of inappropriate lifestyles is the dramatic figure that each week in the USA there are 600 deaths from gunshot wounds. This is largely due to the wide dispersal of guns in US families, and the strong gun lobby in the US Senate, which maintains this 'freedom'. By law, any Texan, unless he or she has been convicted of a criminal offence, can carry a loaded gun down Main Street. Probably 70% of Texan households have guns. Guns are used in 80% of murders and a high proportion of suicides in Texas.

In the European Common Market we spend US $7 million to subsidise farmers who grow tobacco and only one million on all cancer prevention campaigns. With less than a quarter of the US population, smoking in the United Kingdom is responsible for a similar number of deaths per week. In this country, the multinational tobacco industry, and the fear of loss of tobacco tax and employment, has led to a reluctance to implement steps which would lead to a decline in smoking and so reduce these deaths.

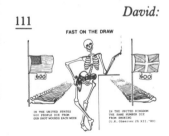

111

FAST ON THE DRAW

In Europe and the US, much less is spent on prevention than on treatment. Effective education to create an illness-preventing and health-promoting attitude is only just beginning.

Hermione: Improved child nutrition and improved housing and sanitation are but two examples of how mortality and health are relatively unrelated to the prevailing pattern of health services in so many countries. Health relates to the way that people live; there are strong pressures on them through advertisement and other means to live in this way. This sort of debate is by no means over. Should we try to control malaria by the traditional methods such as spraying of houses and draining of wet areas? Or should we place reliance on the malaria vaccine being developed? Probably the answer is that we should not rely on either.

Another reason for improved health which is of the utmost importance, and went on throughout this period in Europe and the USA, was a decline in family size so that population growth slowed down. As a result, newly generated capital could be used to raise standards of living which is impossible in countries with rapidly expanding populations.

David: In this discussion on the decline in mortality and the reasons for it, we have been referring to more developed countries. The majority of the less developed countries missed out on the first stage in which decline took place through improved nutrition, sanitation and hygiene. Instead they have tried to reduce mortality largely through steps in the second stage, that is through immunisation and antibiotics, while at the same time trying to develop appropriate methods of water supply and sanitation. Unfortunately for them, due to inequitable international distribution of resources and a rapid population growth, they have difficulty in finding the necessary new resources for investment in their developments. However, countries where even limited resources have been more evenly distributed, such as China, Cuba, S. Korea, Kerala and Nicaragua, have seen a dramatic improvement in the health of their people.

80

DEVELOPMENT : Where the effort goes

MORE DEVELOPED COUNTRIES   LESS DEVELOPED COUNTRIES

Proportion spent on meeting the needs of the INCREASED POPULATION

Proportion spent on GOVERNMENT

Proportion available for raising the STANDARD OF LIVING

Proportion available for INVESTMENT

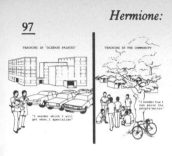

97

Hermione: On reading this chapter again, I think we have given the doctors 'too much stick'. They are not the root cause of the problem. They are the major workers in what we have come to realise is an inappropriate model of health care. The failure of this model in the industrial North is not so serious. Where it has been introduced in the South it gobbles up the limited resources.

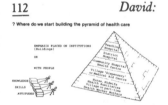

112

David: What disturbs me is that a major proportion of doctors are happy with this system, and for their own self-interest will do all they can to maintain the status quo. This is probably true for those in the large hospitals at the top of the pyramid. Unfortunately, when plans are being made concerning new developments in health care it is their advice which is sought.

Hermione: *Building the health service from the bottom on a foundation of primary health care can only come about through political change and redistribution of resources.* Different people will have different answers. Whatever conclusion we reach, we must accept that health is a highly political matter. So many of our discussions with overseas students end on a hopefully constructive political note.

Health care can be either *people empowering* in the sense that it gives people greater control over the factors that influence their health and their lives, as well as greater leverage over public institutions and leaders: or it can be *people disempowering*, insofar as it is used by the authorities as an instrument for social control. People empowering health care utilises health education, *not* to change people's attitudes and behaviour, but rather to help people to change their situation. Or, as Pablo Friere would say, to change their world.

David: Rather than to become directly involved in politics personally, except as a responsible citizen, I believe the health worker's first responsibility is to make the facts known to those who are making decisions. A number of socio-epidemiological studies described here need to be repeated locally and the results made known to politicians.

To complete this chapter on more appropriate health systems, let us refer to Chinese philosophy:

THE APPROPRIATE EPITAPH

For those who wish to leave behind an effective system of primary health care.

Fig. 113   An appropriate epitaph

But of the
   best of leaders
When their task
   is accomplished
Their work is done
The people all remark
'We have done it
   ourselves'

Hermione: The quotation on the tombstone, partly from Lao Tsu in 500 BC, is incomplete. What James Yen wrote in the 1930s goes like this and could well be posted in the home of everyone concerned to develop primary health care.

Go in search of your people
Love them
Learn from them
Plan with them
Serve them
Begin with what they know
Build on what they have
But of the best of leaders
When their task is accomplished
Their work is done
The people all remark
'We have done it ourselves'.

CHAPTER FOUR
The changing role of health workers

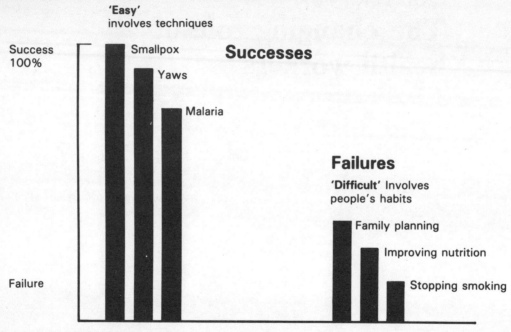

Fig. 114 Successes and failures in health care

'Easy'
involves techniques

Success
100%

Smallpox

Successes

Yaws

Malaria

Failures

'Difficult' Involves
people's habits

Family planning

Improving nutrition

Stopping smoking

Failure

To change habits we need effective communication

The success of health services has been limited to technologies such as vaccination, an injection or house spraying. We have failed in difficult areas involving people's way of life. The role of the health worker must change to meet this need.

Fig. 115 Give a man a fish?

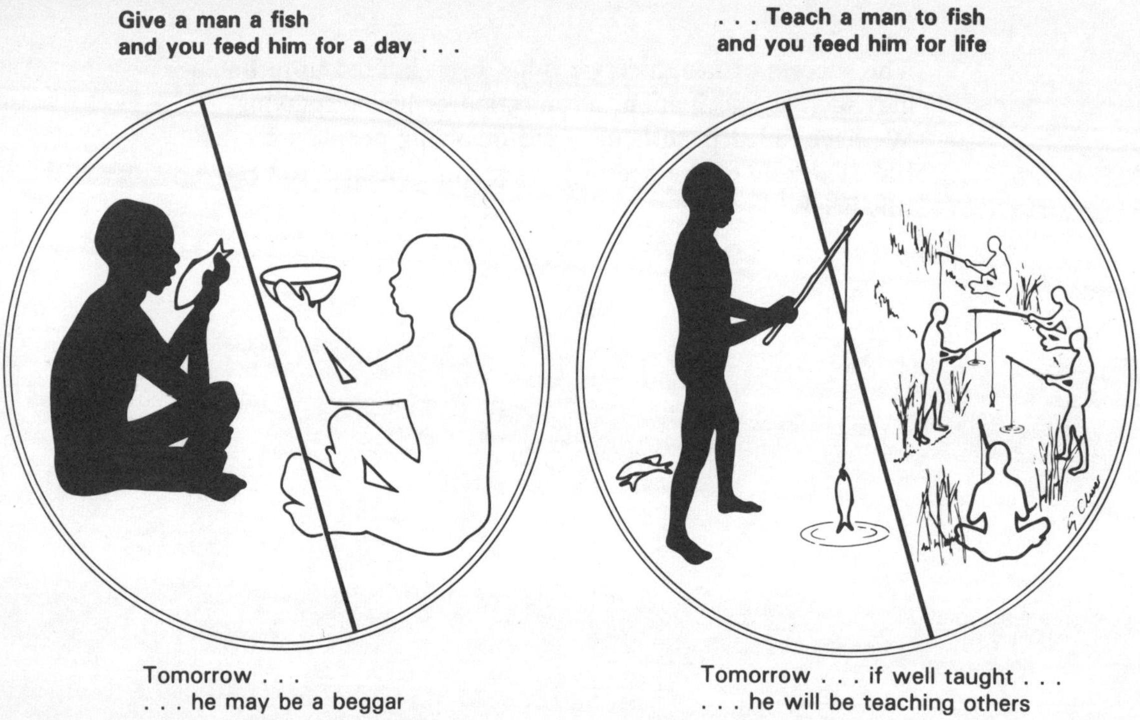

Give a man a fish and you feed him for a day . . .

. . . Teach a man to fish and you feed him for life

Tomorrow . . .
. . . he may be a beggar

Tomorrow . . . if well taught . . .
. . . he will be teaching others

A PILL FOR EVERY ILL?
OR A DISCUSSION ON HOW TO AVOID
ILLNESS NEXT TIME?

Slowly the medical profession is coming to appreciate the
problems of creating dependence. At the same time there is
increasing demand for more action on health. Health is too
important to be left just to doctors.

Fig. 116 Lifestyle and health

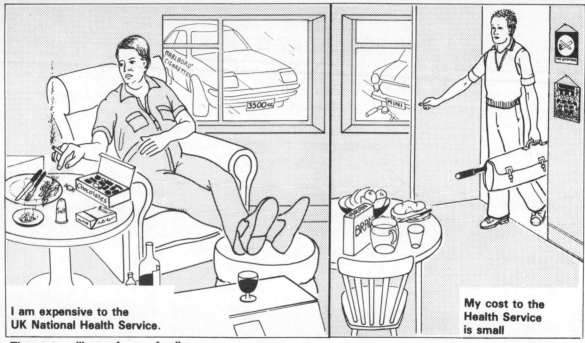

LIFESTYLES ARE AS IMPORTANT AS HEALTH SERVICES

The individual who smokes heavily, drinks too much alcohol, eats an inappropriate diet with much salt, takes too little exercise, drives a large car without seat straps, has put himself at risk of early death. This is 'victim blaming'. Society carries much responsibility in encouraging these 'commerciogenic' illnesses.

David: Around forty years ago, conditions for children and adults in less developed countries of the world started to improve, and there was a decline in death rates with improvement in literacy and life expectancy. Unfortunately, this improvement hardly touched the poorest. That improvement has slowed down, and in some countries even gone into reverse. What would you put this down to?

Hermione: I do not think that we really know the reasons for these trends, we can only make informed guesses. Perhaps the most important was the improvement in economic conditions and the spread of literacy. The low price of fossil fuels made travel over the long distances of less developed countries much easier. However, in those days, we did not realise we were still by-passing the poor; we now appreciate that most of our observations were made from visiting model villages down tarred roads in the dry season, and we were not making the great effort necessary to reach the poor. In the past, we were happy to accept the successes of smallpox eradication, yaws control, the reduction of deaths in areas suffering from malaria, and we forgot about our failures in health care. We easily forget the suffering and the grinding poverty of so many countries as their population increases and outruns their resources, with malnutrition and infective disease becoming rampant. These lead to high child mortality and ensure the parents will want many children.

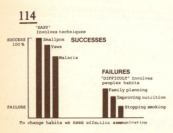

114

'EASY'
Involves techniques

SUCCESS 100 %   Smallpox   **SUCCESSES**
Yaws
Malaria

FAILURES
'DIFFICULT' Involves
peoples habits

Family planning
Improving nutrition
FAILURE   Stopping smoking

To change habits we need effective communication

David: We appreciate how inappropriate it is to 'give a man a fish' instead of 'teaching him how to fish'. We now recognise the importance of teaching and training people to be able to control their environment. Improvement in health in most countries will depend on changes in lifestyle.

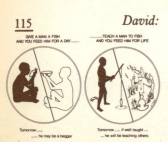

115

GIVE A MAN A FISH
AND YOU FEED HIM FOR A DAY........

........TEACH A MAN TO FISH
AND YOU FEED HIM FOR LIFE

Tomorrow .....
...... he may be a beggar

Tomorrow ..... if well taught ...
... he will be teaching others

Hermione: We need of course to go further; we must try to find out what it is the people want to know. If their 'felt' needs can be met they may be more willing to listen to advice. We must try to help them to be in charge of their own situation. Any help we can provide must be available on their terms.

David: We see this in our own health service in the UK. For years we have been putting so much effort into treating lung cancers, coronary heart disease and high blood pressure. We have assumed that there is nothing we can do about these causes of death. If we only looked to the less developed world, we would find that these conditions do not exist amongst rural peoples there. This implies that they are produced by the environment we have created and are preventable. Only recently have a proportion of doctors become determined to prevent these conditions as a matter of priority.

116

expensive to the
National Health Service
state will care for my family
er my premature death

My cost to the
Health Service
is small

Fig. 117   Communication effectiveness

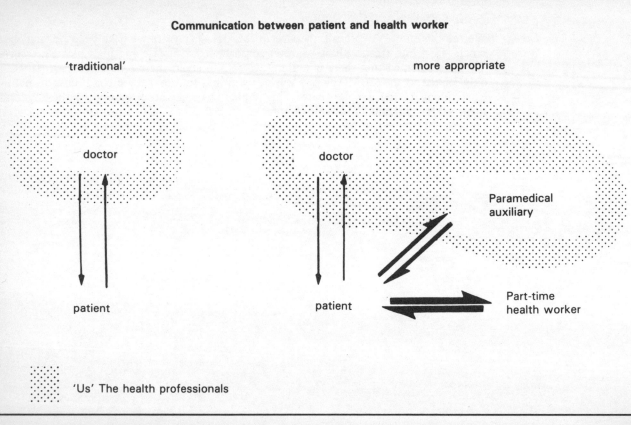

Communication between patient and health worker

WHO COMMUNICATES WELL?

We assume it should be the doctor, but social distance, a different language and a different understanding of the cause of disease makes communication by doctors less effective. The part-time health worker is better placed to communicate effectively.

Fig. 118 Encourage independence

ENCOURAGE INDEPENDENCE

The successful part-time health worker is the liberator of his/her community, not a servant of the health profession.

Fig. 119 The part-time health worker goes to the people

THE PART-TIME HEALTH WORKER

- is chosen by the community to be served
- is trained locally
- is not on any central payroll.

Fig. 120 Share your knowledge

The part-time health workers live and work with the
people they serve. Their first job is to share their
knowledge.

<u>117</u>

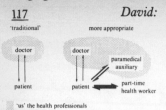

David: Many doctors have no idea how poorly they are communicating with the average patient. If they give any thought to it, their reaction is usually to blame the patient! So often it is other members of the health team who find it is their responsibility to pass on information.

<u>118</u>

Hermione: The success of the part-time health worker, village health worker or whatever the local community health worker is called, must depend on his or her ability to communicate to those in the local family and community circle.

<u>120</u>

David: We can only hope that in the future, doctors will understand the problems of communicating with their patients, and how these can be overcome, particularly through intermediaries such as part-time health workers. These intermediaries do need support and help. Through them, and because they are much closer to the people, we can hope to spread messages to communities such as the need for immunisation, the home management of diarrhoea, a better understanding of nutrition and the spacing of children.

119

David: I have been severely criticised for these illustrations of part-time health workers by a good colleague of mine because I have shown male part-time workers. He quite rightly says that men are inappropriate in this situation, and that mothers who have successfully reared a family can be so much more effective when trained as part-time health workers.

Hermione: This is true, and we must find these women to be part-time health workers, especially in the societies where women cannot move freely, for they will also not easily be able to consult men.

David: We still have so much to learn about these workers, particularly how they can best be chosen. The community, if asked to select who is to become their part-time health worker, have often assumed that they should choose individuals who in the past have been selected to become nurses or medical assistants. After training many are found to be unsuitable. They are asked to look after children, yet are too young to gain the respect of the experienced mother. Their first interest may turn out to be self-interest. They may not be concerned to pass on their knowledge, particularly to those most in need. Work with the local traditional health workers is difficult because they see them as a threat. Frequently their training leads them to find work in the local town.

120

In the majority of successful programmes, very different people have been selected. They are chosen more for their attitude than their education. Many are illiterate but prove to be highly effective as part-time health workers. They usually have deep roots in the community and are respected members. They are usually women who have raised a family of their own. Frequently they have themselves been traditional birth attendants or other traditional providers of health care. If men, they have been successful farmers or herbalists. Their influence is likely to be felt far outside the medical field.

How do you think they are best trained and supervised?

108

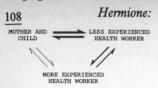

Hermione: Doctors, nurses and other health workers can play some part. But as soon as possible, the training should be taken over by the part-time health workers who have shown themselves to be effective, are respected by their colleagues and have had further training both in health and how the community functions.

David: I know that your colleagues in sociology are most concerned by the way that we use the term 'community' so freely.

Hermione: So often those without experience consider that the communities or villages are fairly simple organisations with leaders recognised by all. This is not so. Villages vary widely and are commonly split by political and other factions.

David: This explains why an experienced colleague of mine from the Philippines spent almost half the time available for training in teaching how to understand the way villages functioned and how the part-time health worker must work if she is to become an agent for change and not just a provider of health care.

Fig. 121 The pyramid on its side

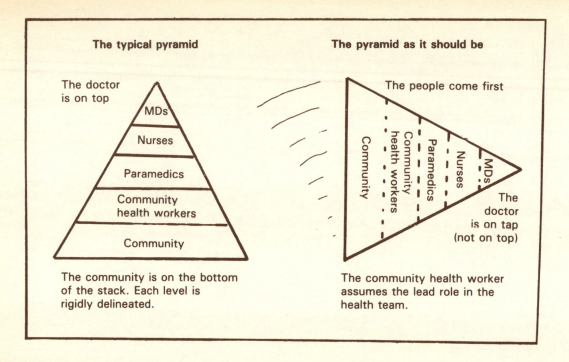

The typical pyramid

The doctor is on top

MDs
Nurses
Paramedics
Community health workers
Community

The community is on the bottom of the stack. Each level is rigidly delineated.

The pyramid as it should be

The people come first

Community
Community health workers
Paramedics
Nurses
MDs

The doctor is on tap (not on top)

The community health worker assumes the lead role in the health team.

Doctors need to develop leadership skills among members of the health team. The doctors and nurses will then have more time to make the best use of their specific medical and caring skills.

Fig. 122   Learning management and delegation

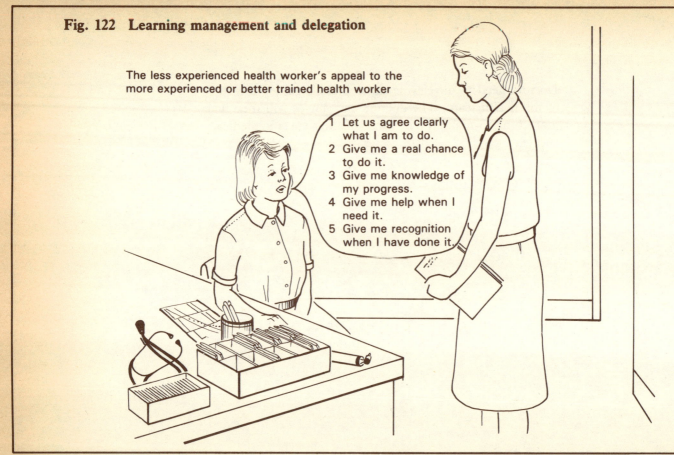

The less experienced health worker's appeal to the more experienced or better trained health worker

1 Let us agree clearly what I am to do.
2 Give me a real chance to do it.
3 Give me knowledge of my progress.
4 Give me help when I need it.
5 Give me recognition when I have done it.

MANAGEMENT AND COMMUNICATION

In a health centre, the ability of the doctors and nurses to manage and communicate are essential. This may be more important than their specific clinical and nursing skills in the value of health care provided.

Fig. 123 'Four-box' health care

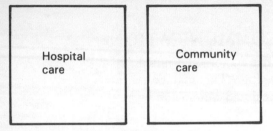

Conventional 'two-box'
view of health care

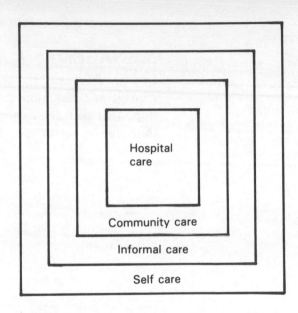

The 'four-box' system of
health care

BRING HOSPITAL AND COMMUNITY CARE TOGETHER

For too long we have considered community and hospital care as separate boxes. They need to be brought together and then the challenge will be to integrate them with informal care and self-care.

Fig. 124 Towards appropriate structures for Primary Health Care

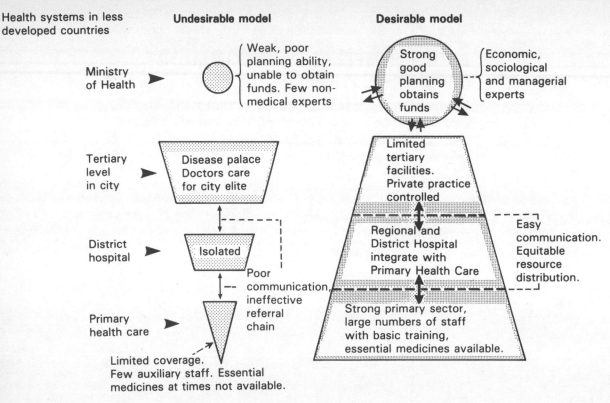

Health systems in less developed countries

Undesirable model

Desirable model

Ministry of Health ▶ Weak, poor planning ability, unable to obtain funds. Few non-medical experts

Strong good planning obtains funds — Economic, sociological and managerial experts

Tertiary level in city ▶ Disease palace Doctors care for city elite

Limited tertiary facilities. Private practice controlled

District hospital ▶ Isolated

Regional and District Hospital integrate with Primary Health Care

Easy communication. Equitable resource distribution.

Poor communication, ineffective referral chain

Primary health care ▶

Strong primary sector, large numbers of staff with basic training, essential medicines available.

Limited coverage. Few auxiliary staff. Essential medicines at times not available.

CHANGING THE STRUCTURE OF HEALTH SERVICES

A management priority must be to restructure the health service model. Emphasis will be placed on a strong primary sector receiving support from all other levels.

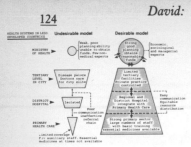

124

David: Over the last few years we have welcomed to the Tropical Child Health Unit a colleague, John Ranken, with specific training in management. His arrival has made a great deal of difference to our thinking and the emphasis we place on management training. The level of health care provided by workers in a primary health centre or small hospital will depend as much on their management skills as on their clinical ability. Unfortunately, these skills are not well taught in medical and nursing schools.

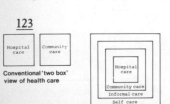

122

123

Conventional 'two box'
view of health care

The 'four-box' system of
health care

Hermione: Yes. Managerial skills are even more required in primary health care than in large hospitals. The primary health care workers are often working in isolation. With the fuel shortage, the local nurse or other supervisor may have great difficulty in helping and supervising their work. There are ways of getting round this. I heard of one place where the nurse in charge arranged for all the local workers to visit her on market day, a day on which they usually travelled to the local town.

The health systems in less developed countries have suffered too long from a narrow-minded view that health care only takes place in hospitals. We need to recognise the network of caring and curing that takes place outside health units, informally, via traditional systems, in the home and by purchase of medicaments. To create more appropriate services and the management which will build them up and maintain them is going to require much rethinking and planning. For too long we have considered community-based health care in terms of only two boxes – hospital care and community care. The challenge is now to involve additionally the informal care that goes on, and self-care, and see how these four can be integrated together.

David: A colleague of ours, Malcolm Segal, believes that the primary health care approach must include three basic ideas:

- That the promotion of health depends fundamentally on improving socio-economic conditions and, in most parts of the world, on the alleviation of poverty and under-development.
- That in this process the mass of the people should be both major activists and the main beneficiaries.
- That the health care system should be restructured to support priority activities at the primary level, because these respond to the most urgent needs of the people.

If we agree with these basic ideas then the structure of health services will have to be changed.

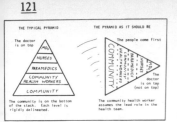

Hermione: Planning in the less developed countries has usually been based on the traditional medical approach of classical epidemiology. What is now required is socio-epidemiological planning which will examine the social side of different conditions. Such epidemiology will particularly examine the deprived groups so that the health service can be restructured to channel services preferentially to those with the greatest need. I know you hope that as a result of this book more health workers will be encouraged to collect information such as depicted in Fig.43 (page 79), Fig.86 (page 149) and Fig.91

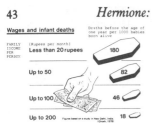

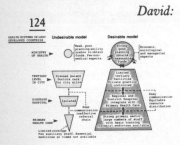

(page 157) for their own city or country. Publication of such local and national figures may lead to action on the problems identified.

David: Many of us think that health care systems in developing countries suffer from a historical development which led the expatriate, and later local, élite to demand that most resources be available for their care through private practice and hospitals. Ministries of Health for the most part are weak and seldom have the government support to make drastic alterations through which health care can be brought to the masses and as a result their health improved.

The most urgent change in most countries is within the government to create a different Ministry of Health. Most existing ministries lurch from one crisis to another. What is required is a ministry capable of planning with economist, sociologist and management experts, capable of standing up against a powerful, well-entrenched and well 'connected' medical fraternity.

Fig. 125 The disciplines that need to work together for health

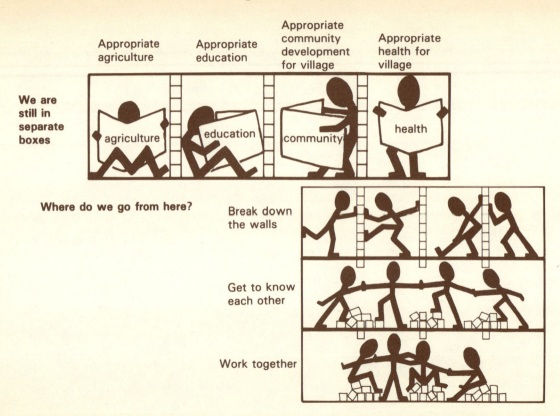

BREAKING DOWN WALLS

We train and work in our boxes. At all levels we need to break down the walls which isolate disciplines.

Fig. 126 Education and health: CHILD-to-child

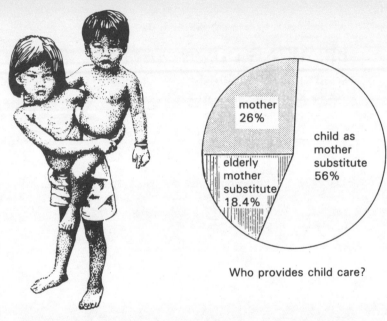

Who provides child care?

The CHILD-to-child programme encourages children of school age to concern themselves with the health, welfare and development of their younger brothers and sisters. It is an attempt by health workers and school teachers to break out of their boxes and work together.

Fig. 127 Networks of information

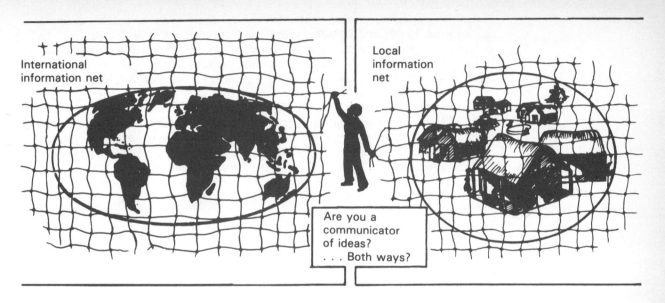

Doctors and nurses have good opportunities to increase their knowledge and ability through the international net. It is their responsibility to strengthen and maintain their links with both nets and to pass ideas both ways.

David: Few doctors have appreciated the importance of effective communication. Unfortunately, the new methods of treatment such as transplant surgery are newsworthy, while the less interesting but far more important declines of mortality through control of infections or improved nutrition do not reach the headlines. To take another example, each day between 10,000 and 20,000 children die from diarrhoea and dehydration. They are buried and mourned by their parents. Most of these children could be alive and healthy if only the parents who are mourning them had been taught a relatively simple message. If they had known how to add the correct quantities of sugar and salt to a cup of water and slowly feed this cup to the child after each stool, these children would be alive and well. This daily tragedy never reaches the headlines; we hear of terrorist actions, war and earthquake where the total deaths are likely to be one percent of the daily tragedy from improperly treated diarrhoea. Those concerned with comprehensive and preventive care (the 'B's in Fig.128) must not allow those concerned with curative care (the 'A's) to continue to dominate the media.

Fig. 128   Whose voice is heard?

In your experience, Hermione, how effective is the communication between the various inputs such as education, health and agriculture in the villages, particularly in Ghana?

Hermione:

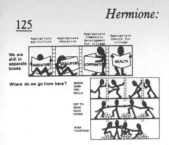

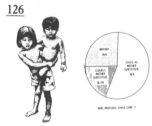

In most countries nearly all these programmes have a vertical structure and there is little communication either at ministry level or in the district or village where it is so important for these groups to work together. However, a few notable projects have been trying hard to work with at least one other sector. There are a number of health and agriculture programmes, also health and community development. What is your experience in this field?

David:

My life has been changed since I became involved with colleagues in education through the CHILD-to-child programme. I now see the immense potential for those in education and health to work together. Through this book there are many examples of how their work is complementary, and I believe this is a responsibility of every health worker from the Minister of Health, the senior medical school teacher, through the district medical officer down to the part-time health worker. Each should know and frequently discuss with a colleague in education, and if possible agriculture and community development, the successes and problems they encounter and how shared activities could achieve much more.

In some communities, more than half the children at any one time are being cared for by older children. CHILD-to-child is an international programme which teaches and encourages children of school age to concern themselves with the health and welfare and development of the younger pre-school brothers and sisters, and other younger children in their community. More than seventeen activity sheets have been developed on such subjects as 'accidents', 'our teeth', 'toys and games', 'understanding children's feelings' and 'a place to play'. One of the experiences of those involved in this programme has been the workshops. At these, those involved in planning primary education sit around a table with health workers, and they come to realise how much those in education and health could depend on, and profit from, close association with other disciplines.

Hermione: The success of the child in the school system will depend heavily on whether she/he has had a stimulating environment in the early years. Many countries are now putting emphasis on pre-school groups with great success in terms of community development, as in Zimbabwe.

127

Information does not flow smoothly in one or two directions but through a most intricate system of nets, by which people gain and pass on information. We particularly need to identify those in developing countries who have some links with the international net, but also have their hands on the local information nets. These are the people through whom ideas on more appropriate primary health care can be brought to the villages and equally important ideas developed in the villages can flow back into the international net. Recently I have been gathering for the WHO a Bibliography of training material on Mother and Child Health Care. I was fascinated to find how much of the more useful material had emanated from those with insight working in the villages. Unfortunately, the links between the nets have tended to become more tenuous, particularly with the increase in energy costs and the shortage of hard currency in so many countries. This has meant that cash is no longer available for books.

David: I am glad that you put this emphasis on books. To me books are, and will remain for some time, the major method of communication. The majority of books in the health field in the past have been written for and by doctors or nurses. The market system for these books means that they are sold through a small number of shops in the capital or big city. These shops are used to a relatively small turnover of books and expect to sell books which cost $50 or $100. If we are to achieve health for all by the year 2000, we shall need large numbers of books in the field of primary health care. These will need to be low cost and readily available through many small bookshops.

Fig. 129

Health workers need and love books

but hate today's prices

Unfortunately, few international organisations have seen this need so far. An exception has been the Swedish International Development Authority, and they have provided Teaching Aids at Low Cost (TALC) with support to provide grants to publishers so that TALC can work with them to bring out low cost books. We are particularly concerned to bring books into the hands of primary health care workers and help them to understand how they can use them.

Fig. 130   The domino theory

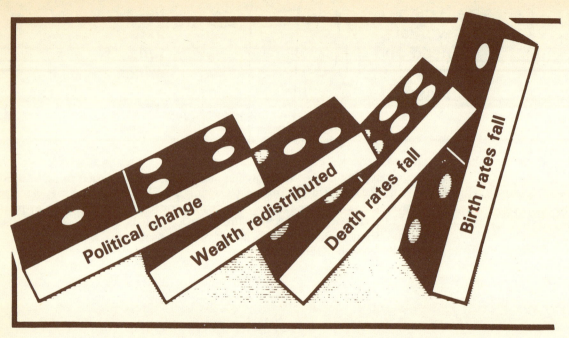

If health workers are concerned to reduce disease and
death, they have a duty to encourage better distribution of
resources through political change.

Fig. 131 Ostriches

When faced with sensitive political
or social issues affecting health . . .

. . . don't stick your neck out
unnecessarily . . .

. . . but don't hide your head
in the sand either.

In the long run, one way can prove as dangerous as the other.

Knock on political doors, but keep out of prison.

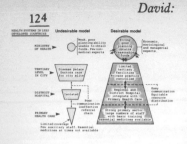

David: If the object of the medical profession is to reduce deaths and bring the birth rate down, then it has to accept that this will only come about in many countries by political change. The political change which brings about redistribution of wealth will affect doctors and their income. For this reason those who 'look for a decline in mortality through wealth redistribution must accept that a large proportion of the health professionals in most countries will resist any change. So often in the Tropical Child Health Unit, either with visitors or with students who come and study with us, our discussion ends on a political note. Segal has suggested some lines along which legislation related to primary health care is needed:

● Economic and tax reform relating to the distribution of wealth and income.
● The establishment of social structures and processes for the democratisation of decision-making.
● The establishment of a national health service.
● Definition of the scope of any private medical sub-sector.
● Education and definitions of health professionals, bonding of graduates to the government service and criteria for career advancement.
● Pharmaceutical and medical equipment.

Hermione: We would all accept that doctors and others in the health profession must come to realise how much politics comes into health provision in their community. Most health workers resist becoming closely involved in politics. However, in all countries health is greatly influenced by politics and the distribution of resources is largely in the hands of politicians. It is not sufficient just to have economic growth to overcome poverty. There must be a more equitable distribution of income. This income includes not only cash and subsistence income but also the 'social wage', which includes education and health care and other public services. Health workers at all levels are gradually collecting more statistics which show the effect on health of income and access to resources.

131

WHEN FACED WITH SENSITIVE POLITICAL
OR SOCIAL ISSUES AFFECTING HEALTH,

DON'T STICK YOUR NECK OUT
UNNECESSARILY,

BUT DON'T HIDE YOUR HEAD
IN THE SAND EITHER.

In the long run, one way can prove as dangerous as the other.

  This and other information on pollution and health related topics must be made available for the politicians and decision-makers in every country. Health care is closely linked with politics. How much people wish to be involved in politics must be the decision of each individual.

CHAPTER FIVE
Where next for children?

'Health is not the only thing, but everything without health is nothing.'
(Mahler '82)

Fig. 132 The priorities for children: Food, health care and play

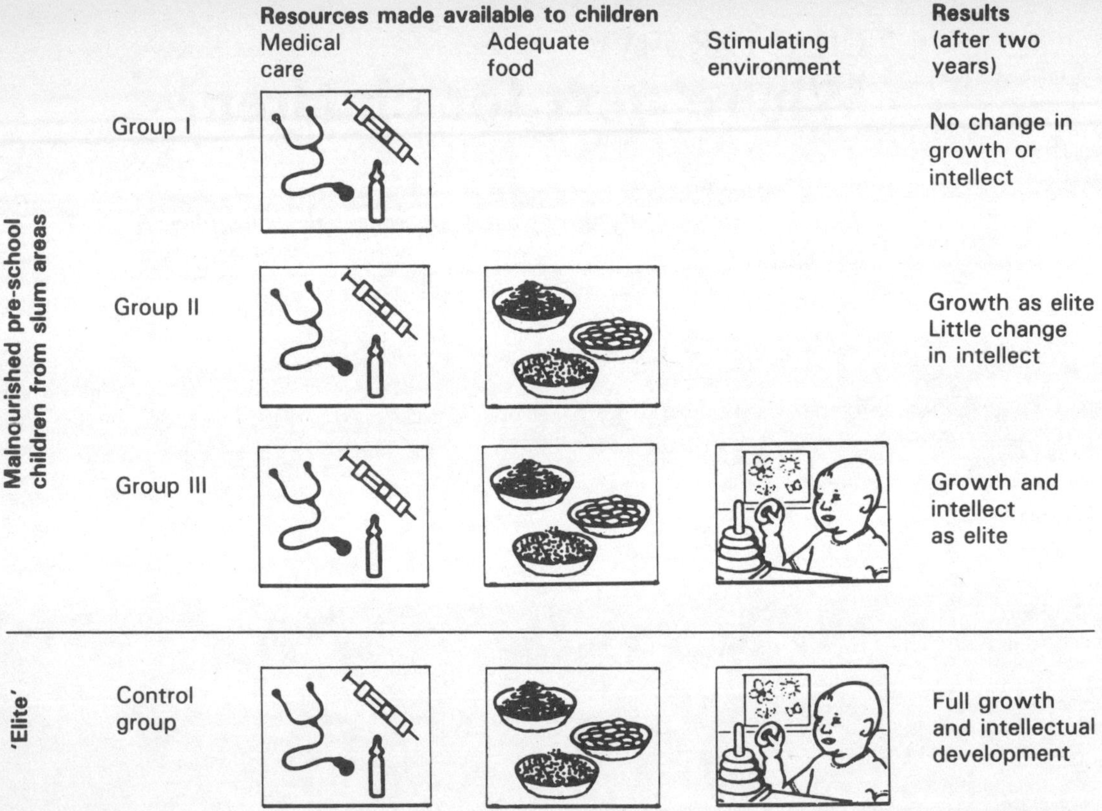

THE PRIORITIES FOR CHILDREN: FOOD, HEALTH CARE, PLAY

Three groups of children were given different services and compared with élite children.

- Health care alone gives no change.
- Adequate food combined with health care gives full physical growth.
- Food, health care *and* stimulation leads to full intellectual development.

Fig. 133   Priorities for improving health

Priority health measures in Third World countries

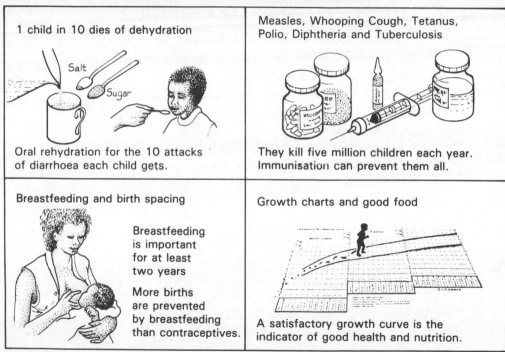

1 child in 10 dies of dehydration

Salt

Sugar

Oral rehydration for the 10 attacks of diarrhoea each child gets.

Measles, Whooping Cough, Tetanus, Polio, Diphtheria and Tuberculosis

They kill five million children each year. Immunisation can prevent them all.

Breastfeeding and birth spacing

Breastfeeding is important for at least two years

More births are prevented by breastfeeding than contraceptives.

Growth charts and good food

A satisfactory growth curve is the indicator of good health and nutrition.

UNICEF has proposed four priorities:
- Oral rehydration
- Immunisation
- Breastfeeding and birth spacing
- Growth charts and adequate feeding.

Hermione: David, it must be now fifteen years since you started to write your book *Paediatric Priorities in the Developing World*, which you have often said changed your life, and more recently led to your being awarded the King Faisal award for your work in primary health care. During these fifteen years, how have your ideas changed on this question of paediatric priorities?

David: I think they have simplified. Visiting the experiment in Cali, Colombia, made me realise that there are priorities other than just providing medical care. In this South American study, three groups of under-nourished children were provided with different resources and compared with a group from well-off élite families.

- Those who received health care alone showed little change after two years.
- Those who had health care and adequate nutrition caught up with their growth, but showed little catch-up in their intelligence.
- Those who had health care, adequate nutrition and a stimulating environment were able to catch up in almost all respects with the élite in the community.

132

Hermione: From this study and many others, we now believe that an adequate food intake is the most important priority for children. However, they also need simple medical care to treat sickness promptly so that the children will maintain their appetite and make best use of the food. At the same time, the children need a stimulating and loving environment.

David: I do not believe it is the job of health professionals to be handing out foods or even food supplements. The whole concept of offering one child in a family a supplement is questionable. This may disrupt the family and there is little evidence of beneficial effects of food supplements on the growth of individual children. We do have an important job in helping mothers to realise whether their children are having enough food by the way they are growing. Doctors together with all health workers have a responsibility, with guidance from nutritionists, in helping mothers to see that the child has the right foods in sufficient quantities, and to make feeding of children during and after illness a priority of treatment. I think we have a responsibility too to

133

Priority Health Measures in Third World Countries (GOBI-FFF)

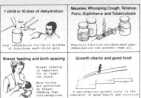

1 child in 10 dies of dehydration	Measles, Whooping Cough, Tetanus, Polio, Diphtheria and Tuberculosis
Oral rehydration for the 10 attacks of diarrhoea each child gets	They kill 5 million children each year. Immunization can prevent them all
Breast feeding and birth spacing	Growth charts and good food
Breast feeding is important for at least two years. More births are prevented by breast feeding than contraceptives	A satisfactory growth curve is the indicator of good health and nutrition

help educationists and parents in less developed countries to see that children have a secure, loving and stimulating environment.

In this chapter we shall be looking at priorities. We will take the four priorities of UNICEF, which are central to the child survival and development revolution; Growth Charts to monitor health and adequate food intake, Oral Rehydration, Breastfeeding with Birth Spacing and Immunisation. These four priorities spell out part of the acronym 'GOBI' — FFF. We will discuss them in a different order taking the most urgent first.

The letters FFF stand for Female literacy, Family planning or birth spacing and Food supplementation. Of these, Female literacy has already been dealt with, as has birth spacing. Food supplementation will be linked with growth monitoring and the use of growth charts.

Small children are often sick and lose their appetite. They need easily accessible health care; basic but comprehensive health care need not be costly. Children need a stimulating environment if they are to reach their full intelligence. Parents, with the health worker and all those caring for small children, need to work together, for these young children are the future of the nation.

Fig. 134 Each child under five in less developed countries has 10 attacks

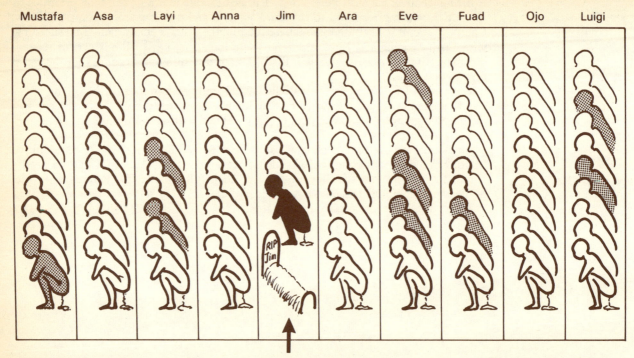

Mustafa   Asa   Layi   Anna   Jim   Ara   Eve   Fuad   Ojo   Luigi

Each figure represents
one attack of diarrhoea

1 in 10 children die of
diarrhoea and dehydration

10% have significant
dehydration

DIARRHOEA IS SO COMMON

The very frequency of diarrhoea deceives parents and health workers.

In the less developed countries, one in ten of the attacks leads to significant dehydration.

Only one in a hundred episodes is fatal —

BUT ONE IN TEN *CHILDREN* MAY DIE FROM DIARRHOEA.

Fig. 135   Diarrhoea kills 1 child in 10

Each child has 10 attacks before the age of 5

Fig. 136 Water, sugar and salt, not dangerous diarrhoea medicines

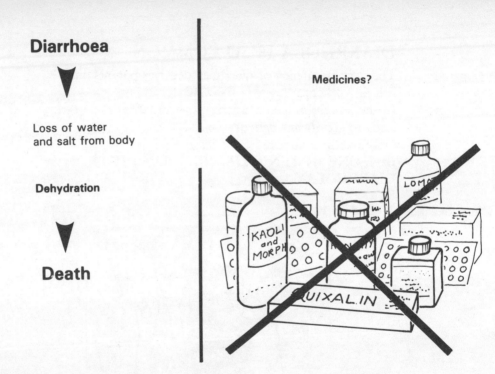

Diarrhoea

Loss of water
and salt from body

Dehydration

Death

Medicines?

Diarrhoea is caused by bacteria, viruses and their toxins. The body's defence is to wash these out as diarrhoea. We need to replace the water and salt. Sugar is also needed for these to be absorbed. Medicines seldom help.

Fig. 137 Sugar carries salt into the body

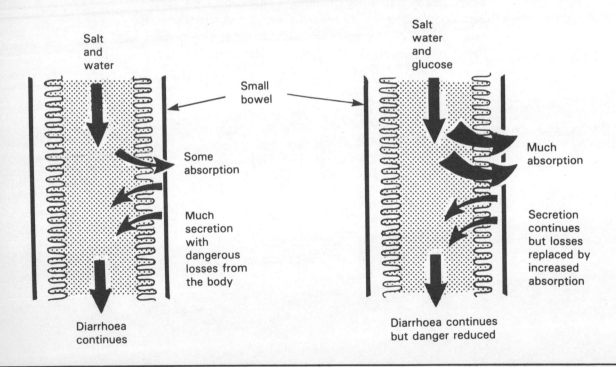

Replacement of fluids by mouth in acute diarrhoea

Salt and water

Salt water and glucose

Small bowel

Some absorption

Much secretion with dangerous losses from the body

Diarrhoea continues

Much absorption

Secretion continues but losses replaced by increased absorption

Diarrhoea continues but danger reduced

Diarrhoea takes away water from the body. Like a flower without water, the body droops.
Unlike a flower the child's body also needs salt. Sugar is required to help the body to absorb the salt and water.

Fig. 138 Flowers need water

Fig. 139 Sugar and salts for diarrhoea

UNICEF
ORAL
REHYDRATION SALTS

Sodium Chloride	3.5 g
Potassium Chloride	1.5 g
Sodium Bicarbonate	2.5 g
Glucose	20.0 g
Flavouring	0.5 g
Total weight	28.0 g

Directions
Dissolve in ONE LITRE of drinking water
To be taken orally—

Infants — over a 24 hour period
Children — over a 6 to 8 hour period
Or as otherwise directed
under medical supervision

CAUTION
DO NOT BOIL SOLUTION

مسجل بوزارة الصحة رقم ١٣١٣٨

For 1,000 cc of water

For 200 cc of water

Governments with help from UNICEF and WHO produced 200 million packages in 1985. In many countries the smaller package for just a cupful has proved more acceptable but is more expensive to produce.

Fig. 140 Managing diarrhoea in the home

Simple ways of measuring salt and sugar

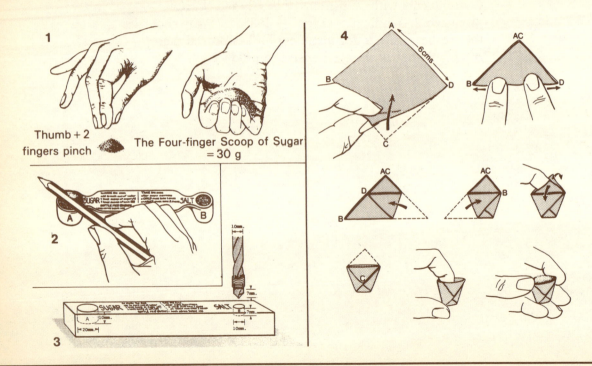

Thumb + 2 fingers pinch

The Four-finger Scoop of Sugar = 30 g

Most episodes of diarrhoea can be managed at home with a simple salt and sugar solution.

1 Some countries use a two-finger pinch of salt and 'fistful' of sugar.

2 A two-ended spoon can be made in plastic.

3 The same can be made locally in wood.

4 A 6 cm (sugar) and 3 cm (salt) square of paper can be folded to make a measuring cup.

Fig. 141 Local measures for making salt and sugar rehydration solution

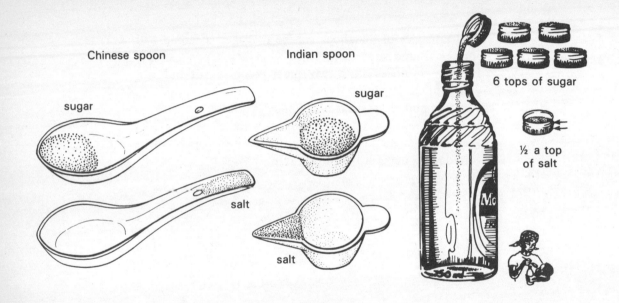

Chinese spoon

sugar

salt

Indian spoon

sugar

salt

6 tops of sugar

½ a top
of salt

LOCAL MEASURES

In Asia, local spoons have been used: in Africa, a bottle and top.

For those children who do not get oral rehydration soon enough, the parents must know the signs of dehydration.

Fig. 142 Parents need to know signs of dehydration

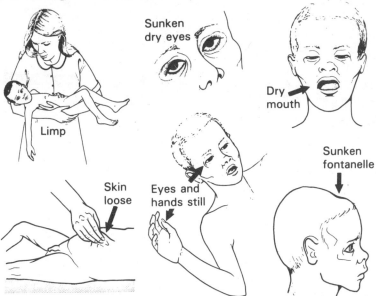

Sunken dry eyes

Dry mouth

Sunken fontanelle

Limp

Skin loose

Eyes and hands still

Fig. 143 Oral rehydration in home and hospital

Valuable in hospital

Invaluable in home

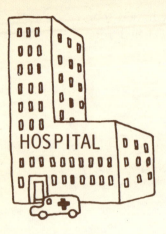

Reduces cost
Increases safety

No intravenous treatment
available or necessary

The revolution in management of diarrhoea has occurred in home and hospital.

Fig. 144 Rehydration therapy, University Hospital, Haiti

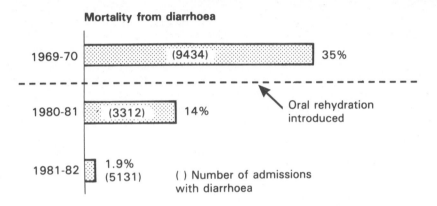

Mortality from diarrhoea

1969-70   (9434)   35%

Oral rehydration introduced

1980-81   (3312)   14%

1981-82   1.9% (5131)

( ) Number of admissions with diarrhoea

- Malnutrition in 60% of those admitted.
- About 15% with severe dehydration get three hours intravenous treatment.
- Remainder get *oral rehydration only*.

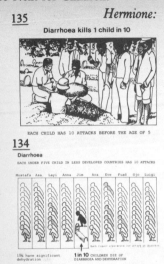

135

Diarrhoea kills 1 child in 10

EACH CHILD HAS 10 ATTACKS BEFORE THE AGE OF 5

134

Diarrhoea

EACH UNDER FIVE CHILD IN LESS DEVELOPED COUNTRIES HAS 10 ATTACKS

Mustafa Asa Layi Anna Jim Ara Eve Fuad Ojo Luigi

10% have significant dehydration

1 in 10 CHILDREN DIE OF DIARRHOEA AND DEHYDRATION

Hermione: Of all the simple comprehensive health care messages that people need, oral rehydration is the most important. Every tenth child born in some less developed countries is likely to die of diarrhoea. Around 5 million die each year from diarrhoea and dehydration. However, as every child is likely to have around 10 attacks during the first five years of life, there may be 99 attacks of diarrhoea before there is a fatality. An important discovery has been the relationship between severe episodes of dehydration and the subsequent incidence of cataract many years later. Management of dehydration saves lives, prevents malnutrition and means that cataract and years of impaired sight and blindness will be prevented. We know villages around the world where for practical purposes every episode of diarrhoea is treated within the home by the mother, sometimes with support and help from the village health worker. The very frequency of diarrhoea makes it almost mandatory that it has to be treated simply at home and the exciting new message we need to make known is that this treatment is very satisfactory, in fact better than that offered by hospitals and doctors in the past.

136

DIARRHOEA

▼

Loss of Water and Salt from Body

DEHYDRATION

▼

Death

MEDICINES ?

David: We have good evidence that so called diarrhoea medicines are at times harmful. The aim of most medicines is to stop the movements of the gut so the diarrhoea stool stays within the body. As a result the child absorbs more of the toxins produced by the germs in the bowel. Diarrhoea is the way that nature 'flushes out the germs and their toxins' from the bowel. Our job must be to see that the water and salt lost from the body is quickly replaced in adequate quantities. Mothers who are given medicines for their child's diarrhoea think these are important and do not put the emphasis where it is needed, that is on drinks of water with salt and sugar. The great development has been the research which shows that the salt lost with water causing the dehydration cannot be treated with salt water alone. For the salt and water to be absorbed, our bowel also needs glucose. However, sugar or any cereal is broken down quickly by the gut into glucose. Each molecule of glucose carries a molecule of salt into the body. The

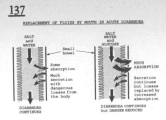

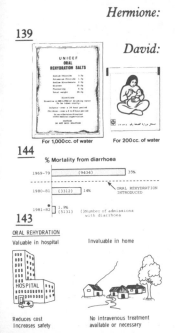

medicines commonly used are of no value and some are harmful. If we could stop doctors giving medicine and instead get them to teach the mothers to give water with salt and sugar in the right quantities, then the mortality around the world from diarrhoea would be greatly reduced. Perhaps in the future we may have medicines which will stop the secretion of water from the bowel but even these may not necessarily be as good, as we need the water to flush out the toxins from the body. The important message will always remain that we have to put the water, salt and sugar back.

Hermione: The response to this message has been tremendous in the way that governments have produced oral rehydration packets.

David: The United Nations Organisations have excelled themselves in the speed of getting these packages around, and teaching about their use. This has saved many lives. An example of what can be achieved is shown by this diagram from Haiti University Hospital. The mortality from diarrhoea in the wards was reduced from 35% to under 2% and the majority of patients are treated just with oral rehydration. Only around 15% of the severely dehydrated children required three hours of intravenous therapy. Also the incidence of severe dehydration is becoming less as the mothers who are taught to rehydrate children, both in hospital wards and clinics, take the message home and start to rehydrate their children even before they are brought to hospital. We hope that soon many of them will be able to manage diarrhoea in their own home using salt, sugar and water, and keeping the packages for severe cases.

140

Simple ways of measuring Salt and Sugar

141

Local measures for making salt and sugar rehydration solution

Chinese Spoon   Indian Spoon

SUGAR   SUGAR
SALT   SALT

6 Tops of sugar
½ a Top of salt

142

Sunken dry eyes
Dry mouth
Limp
Skin loose
Eyes and hands still
Sunken fontanelle

Hermione: The production of these packages has of course not gone without criticism. By using packages we are still depending on the drug industry to produce the packages and so we are not putting the responsibility where it belongs, back into the community and with the mother. Probably more important than the question of distributing the packages is getting the message to people so that they can manage this condition themselves. They can learn to produce their own oral rehydration solutions and recognise the signs of dehydration.

David: The newer so-called 'Cereal O.R.S.' replaces the glucose with rice powder and is similar to the 'kunjee' used in many parts of Asia. In the past, rice water has been traditionally used for the treatment of diarrhoea. Unfortunately the amount of starch in rice water is very variable and so it is better to teach to use actual rice powder. The quantity of this is 50 grams per litre. This means that if we are making it up in a cupful of 250 cc, we need approximately 12 gm, or 3 of the sugar-measures, of starch.

This of course needs to be cooked and needs the usual quantity of salt added to it (0.9 gm). Using this, the volume of faeces in the diarrhoea is reduced by about a quarter and the amount of vomiting may be reduced by half. There is now plenty of research to show that children with diarrhoea need to be fed just as soon as they will take food. In the past, both grandmother and doctor thought food should be restricted during episodes of diarrhoea. In fact a child needs more food not less when it is fighting an infection. Food helps the gut return to normal more rapidly.

138

137

REPLACEMENT OF FLUIDS BY MOUTH IN ACUTE DIARRHOEA

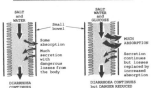

Hermione: When teaching we need to start from what people already know and understand. Show them two flowers, one which has been left in a glass without water for 24 hours and the other which has had water. Go into the difference and how water is needed by flowers. Then suggest that children or adults who have diarrhoea also need water, but need salt as well. Remind them that body fluids like sweat and tears taste salty.

In the future when parents see a child with diarrhoea, they need to understand that the child's body is trying to wash out dirty material from inside. The child will require extra fluid so that it can wash the material out well. For this reason they need to give water and the right amount of salt and sugar, so as to help the child.

141

Local measures for making salt and sugar rehydration solution

David: We also need to look around homes in every community to find out which measures the mothers will find most easy to use for measuring sugar and salt.

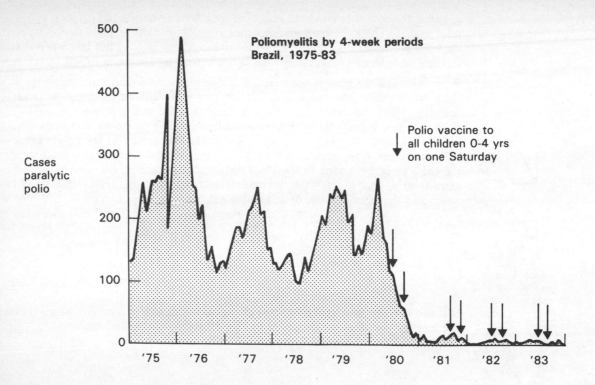

Fig. 145 Poliomyelitis decline in Brazil

Poliomyelitis by 4-week periods
Brazil, 1975-83

Cases paralytic polio

Polio vaccine to
all children 0-4 yrs
on one Saturday

'75 '76 '77 '78 '79 '80 '81 '82 '83

Fig. 146 Polio: a disease of antiquity that now should be stopped

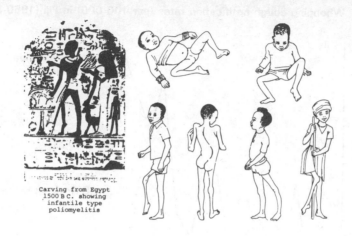

Carving from Egypt
1500 B.C. showing
infantile type
poliomyelitis

IMMUNISATION: STOP POLIO

Of all public health measures, immunisation has the
greatest potential. Immunisation can eradicate a disease like
polio, present since ancient times, in one year.

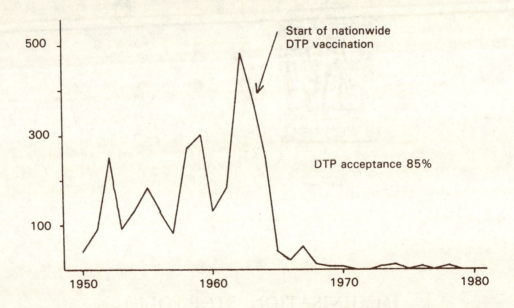

Fig. 147 Whooping cough eradicated in Fiji

Whooping cough notification rates (per 100 000) in Fiji (1950-80)

Start of nationwide
DTP vaccination

DTP acceptance 85%

An island such as Fiji can eradicate whooping cough by immunisation. Eradication in other countries is more difficult due to unjustified fears of a reaction to the vaccine making it less popular with health workers and mothers. If the relative frequency of adverse reaction to DPT immunisation is compared with the complications from natural whooping coughs, health workers will realise their responsibility in strongly advocating the use of this vaccine.

	Whooping cough per 100,000 cases	DPT vaccine per 100,000 doses
Permanent brain damage	600 – 2,000	0.2 – 0.6
Death	100 – 4,000	0.2
Encephalopathy, encephalitis	90 – 4,000	0.1 – 3.0
Convulsions	600 – 8,000	0.3 – 90
Shock	—	0.5 – 30

(source WHO)

Fig. 148 Decline of tetanus of the newborn

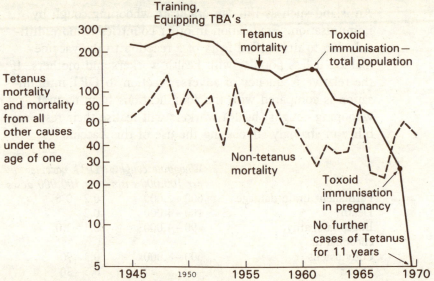

**Census tract (pop. ≃9000) Schweitzer Hospital, Haiti
Tetanus and non tetanus mortality**

Training, Equipping TBA's

Tetanus mortality

Toxoid immunisation— total population

Tetanus mortality and mortality from all other causes under the age of one

Non-tetanus mortality

Toxoid immunisation in pregnancy

No further cases of Tetanus for 11 years

Tetanus of the newborn became less common when the traditional midwives were trained. It was dramatically reduced after offering tetanus immunisation in pregnancy and was eliminated when offered to all women.

Fig. 149 Measles decline in the US

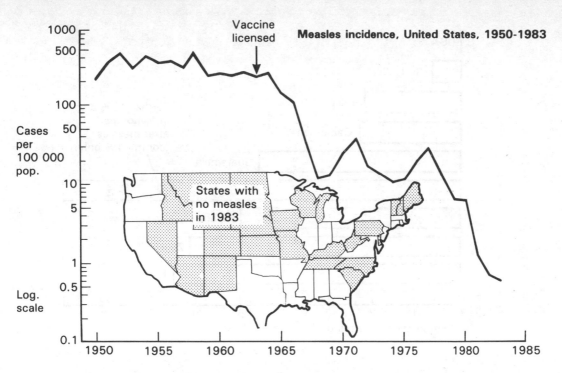

The US has almost got rid of measles.
This suggests that eradication worldwide is possible.

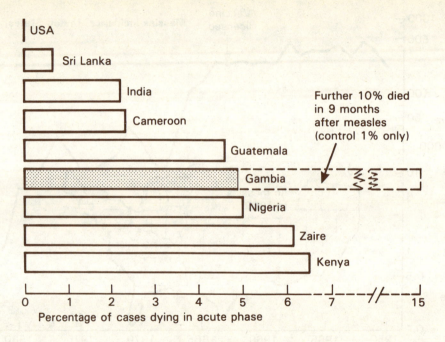

Fig. 150   Child deaths during and following measles

Further 10% died in 9 months after measles (control 1% only)

Percentage of cases dying in acute phase

PREVENTING THE LONG-TERM EFFECTS OF MEASLES

Not only is there a high mortality and much permanent disability from measles, but measles also upsets the immune system of the child and this may lead to many more deaths in the months following measles.

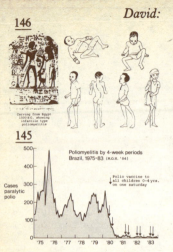

146

Carving from Egypt
1500 B.C. showing
infantile type
poliomyelitis

145

Poliomyelitis by 4-week periods
Brazil, 1975-83 (M.O.H. '84)

Cases
paralytic
polio

Polio vaccine to
all children 0-4 yrs.
on one saturday

'75 '76 '77 '78 '79 '80 '81 '82 '83

David: Of all the technologies that can help children in the less developed world, immunisation must be a priority. Poliomyelitis is an ancient disease and was depicted in the drawings on the Egyptian temples. Oral poliomyelitis vaccine has led to the disappearance of the disease in most developed countries. A number of South American countries, including Brazil, have undertaken a policy of mass immunisation of all small children and pregnant women twice a year, with a dramatic disappearance of the disease. This was achieved by turning immunisation from being a health measure and making it a political issue. In a number of countries now, programmes have been developed involving political parties, the army, the religious groups, as well as voluntary agencies. On the appointed days, these groups co-operate to take the immunisation programme to both the most remote and also the least privileged children in the country.

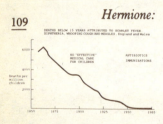

109

DEATHS BELOW 15 YEARS ATTRIBUTED TO SCARLET FEVER,
DIPHTHERIA, WHOOPING COUGH AND MEASLES. England and Wales

NO 'EFFECTIVE'
MEDICAL CARE
FOR CHILDREN

ANTIBIOTICS
IMMUNISATIONS

Deaths per
million
children

1850   1875   1900   1925   1950   1985

Hermione: I think it may seem strange to our readers that we are putting great emphasis on immunisation. Surely we have already shown that in Europe the mortality from the common diseases of children for which we have vaccines declined long before these vaccines were made available.

David: Yes, this is true, but it is also true that vaccines along with comprehensive care can dramatically reduce the mortality of existing underprivileged populations. The following gives some idea of the size of the problem. Of every 1,000 children born in developing countries, WHO estimate that:
● five will grow up disabled with poliomyelitis

- ten will die of neonatal tetanus
- twenty will succumb to whooping cough
- thirty will die as a result of measles.

I like the following quotation:

'In the hands of able leaders and in populations of up to 60,000–70,000, well-designed and effectively operated projects can reduce infant mortality and child mortality rates by one third to one half or more within one to five years, at a cost of less than the equivalent of 2 per cent of per capita income — an amount no greater than that currently being allocated to health nationally.' (Gwatkin 1980)

I was fortunate enough to be involved in one of the ten projects described in that account, and to me it is clear that immunisation, and particularly that against measles, whooping cough and tetanus, can have a dramatic effect on the mortality in a village.

Recently fresh emphasis has been placed on neonatal tetanus. New studies have shown that up to 60 in every thousand children born in some countries may die within the first two weeks from neonatal tetanus due to infection of the umbilical cord. This may be reduced by improving the methods used in caring for the cord by the traditional birth attendant. However, the practical and cost-effective method is the immunisation of all women against tetanus as was shown in this study in Haiti. More countries are now aiming to eradicate this disease by a programme to immunise all women.

148

Hermione: I know that you have made a special study of measles and you were perhaps the first to write in detail about the 'severe measles' of Africa. How important is this in the overall mortality of children?

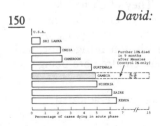

150

David: In less developed countries, measles is the most severe of the common diseases of children. Around 2–5% or even more may die in the severe acute stages. Death occurs due to diarrhoea, pneumonia or a number of other manifestations. We used to call these 'complications' but we now understand them to be part of the severe disease. However, deaths and permanent disability from acute measles may be only half the problem the disease creates. Due to its effects on the nutrition of the child and the immune system of the body, there may be as many additional deaths in the nine months after the disease as during the acute stage.

281

5 Where Next for Children?

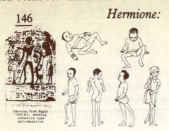

146

Carving from Egypt
1500 B.C. showing
infantile type
poliomyelitis

148

CENSUS TRACT (pop. 25000) SCHWEITZER HOSPITAL HAITI
TETANUS AND NON TETANUS MORTALITY, Maternal Histories [Berggren '80]

Hermione: A few years ago, 'lameness surveys' were developed, produced by school teachers. They gave us a rapid and reasonably accurate method for assessing the prevalence of poliomyelitis. Now a new method of enquiring about deaths of newborns is giving us figures from many countries about neonatal tetanus. We shall never eradicate this disease, as tetanus spore will always be around, but as shown in Haiti, and many countries, we can make it a rarity.

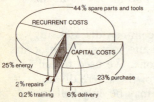

87

Breakdown of Lifetime Costs of Cold Chain Equipment Over 10 year period (WHO/EPI/GAG/'83/WP.1)

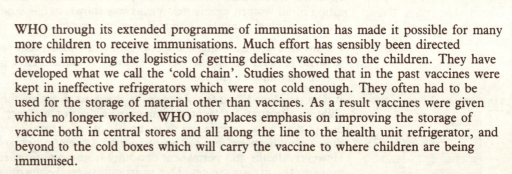

44% spare parts and tools
RECURRENT COSTS
CAPITAL COSTS
25% energy
2% repairs
0.2% training
6% delivery
23% purchase

David: WHO through its extended programme of immunisation has made it possible for many more children to receive immunisations. Much effort has sensibly been directed towards improving the logistics of getting delicate vaccines to the children. They have developed what we call the 'cold chain'. Studies showed that in the past vaccines were kept in ineffective refrigerators which were not cold enough. They often had to be used for the storage of material other than vaccines. As a result vaccines were given which no longer worked. WHO now places emphasis on improving the storage of vaccine both in central stores and all along the line to the health unit refrigerator, and beyond to the cold boxes which will carry the vaccine to where children are being immunised.

Hermione: Do you think we can hope to eradicate any other disease as we have eradicated smallpox?

David: The only one that I can see which is at all possible, and I think even probable, is measles, which we might eradicate by the end of the century if not this decade. Measles was estimated to have been responsible for the deaths of 2.5 million children in 1983. Of all public health measures, the most cost-effective is measles vaccine if successfully used. The USA and a few other countries are leading the way on the eradication of measles. We in the UK are lagging behind.

Hermione: Governments and WHO have already gone a long way in spreading immunisation to where it is needed. India protects 6 million of her 25 million children from whooping cough and prevents 80,000 deaths. Brazil protected half of its children by giving 2.5 million doses of measles vaccine in 1983 and prevented at least 50,000 deaths.

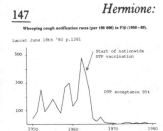

147

Whooping cough notification rates (per 100 000) in Fiji (1950–80).

Lancet June 18th '83 p.1381

Start of nationwide DTP vaccination

DTP acceptance 85%

Fig. 151 A refrigerator for vaccines only

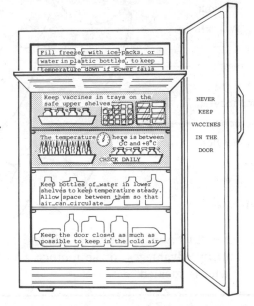

Fill freezer with ice packs, or water in plastic bottles, to keep temperature down if power fails

Keep vaccines in trays on the safe upper shelves

The temperature here is between 0°C and +8°C

CHECK DAILY

Keep bottles of water in lower shelves to keep temperature steady. Allow space between them so that air can circulate

Keep the door closed as much as possible to keep in the cold air

NEVER KEEP VACCINES IN THE DOOR

Fig. 152 Suckling has advantages to the mother and child

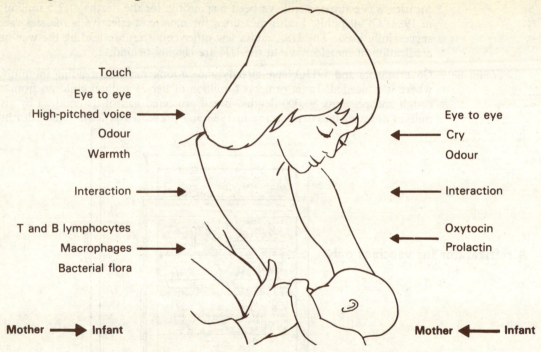

Touch
Eye to eye
High-pitched voice
Odour
Warmth

Interaction

T and B lymphocytes
Macrophages
Bacterial flora

Eye to eye
Cry
Odour

Interaction

Oxytocin
Prolactin

Mother ➔ **Infant**

Mother ⬅ **Infant**

Recent research has revealed, and still is revealing, the
many advantages to the mother who suckles and the infant
who is suckled.

Fig. 153 Frequent suckling in a traditional society

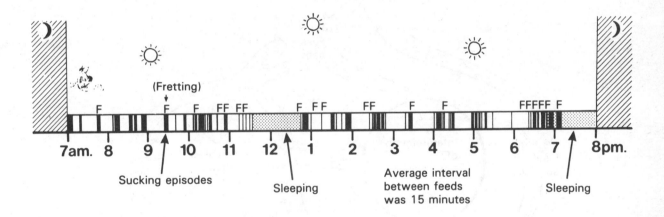

A day's observation of breastfeeding
(female infant aged 1 year)

(Fretting)

F   F   F   FF FF   F   F F   FF   F   F   FFFFF F

Sucking episodes

Sleeping

Average interval
between feeds
was 15 minutes

Sleeping

7am. 8   9   10 11 12   1   2   3   4   5   6   7   8pm.

In the traditional societies from which all societies have
developed, suckling is frequent.

Fig. 154   Too little suckling leads to problems

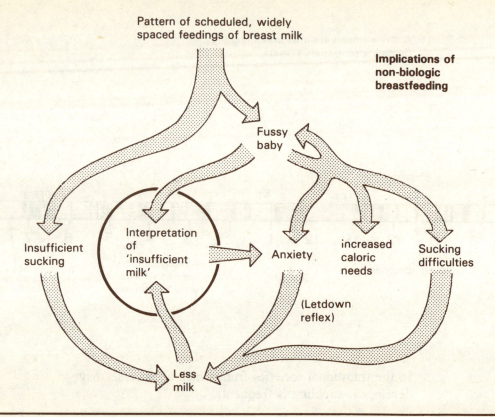

Pattern of scheduled, widely spaced feedings of breast milk

Implications of non-biologic breastfeeding

Fussy baby

Insufficient sucking

Interpretation of 'insufficient milk'

Anxiety

increased caloric needs

Sucking difficulties

(Letdown reflex)

Less milk

For small babies, attempting to allow suckling at only two-
to three-hour intervals is a new development over the last
100 years. It is non-biologic and is responsible for many of
the difficulties encountered by 'westernised' women in
establishing and maintaining effective breastfeeding.

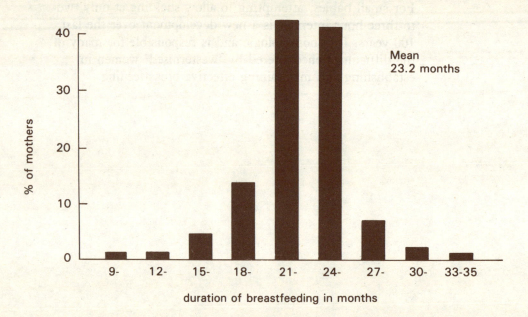

Fig. 155 Duration of suckling in months

Duration of breastfeeding: 291 mothers in a West African village

Mean
23.2 months

% of mothers

duration of breastfeeding in months

In traditional societies, mothers suckled for two to three years.

Fig. 156   Suckling and conception

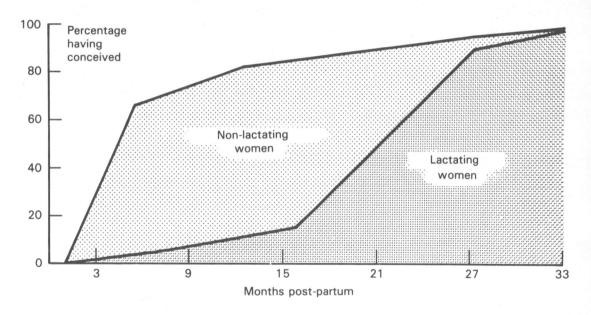

**Conception rates post-partum in lactating
and non-lactating Eskimo women**

Suckling delays the birth of more infants in our world than
all contraceptive measures.

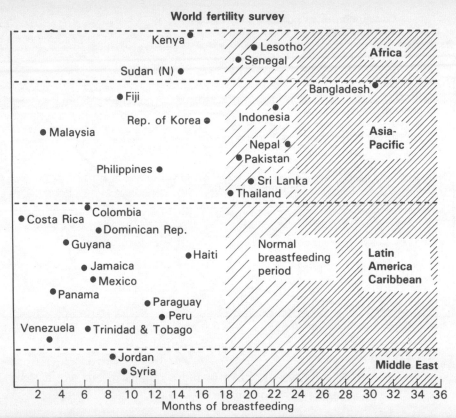

Fig. 157 Median length of breastfeeding

DECLINE OF SUCKLING WORLD-WIDE

Few countries remain unaffected by this trend. Closely associated with this is a shortening of the birth interval.

Fig. 158 Return to suckling in the North

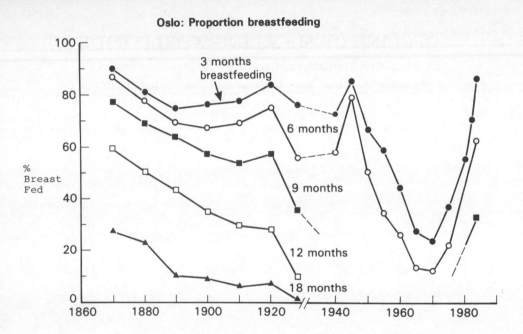

Oslo: Proportion breastfeeding

SUCKLING RETURNS IN THE NORTH

The duration of breastfeeding fell rapidly between 1940 – 1960. This trend has been reversed. Many European mothers now suckle their infants for 1 – 3 years.

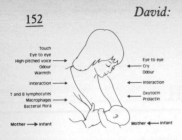

152

David: Breastfeeding has many advantages to the mother and the child and is of great importance in the development of the infant and its relationship with the mother and the outside world. If full physical development is all that parents are looking for, then this can be achieved in the **developed** world by the use of breast milk substitutes. However, in the situation of developing countries, even simple physical growth is difficult to achieve through the use of breast milk substitutes. The environment is only rarely suitable for preparing breast milk substitutes in a clean way, free from dangerous germs. In a traditional society such as in parts of **West Africa** suckling continues for two years or more.

Hermione: Much has been said over the last few years of the ill-effects of breast milk substitutes which have been exported to the less developed countries of the world in such large quantities. Only now are we beginning to realise that the important message is the *advantages* to mother and child of normal suckling.

David: We have, I think, put too much emphasis on the measurable advantages of breast-feeding such as the increased contact and interaction and the macrophages, the hormones and bacterial flora. Have we been reticent in bringing forward the question of 'sexual pleasure to the mother'? I well remember a friend of mine saying that she thought feeding in public was like having 'sex on a park bench'.

Hermione: I think that is fairly strong language. It is also muddling any pleasure in breastfeeding, with the prudity felt by some women in feeling they have to get half undressed to feed the baby! The important thing about breastfeeding is the mother's attitude. It can be done so discreetly that no-one knows there's a baby around. I suspect women who are comfortable with themselves and their bodies are also those who have no problem with breastfeeding: whereas those whose self-image has been dominated by media emphasis on breasts as sexual objects find it more difficult and, like your friend, not something they want to do in a public place. I enjoy being in many developing countries (and also Scandinavia) where it seems breastfeeding is widely accepted as the norm and no-one takes any notice.

Much more important than any pleasure in breastfeeding is the convenience. Once breastfeeding is well-established, feeding takes only a few minutes; there is no crying as when a bottle is being prepared and most mothers find they can continue with what they were doing or soon return to it with relatively little interference. Certainly breast-feeding can be pleasurable, although it is also at times exhausting and, when things go wrong, uncomfortable and painful. This is where we need more help for mothers; particularly in the early weeks after delivery. Women who have delivered in hospital may be without local support or appropriate medical advice if problems arise. Of all the advice and help she needs, the most important is that of increasing the number of times the baby needs to be allowed to suckle.

<u>153</u>

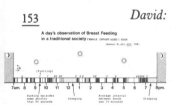

A day's observation of Breast Feeding in a traditional society FEMALE INFANT AGED 1 YEAR

David: In the past, when I have spent years in less developed countries helping mothers with their children, I of course saw mothers breastfeeding frequently. However, I did not understand how frequent this was nor the significance until I came across these observations on an infant in Southern Africa.

Hermione: This one observation you quote may be misleading. I wonder if this child had a mild fever and is thirsty or has been unwell and is now getting better. Neither of my children suckled so frequently except when there was something wrong or they were recovering.

David: You may well be right; unfortunately it is the only study I know where suckling was observed for a whole day. Unfortunately even this one omitted the important night time feeding. Almost certainly this child was not getting sufficient and was not getting much other food and this encouraged it to suckle frequently. Probably the child had had a recent infection and due to less suckling during that time, the child on the day of the study was making good this previous shortage.

Hermione: It is extraordinary how the medical profession has picked up the strange idea that mothers who are well nourished could have insufficient milk. There is plenty of evidence that less well-nourished mothers, and in fact very malnourished mothers, in less developed countries succeed in breastfeeding very well.

David: Breastfeeding rigidly spaced every three to four hours as practised by some women in Western countries leads to many difficulties and the assumption by many that they are unable to produce sufficient milk. Mothers breastfeeding in this way are not protected against pregnancy and half of them will be pregnant within a year. In traditional cultures, the mother carries the infant around with her and expects frequent suckling.

Fig. 159 Prolactin levels defer ovulation and menstruation

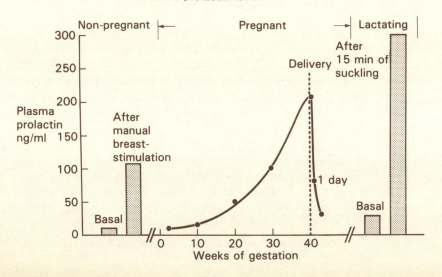

156

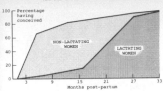
CONCEPTION RATES POST-PARTUM IN LACTATING AND NON-LACTATING ESKIMO WOMEN

As a result, a high level of prolactin is present in her plasma, and ovulation and menstruation do not occur. Such women are more likely to have an adequate supply of milk and to be protected from becoming fertile. This frequency of suckling has been in the past responsible for the long interval between births found in so many traditional societies.

154

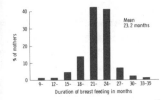
DURATION OF BREAST FEEDING 291 mothers in a West African village

Hermione: At the root of the problem of insufficient milk is insufficient suckling of the infants timed by the clock rather than when the infant requests it.

155

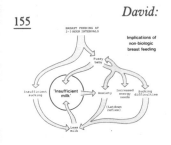

David: The histogram records the duration of breastfeeding in the village of Imesi-Ile and where a study was undertaken of African children from before birth till the age of five. In these traditional societies children benefit from two years at the breast. Historically this was true of all societies. El Qur'an (11.233) states:
'Mothers shall suckle their infants for two whole years'.
Parents in less developed countries yearn for the better health and material benefits they see in more developed countries for their children. Unfortunately, some have assumed breast milk substitutes could be a possible step towards this goal. I am a firm believer that mothers should be allowed to decide for themselves how long to breastfeed. However they should be encouraged to breastfeed for around two years or perhaps until their infant weighs more than 10 kg, or until the infant weans itself from the breast.

The human baby puts on about 30 gm (1 oz) every day for the first 100 days of life. Compare this with the grey seal pup who puts on 2 kg a day while the mother seal loses 4 kg a day!

Hermione:

I find it interesting to compare the huge amount of research on lactation in animals and the very small amount of work that has so far been done on human lactation. In animals the focus has been on the economic need to produce healthy young or milk for sale. There has been a growing awareness that animals suckled by the mother are likely to be ill less frequently. In many species the young grow better on their mother's milk than on artificial food. In animals the fat content and volume of milk is known to be related to food intake. Thus in the **Anand** dairy project in India the price paid to women depends on the fat content of their buffalo milk. This encourages the family to feed the buffalo well.

Traditionally in some societies the lactating woman has always received extra food and relief from some of her work and chores which involve heavy energy expenditure, for a year or more post partum. Yet in other places this help is limited to one or a few months after birth and does not cover the important weaning period when the baby still depends heavily on breast milk. We do not yet know the pattern of weight loss in the mother at this time. All we know is that for some later pregnancies she is likely to start off very thin.

The normal period of breastfeeding in women in the past was probably around two years, although many infants were breast fed until the age of three or four. A recent worldwide survey showed that only in one country, Bangladesh, was the average period of breastfeeding over two years. In most of the countries studied, the median period is now under eighteen months, and in many countries, breastfeeding does not continue longer than nine months. As will be seen, the non-lactating mother is much more likely to conceive between six and eighteen months after delivery, leading to a short birth interval with ill effects on the family and acting as a brake holding back national development. Elsewhere in this book (Fig. 25, page 46) we emphasised mother education as the most important single factor in reducing child mortality rates. Unfortunately, some educated mothers are more likely to be persuaded to give breast milk

157

Median length of breast feeding
World fertility survey (Ferry B. Smith D. 1982)

substitutes. If only these mothers could realise the value to their child of breast milk then education could even further lower the mortality.

David:

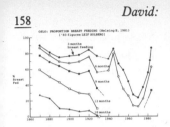

OSLO: PROPORTION BREAST FEEDING (Helsing E. 1981)
('83 figures LEIF SOLBERG)

At a time when mothers are tending to put their babies on the bottle in less developed countries, in many advanced countries the mothers are discovering the value and the pleasure of successful breastfeeding. Particularly in northern Europe now, the majority of mothers successfully breastfeed and many will be breastfeeding over nine months and into the second year of life.

Hermione:

The swing to the use of breast milk substitutes has led to a shortening of the interval between births. Many of the problems that we see arising with a short birth interval must be blamed on the use of these breast milk substitutes.

Fig. 160 Bottle feeding: the unplanned experiment of the last 50 years

| Homo genus established | Fire and shelter | Agriculture and settlement | Fair housing and hygiene |

| Years | 2 million | 100,000 | 10,000 | 50-100 |

The last 100 years have seen many dramatic changes. The availability of breast milk substitutes has and can save lives. But their widespread use to replace suckling has created severe problems for both mothers and children.

Fig. 161 Breast milk substitutes

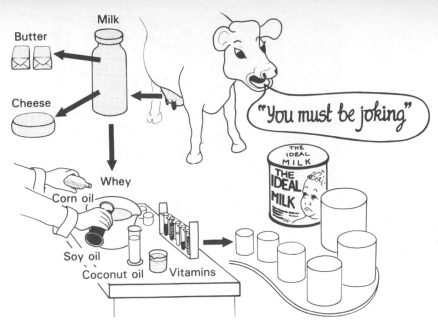

BREAST MILK SUBSTITUTES

These have been developed by, and have produced
enormous profits for, the international milk industry.
They remain inferior substitutes.

Fig. 162 A symbol of failure

A SYMBOL OF FAILURE

Poor mothers throughout the world struggle to achieve
health and a better life. Breast milk substitutes have been
presented to them as a prestige symbol. They are a symbol
of the failure of suckling which is so beneficial to mothers
and infants.

Fig. 163   Less infections in newborns fed raw human milk

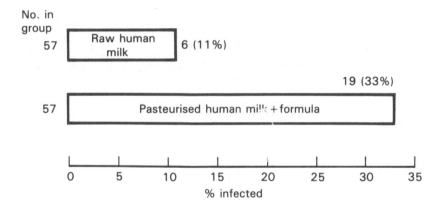

Occurrence of infection in high risk neonates fed formula and breast milk

No. in group

57 — Raw human milk — 6 (11%)

57 — Pasteurised human milk + formula — 19 (33%)

0   5   10   15   20   25   30   35

% infected

This study compares feeding infants known to be at risk from infection on human milk and formula. Children fed untreated breast milk had three times less infection.

5 Where Next for Children?

Hermione:

Over the last two million years there have been slow changes in the environment of the child. These changes have become dramatic and rapid in the last hundred years, but no change has been more significant and perhaps more damaging than the introduction of bottle or formula feeding.

David:

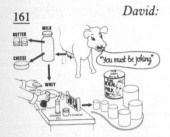

Cow's milk formulas are chemically inferior to breast milk, and they lack immuno-globulins, white blood cells and other anti-infective substances. Cow's milk and other foods introduced too early to children in the more developed countries play a part in causing eczema, asthma and other allergic conditions previously uncommon in traditional societies, though they are now beginning to be seen there.

Hermione:

The mother in less developed countries is reaching out for something that will take her child into what she sees as the wonders of more developed countries. One possibility which is available easily to her is to buy breast milk substitutes. Through many channels she is made to believe that these will produce strong infants. She is easily tempted to buy just one of these tins of milk and unwittingly deny her infant permanently the safety and assurance of her own breast milk.

163

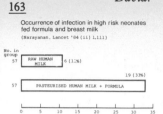

Occurrence of infection in high risk neonates
fed formula and breast milk
(Narayanan, Lancet '84 (ii) 1,111)

David: This study from New Delhi on newborns is particularly significant. In this hospital there was not enough mother's milk for some infants and in the past many hospitals used to pasteurise or heat-treat the mother's milk to destroy any bacteria. Unfortunately, this treatment caused destruction of the many living cells and the globulins which protect infants from infection. This study shows that babies given pasteurised breast milk were three times more liable to suffer from infections as those given natural 'raw' breast milk.

Hermione: The return to breastfeeding in more developed countries has followed the usual pattern of change. It starts with better-off mothers who include the opinion leaders and many of the innovators: they also have more access to the media and medical advice. The less privileged and poor mothers are likely to change later. For this reason, persuading the wife of the president or other leading personality, particularly one well-known in the media, both to breastfeed and publicly say she does so has proved successful. One successful way to encourage this is a duplicated or printed newsletter circulating amongst leading women.

Governments by legislation can also achieve change. In Papua New Guinea a certificate from a health worker is required to purchase breast milk substitutes or feeding bottle teats. The legislation requires the health worker to take on the responsibility of teaching the use of the bottle; failure to do this can lead to a fine. Surveys show that this action was followed by a fall in child admissions to hospital with diarrhoea and malnutrition as well as a return to breastfeeding.

Fig. 164 Adequate food — adequate growth

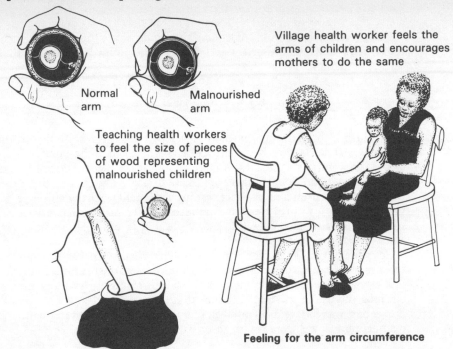

Normal arm

Malnourished arm

Teaching health workers to feel the size of pieces of wood representing malnourished children

Village health worker feels the arms of children and encourages mothers to do the same

Feeling for the arm circumference

How can we help mothers to measure their child's growth? Feeling for the size of arm circumference may be the most acceptable means.

Fig. 165 Measuring round the arm

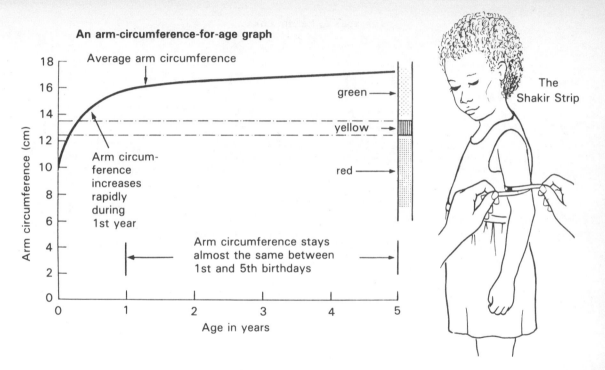

An arm-circumference-for-age graph

Average arm circumference

Arm circumference (cm)

18
16
14
12
10
8
6
4
2
0

Arm circum-
ference
increases
rapidly
during
1st year

Arm circumference stays
almost the same between
1st and 5th birthdays

green

yellow

red

The
Shakir Strip

0   1   2   3   4   5

Age in years

From the first to the fifth birthday, a coloured strip has
proved a simple but satisfactory assessment of nutrition.

Fig. 166 Weight charts

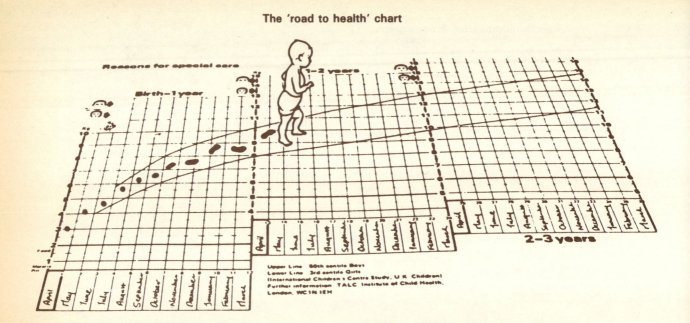

Simple weight-for-age charts are widely used to monitor the growth of small children.

Fig. 167   Two children born in the same month in the same village

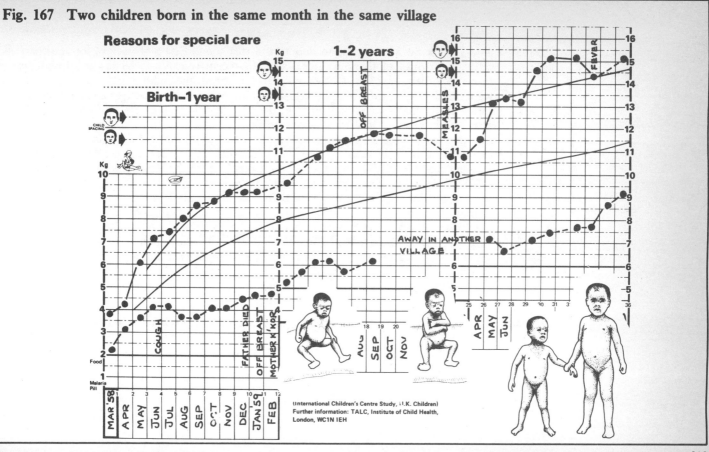

(International Children's Centre Study, U.K. Children)
Further information: TALC, Institute of Child Health,
London, WC1N IEH

Hermione: When I first joined the Unit seven years ago, the emphasis was on growth charts. I am pleased that we have now changed our emphasis to consider other measurements, particularly those that the mother herself can easily understand and perhaps undertake.

David: Yes. It took me a long time to understand that the old type of 'weight-for-age chart' is difficult for most mothers to understand. As recent research in Ghana and India has shown, mothers have many other ways of measuring their children's growth. I think we were all impressed when we heard of the mothers who expect to change the beads round their child's waist five times in the first five months of life, adding further beads as the child grows. Of all the measurements that mothers use, I think we can develop the limb circumference as the most useful. Because the normal arm circumference increases so little between the first and fifth birthday, we can use a coloured strip right through this period. This is suitable for a quick check to identify wasted children.

Whilst the strip is very popular, I suggest people routinely use their fingers. They need to be able to 'calibrate' where their forefinger-nail comes on the ball of their thumb. To help with this, TALC has produced a set of 'plastic arms' of graded circumference. After learning the 'feel' of 12.5 cm, the health worker tries to learn the 'feel' of other sizes in a bag. After this she should 'greet' a child between one and five years by slipping her finger around the child's upper arm and assess the size of the arm.

The arm circumference cannot monitor the growth of children in the way a growth curve will on the child weight-to-age chart.

Hermione: I think that you still favour this weight-for-age chart. Perhaps now that in some countries, notably Indonesia, mothers themselves are learning to weigh their children, more mothers will come to understand that this is a useful tool for measuring their child's growth.

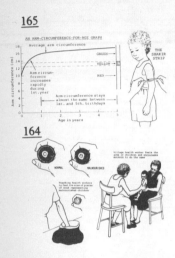

165

164

166

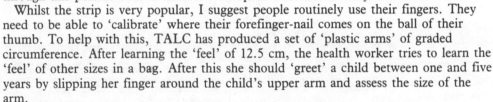

David: This is an important development. The weight chart can show so much that can be related to the child's growth curve, for example the time of illnesses and important changes such as when the child comes off the breast. We want the mother, with help from other mothers, to come to understand her child's growth curve and how breast-feeding and the food she gives can influence the growth of her child.

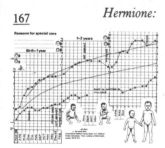

167

Hermione: Growth of the child's brain and the implications for national development still seems an almost taboo aspect of malnutrition of mothers and children. Growth in utero and in the first three years of life is not just something of importance to health workers but is of considerable importance to anyone concerned with policy and development.

Perhaps mothers will come to understand their child's weight curve if the new TALC scale proves practical. The TALC spring stretches exactly one centimetre for each kilogram and promises to revolutionise the understanding of weighing by mothers. She will see her child's weight stretching the spring up her child's chart each month and a dot placed opposite the pointer on the spring to create a growth curve. Perhaps we will move away from 'weight gain', which for mothers must be a nebulous idea, to the concept of 'spring stretching', which is visible. With this technique we hope that weighing will become much more of a community activity taking place in people's homes.

Fig. 168 A new method of weighing

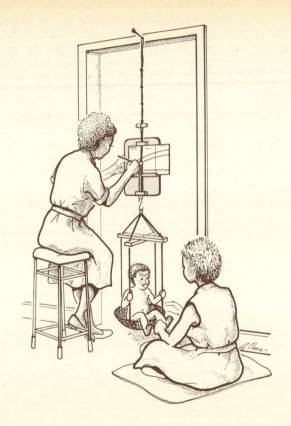

Fig. 169 Brain growth

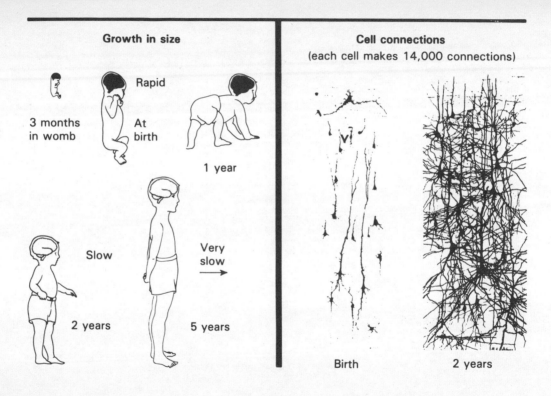

Growth in size

3 months in womb

At birth — Rapid

1 year

2 years — Slow

5 years — Very slow →

Cell connections
(each cell makes 14,000 connections)

Birth

2 years

For every parent, adequate growth of their child's brain in the first two years of life should be a priority. Adequate growth of a child as shown by a weight curve is the only practical way to ensure adequate brain growth.

Fig. 170 More food produces more activity

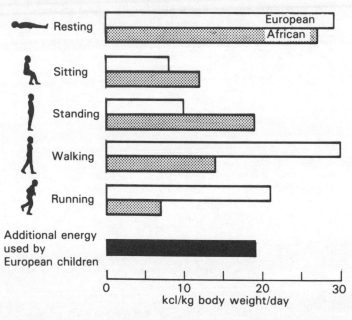

Saving energy for growth:
energy expenditure of European and African children
calculated as observed activity

A study of children eating too little food showed that they conserved energy. More food leads to more activity and better intellectual development.

5 Where Next for Children?

Hermione: Isn't it surprising that although it is only the brain that makes human beings different from other animals, most societies pay so little attention to the development of the child's brain.

David: Yes. But I think the problem has been that only recently have scientists realised that the growth of the brain is almost completed by the time the child is two years old. The important time for cell multiplication is before birth. Between birth and the second birthday is the time when the cortical brain cells build up their many links. The best indication that the brain has grown normally during this period is the growth of the whole child. This can be best ensured by monitoring growth using a weight-for-age chart.

169

GROWTH IN SIZE — CELL CONNECTIONS

3 months in womb — At birth — 1 year — 2 years — 5 years

BIRTH — 2 YEARS

Hermione: Inadequate brain growth is not the only way poor nutrition may affect the child's future intelligence. We also know that the child who is deficient in energy food is less active, yet these early years are the time when a child needs to develop skills and abilities by running about and playing.

David: There is of course controversy as to whether nutrition or stimulation is more important. There is little doubt that the two are so intimately bound together they cannot be separated.

170

SAVING ENERGY FOR GROWTH:
ENERGY EXPENDITURES OF EUROPEAN AND AFRICAN CHILDREN
Calculated as observed activity

Resting — Sitting — Standing — Walking — Running

European
African

Additional energy used by European children

0   10   15   20   30
kcl/kg body weight/day

Hermione: In less developed regions where children have an inadequate food intake, their bodies conserve energy for growth. Adequate activity is important for development of the brain and the skills of the adult. In countries where the health workers are concerned for the regular growth of children, simple growth charts along these lines have been introduced. The steady upward curve of a child's growth is the most valuable assurance of optimal brain growth. A satisfactory curve also suggests that the child is eating enough energy to play and learn. The need for such charts was brought out by a detailed review of several hundred nutrition programmes, conducted by the Harvard Institute for International Development. This concluded that: *'The average moderately*

Growth of the Intellect

malnourished child in the 6 — 24 month age range looks entirely normal but is too small for his or her age, has lowered resistance to infection, and therefore easily succumbs to illness. The child receiving only 60% of caloric requirement may give no outward sign of hunger, beyond a frequent desire to breast feed. In the Philippines study, 58% of the mothers of second- and third-degree malnourished children said they thought their babies were growing and developing well.'

The need was shown equally well in the State of the World's Children 1984: *'An invisible malnutrition touches the lives of approximately one quarter of the developing world's young children. It quietly steals away their energy; it greatly restrains their growth; it gradually lowers their resistance.'* I would like to add *'it impairs their intellectual attainment.'*

Fig. 171 Prestigious foods — not essential

Health workers have over-emphasised the importance of meat, eggs and fish. These are not available for most of the world's poor, nor are they essential for growth and good health.

Fig. 172 Bulky food and small stomachs

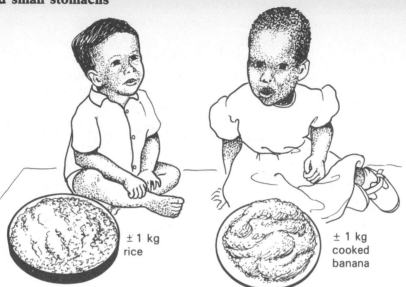

± 1 kg
rice

± 1 kg
cooked
banana

THE VOLUME CHILDREN HAVE TO EAT TO CONSUME 1,000 CALORIES OF BULKY FOOD IS VERY LARGE

As their stomachs are no larger than their fists they cannot eat enough to meet their energy requirements. Just giving extra protein will not help.

Fig. 173 More fats and oils is the priority

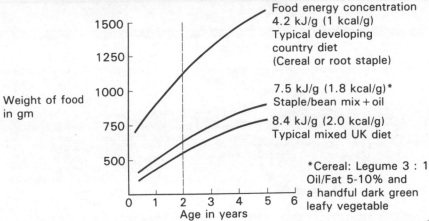

Food intakes in relation to energy concentration

Weight of food in gm

Food energy concentration
4.2 kJ/g (1 kcal/g)
Typical developing
country diet
(Cereal or root staple)

7.5 kJ/g (1.8 kcal/g)*
Staple/bean mix + oil

8.4 kJ/g (2.0 kcal/g)
Typical mixed UK diet

*Cereal: Legume 3 : 1
Oil/Fat 5-10% and
a handful dark green
leafy vegetable

Age in years

As the graph shows, many children have to eat a kilo of staple to get enough energy (calories). Adding oil
- softens the food
- reduces the need to add so much water
- provides additional calories.

5 Where Next for Children?

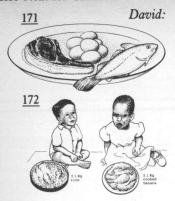

171

172

± 1 Kg rice

± 1 Kg cooked banana

David: Unfortunately, nutritionists have placed too much emphasis on the prestigious foods such as meat and fish and dairy products. We now know that in malnutrition the energy (calorie) deficit is more important than the shortage of protein. This is not because parents do not give children enough to eat, but because the food is so bulky that they cannot eat enough to achieve the energy intake they need. The children in the drawing have to eat a plateful like this every day. The stomach when empty is the size of their fist. *The nutritional problem for most small children in less developed countries is that the foods they are being fed are too bulky.*

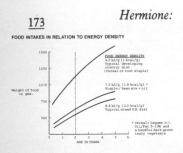

173

FOOD INTAKES IN RELATION TO ENERGY DENSITY

Weight of food in gms.

FOOD ENERGY DENSITY
4.2 kJ/g (1 kcal/g)
Typical developing country diet
(Cereal or root staple)

7.5 kJ/g (1.8 kcal/g) *
Staple / bean mix + oil

8.4 kJ/g (2.0 kcal/g)
Typical mixed U.K. diet

* Cereal: Legume 3:1
Oil/Fat 5-10% and a handful dark green leafy vegetable

AGE IN YEARS

Hermione: It is important for the community and the family to know, for example, that the growing body of a young child needs three times as much energy (calories) and twice as much protein per kilo of body weight as an adult. *We must teach that a child needs HALF the TOTAL food of an adult.* Because a young child's stomach is smaller, feeding needs to be more frequent. Can the mother or someone else give the child an extra meal every day? There is a real problem for the mother and the health worker which has been well-named the 'Weanling's Dilemma'. If foods other than breast milk are delayed, the child will get malnourished; if introduced too early, the child may suffer from repeated episodes of diarrhoea and becomed malnourished. Helping mothers provide their children with diets that have a reasonably high energy concentration is so important. However, if we can get across to mothers the importance of oils and fats in their children's diets, will they be able to obtain them?

David: Yes. These are expensive but if we think of them in terms of the calories or energy they produce, then the price is small and of course children only need relatively small quantities. In many societies there were traditional foods which were recognised to be particularly useful for children in the weaning period. In Pakistan the mothers

Fig. 174   The Weanling's Dilemma

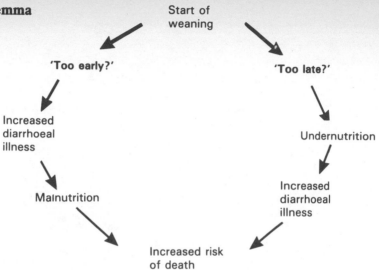

recognise that chippatees made with ghee (butter fat) will help their children to grow strong. Another example of this is the porridge produced from malted (sprouted) grains in parts of India. These have a much higher energy concentration than unsprouted grains.

Hermione: We need to learn more about the many excellent traditional weaning foods. In northern Ghana, a nutritionist friend of mine did a study of the bacterial count in traditional (yoghurt-based) weaning food and in a 'modern' weaning food based on skimmed milk powder. She found that a bowl of the 'modern' multimix was crawling with bacteria when left for the child's next snack. The traditional food, also left in the same circumstances till the child wanted some more, was in much better condition with fewer bacteria present.

Fig. 175 Breast milk: valuable in the second year

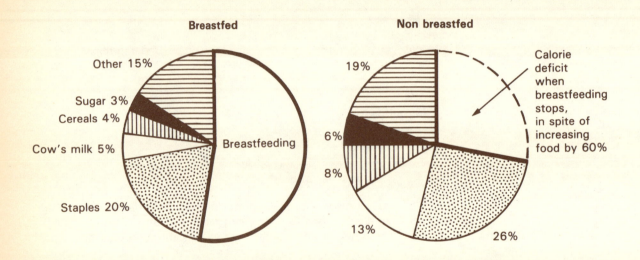

Breastfed

Other 15%

Sugar 3%

Cereals 4%

Cow's milk 5%

Breastfeeding

Staples 20%

Non breastfed

19%

6%

8%

13%

26%

Calorie
deficit
when
breastfeeding
stops,
in spite of
increasing
food by 60%

The child who is breast fed during the second year is less
likely to be short of energy than the child who has been
removed from the breast.

Fig. 176 Most people are short of energy — not protein

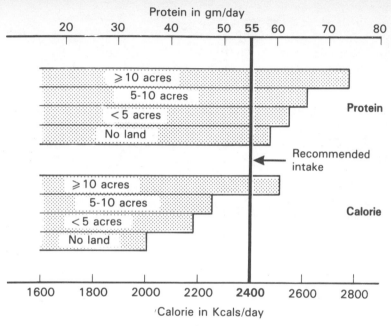

Land holdings and protein/calorie intake — Maharashtra, India

In India, as in most of the world's villages, only the privileged few have an adequate energy intake.

Fig. 177 Fats and oils: North and South

	grams per day	Proportion of total calories consumed
Industrialised countries	126	34%
Developing countries	41	16%

The average person in the North eats three times more oils
and fats than the average person in the South.

5 Where Next for Children?

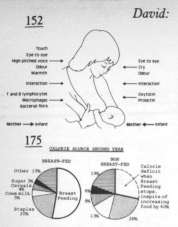

152

175

CALORIE SOURCE SECOND YEAR

David: For children in the South, in the less developed communities, breastfeeding is the only basis on which good nutrition can develop. If I look back ten or fifteen years to when I was lecturing to students, I remember saying that breastfeeding in the second year of life is important for the first-class protein that this provided for the child. As in so many things, I have now changed what I say and I now put the emphasis on the energy, particularly since I saw this study in East Africa where children who were no longer breastfed had 25% fewer calories than those who were still being breastfed. The importance of breastfeeding in the second year of life now seems to me largely to do with the fact that this provides an excellent source of easily absorbed calories.

Hermione: To return to the question of calories and protein, not only the child but the whole community, except for the wealthy, may be deficient in their energy intake. The protein intake may be sufficient even for the poor, as shown in many studies from India. I wonder how they exist on so little energy food?

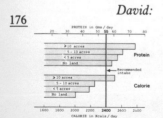

176

David: The Harijans and others who own no land are the smaller individuals, partly because they have grown less well as children. Their requirements are less, their children tend to grow less well and they will become small adults. For the whole of India, consumption of fat is 15 gm per day; this is half the recommended intake. The less well-off group are particularly deficient in fats and oils.

Hermione: The nutritional deficits in India might be much greater if all Indians were the same size as Europeans or Americans! Unfortunately, however, this lack of energy intake will also mean a deficiency in the activity of these people, leading to the cycles of malnutrition we have described amongst girls and women, and the cycle of deprivation in men and their families.

46

THE CYCLE OF UNDERNUTRITION

David: Too much emphasis has in the past been placed on a deficient protein intake in less developed countries. Although the consumption of foods from animal origin is much lower, this may be made up by protein from vegetables if enough of the existing diet is eaten to supply the energy requirement. The difference in the consumption of fats and oils between more and less developed countries is considerable. In the more developed, we may eat too much of these. In the less developed countries an increased intake by children of oils and fats would do much to increase the energy intake and reduce the incidence of malnutrition.

177

	grams per day	Proportion of total calories consumed
INDUSTRIALISED COUNTRIES	126	34 %
DEVELOPING COUNTRIES	41	16 %

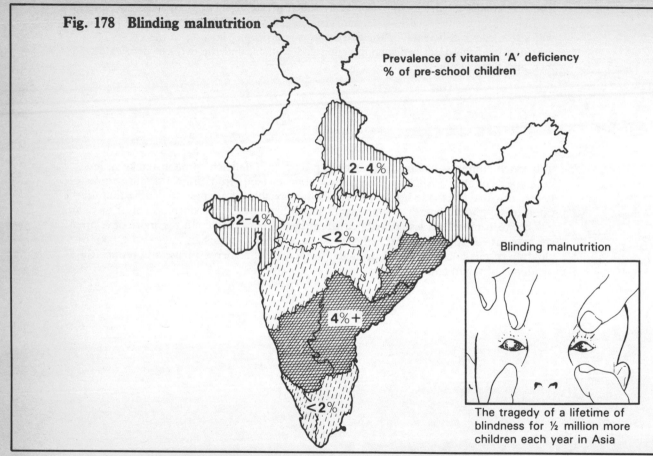

Fig. 178 Blinding malnutrition

Prevalence of vitamin 'A' deficiency
% of pre-school children

2-4%

2-4%

<2%

4%+

<2%

Blinding malnutrition

The tragedy of a lifetime of
blindness for ½ million more
children each year in Asia

Vitamin A is found in dark green leafy vegetables. Each year 14,000 Indian children go blind for the rest of their lives because they are not fed these foods.

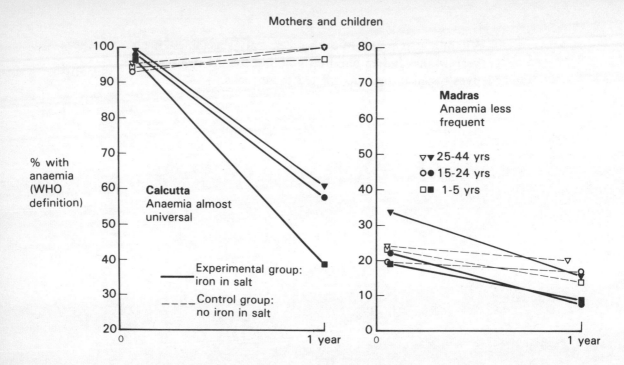

Fig. 179 The decline in anaemia on adding iron to salt

Mothers and children

% with anaemia (WHO definition)

Calcutta
Anaemia almost universal

Experimental group: iron in salt

Control group: no iron in salt

Madras
Anaemia less frequent

▽▼ 25-44 yrs
○● 15-24 yrs
□■ 1-5 yrs

IRON DEFICIENCY

The anaemia due to iron deficiency affects all age groups.
With iron there is less illness, better performance at school,
a higher work output and safer pregnancy. All these can be
achieved by adding iron to the diet where this is deficient.

Hermione:

178

Hermione: Although energy protein malnutrition is the major problem, it is by no means the only problem, particularly in the Indian subcontinent. Other substances such as vitamins, iron, iodides and zinc may also be lacking. In many countries, insufficient dark green leafy vegetables are eaten. Most children have multiple deficiencies and when these include Vitamin A, blindness may follow. In India alone 14,000 children a year go blind due to the lack of Vitamin A causing a blinding malnutrition. World-wide it is believed that 10 million children have symptoms and 0.5 million go blind each year. Research also suggests that children who show signs of Vitamin A deficiency, unless treated, have a high mortality. For this reason an increased consumption of Vitamin A-containing dark green leafy vegetables will prevent blindness and reduce mortality.

David: Unfortunately, energy protein malnutrition may be linked to a shortage of Vitamin A due to a diet lacking green leafy vegetables. If we were to enable every parent to feed their children a handful of dark green leafy vegetables along with their other food, this illness would disappear and 14,000 children would keep their sight and mortality in childhood would be much reduced.

Hermione: But getting this message across is difficult because those who need to hear it are the deprived and the least likely to receive health messages. The Royal Commonwealth Society for the Blind is running a programme to overcome blinding malnutrition. They are trying to provide women village health workers to go in regularly to these under-nourished and often socially isolated families to encourage the mothers. This use of local well-respected mothers to encourage the less fortunate and less capable mother to give her children dark green vegetables is an important step.

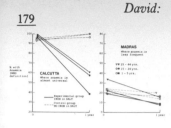

179

David: The Indian study on the frequency of anaemia shows how a government may significantly improve the health of a people through legislation, in this case by adding iron salts to table salt.

Hermione: Yes, unfortunately there is the danger that an additive such as this which does enormous good for the masses will do some harm to a few members of the community and they may then seek damages from the government in the courts.

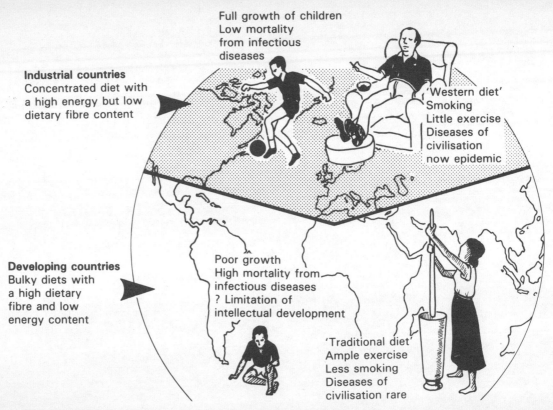

Fig. 180 Nutrition and lifestyles: North and South

Full growth of children
Low mortality
from infectious
diseases

Industrial countries
Concentrated diet with
a high energy but low
dietary fibre content

'Western diet'
Smoking
Little exercise
Diseases of
civilisation
now epidemic

Developing countries
Bulky diets with
a high dietary
fibre and low
energy content

Poor growth
High mortality from
infectious diseases
? Limitation of
intellectual development

'Traditional diet'
Ample exercise
Less smoking
Diseases of
civilisation rare

MALNUTRITION NORTH AND SOUTH

One is the reverse of the other.
In the South the children are energy-deficient.
In the North the adults eat too much.

Fig. 181 Temptation of high energy food for those already fat

Fig. 182 Small children are often sick and refuse to eat

Small children are often sick

SICK CHILDREN REFUSE FOOD

For ten days each month, illness is likely to reduce a child's appetite. During the other twenty the child needs to eat even more.

180

Nutrition and Life Styles:

Hermione: The concept that what we suffer from in the North is the reverse of what those in the less developed countries of the South suffer from, is one which should be more widely understood. The excess calories and deficient exercise of adults in the North, with an over-refined diet containing too much salt and far too little dietary fibre, are compounded by smoking to create a situation where we now have many degenerative diseases related to this lifestyle. These diseases are hardly seen in the villages of the less developed world.

David: Yes, Dennis Burkitt said to me recently, *'David, if only we could persuade people to stop smoking and pass stools that float we would reduce the incidence of cancer by two thirds'.* This rather surprising statement arises from a detailed study by Doll and Peto of Oxford on cancer in the USA. Their 'best estimate' on largely epidemiological grounds

Fig. 183 Grain the main source of dietary fibre

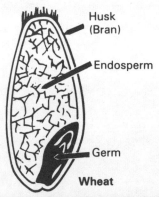

Husk (Bran)

Endosperm

Germ

Wheat

is that in the US, 30% of cancers are related to smoking and 35% to inappropriate diets. Burkitt is assuming that a low level of cereal dietary fibre is the major dietary factor. On a high dietary fibre intake, the time from eating to passing food residue as faeces may be reduced from five to seven days to one to two days. The stools are more bulky due to a higher bacterial content and they float because they contain more gas. The principal source of dietary fibre is the bran that covers all grains. When wheat or any other grain is milled this is removed.

Hermione: So in the North we need to reduce our oil, fat and salt intake and increase our dietary fibre as an initial step towards improving health. In the South more foods with a high energy concentration are needed by the children.

182

Small children are often sick

However, the problem of energy protein deficiency will not be understood if we do not also take into consideration the serious effects of infections and their frequency. Many of the common illnesses are likely to be much more severe in children who are undernourished. Measles particularly demonstrates this difference. In a well-fed population in the North, only one child in every 10,000 who catches the disease is likely to die. In the South, this size of epidemic may cause 400 deaths. Fig. 184 demonstrates this interaction. We know well how major illnesses such as measles also drive children into malnutrition, but there are also the multiple small illnesses which play their part. Management of these, and particularly emphasising the food intake of the child who is or has been slightly ill, is so important in improving their health.

Fig. 184 Infection and malnutrition

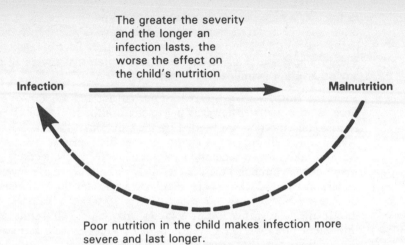

The greater the severity
and the longer an
infection lasts, the
worse the effect on
the child's nutrition

Infection → **Malnutrition**

Poor nutrition in the child makes infection more
severe and last longer.

David: Yes. We have now with a few diagrams emphasised the importance of adequate food which we saw as the priority for children. However, management of diarrhoea to prevent dehydration, immunisation against common diseases of children and successful breastfeeding are also important. I hope our reader can appreciate how these priorities all work together to help the child.

Fig. 185　The need for a stimulating environment

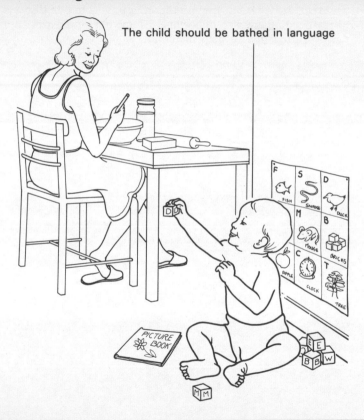

The child should be bathed in language

A STIMULATING ENVIRONMENT

Good food, adequate growth and maintenance of health are important but growth of the intellect is essential. Play is the vital schooling of the young child.

132

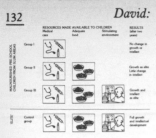

David: There is much that we could have included in this book. I am however sad that there is not more on the need for the child to have a stimulating environment.

185

Hermione: I would agree with this. There is much encouragement to be found. We now know what a huge difference stimulation makes to the development of the handicapped child. We also know that malnourished children (e.g. children with coeliac disease) are not intellectually stunted if they have been in an environment which has been caring and interested in them developing. For me this means that in developing countries even while we know food shortages continue, there is hope that with a good environment for the children, their brains can still grow well. Countries such as Venezuela who have now appointed a Minister of Intelligence specifically to encourage brain growth of children through play centres and to teach *thinking* in schools, may well be seen in retrospect to have led the way to the twenty-first century.

Fig. 186 A fable for the Nations

'THE TWO MULES'

A fable for the Nations

CO-OPERATION

IS BETTER THAN CONFLICT

If nations would pull together, most of the world's problems would be solved.

Fig. 187 Employment when they grow up

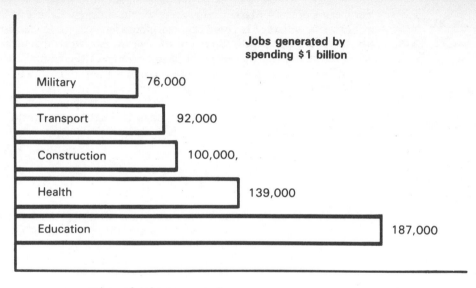

Jobs generated by
spending $1 billion

Military — 76,000

Transport — 92,000

Construction — 100,000,

Health — 139,000

Education — 187,000

number of jobs generated

Unemployment and underemployment are the blight of
both the North and the South. Let's generate jobs where
they are desperately needed, in health and education.

5 Where Next for Children?

Hermione:

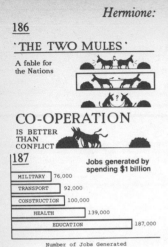

186

'THE TWO MULES'

A fable for
the Nations

CO-OPERATION

IS BETTER
THAN
CONFLICT

187 Jobs generated by
spending $1 billion

MILITARY	76,000
TRANSPORT	92,000
CONSTRUCTION	100,000
HEALTH	139,000
EDUCATION	187,000

Number of Jobs Generated

Coming to the end of any book is difficult. I hope our readers will agree with us in putting the hope of better co-operation between races as the first priority. We in Europe have many grumbles at the bureaucracy, the waste and the injustices of our European Common Market. However, we do sincerely believe it has made further wars in Europe less likely. Let us hope that politicians can produce some formula through which we, the privileged nations of the North, can work together with the less privileged nations of the South in tackling some of their immense problems. As the title of this book suggests, the better care and upbringing of children in all countries should start 'today' rather than 'tomorrow'.

As we tackle the world-wide problems of unemployment let us consider the 'powerless', the 'flowers of the future', the small children of our world and their needs for health and education.

David:

Much of the content of this book arises from ideas expressed at the Alma Ata Declaration. Bailey, the editor of the Journal of the Royal College of General Practitioners in the UK, found two 'translations' of this by Duke and Fendall:

'In some parts of the world, people are much less healthy than in others. That is unjust; it is also dangerous, because health, peace and economic development depend world-wide on one another. If we are to put things right by the end of the century, we must all work and plan together in freedom and equality, governments and individuals alike. By spending less on guns, we can spend more on caring for the ill, but also on eradicating disease, feeding and housing people properly, and teaching them how to live in a healthy way.'

and this definition of primary health care:

'Primary and intimate contact with the community; an adequate range of services; co-ordination of those services; a capacity for health assessment of both the individual and the community; continuity of care; a progressive care support structure; a family orientation; and a non-institutional outlook.'

INDEX OF TOPICS

INDEX OF COUNTRIES

Introduction

Fig. 1

From ACTION, World Association of Christian Communication, 122 King's Road, London, SW3 4TR, with small adjustment.

Abbat, F., McMahon, R. (1985) Teaching health care workers. London: Macmillan.

Bligh, D., Ebrahim, G.J., Jaques, D., Warren Piper, D. (1975) Teaching students. Exeter: EUTS Production.

Chapter 1: Our Children's World

Fig. 2

From: King, M., King, F., Soebagio Martodipoero (1978) Primary child care. Vol 1. Oxford: OUP.

In many countries the Government or a paediatric association has tried to draw up plans for children. This was undertaken in 1978 in the UK in what has become known as the Court Report. Great Britain. Committee on Child Health Services (1976) Fit for the future: report. (Chairman, S.D.M. Court). 2 vols. London: HMSO.

Fig. 3

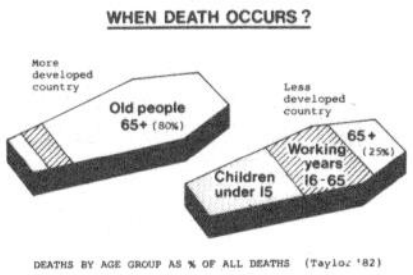

This illustration comes from figures produced by the UK Office of Health Economics, 12 Whitehall, London, SW1.

Of 35,095 deaths in the Inter-American investigation of mortality, 78.6% were infants.
Puffer, R.R., Serrano, C.V. (1973) Patterns of mortality in childhood. Washington D.C.: PAHO/WHO: 154–5. (PAHO Scientific Publications; 262).

Vallin, J. (1976) World trends in infant mortality since 1950. World Health Statistics Rep. **29**: 11.

Gwatkin (1980) Deaths in developing countries. Am. J. Public Health. **70**: 1286

(1978) Primary Health Care: Report of the International Conference on Primary Health Care. Alma Ata. Union of Soviet Socialist Republics, 6–12, September 1978, Geneva: WHO.

Fassin, D., Badi, I. (1986) Ritual Buffoonery: A social preventive measure against childhood mortality in Senegal. Lancet i: 142.

Fig. 4

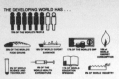

This was taken from Cajanus, the Journal of the Caribbean Food and Nutrition Institute, PO Box 140, Kingston 7, Jamaica. The source of the illustration was not indicated and has not been elicited by correspondence.

For information and books on this subject: World Watch Institute, 1776 Maddison Avenue, Washington DC, 20036, USA.

Fig. 5

Taken from People, the Journal of the International Planned Parenthood Federation (IPPF), 18-20 Lower Regent Street, London, SW1Y 4PW.

Fig. 6

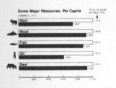

Histogram from figures extracted from: Brown, L. (1984) The state of the world. London: Norton & Co., for the World Watch Institute.

Anyone interested in the background to resources in our world should obtain Worldwatch publications, World Watch Institute, 1776 Maddison Avenue, Washington DC, 20036, USA.

Fig. 7

This drawing is a variation of one received from a French colleague, source unknown.

For a useful collection of world maps and data on numerous north/south topics, see: Kidron, M., Segal, R. (1981) The state of the world atlas. London: Pan Books and Heineman.

Fig. 8

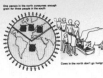

This was adjusted from a diagram in a paper produced by Christian Aid of the UK. Source requested but unknown.

The Food and Agricultural Organisation (FAO), Via Delle Terme di Caracalla, 00100 Rome, Italy, is an excellent source of information on food production and distribution in our world.

Fig. 9

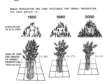

This drawing was modified from an Indian paper. Taken from Brown, L. (1984) The state of the world 1984. London: Norton & Co.

Lancet Leader (1985) Food and population. Lancet i: 793. Examines particularly the problem faced by the African continent.

Fig. 10

Source: Human Story. A booklet illustrating a travelling display prepared by IBM for the Commonwealth Institute used by kind permission of the Director.

As pressures on the land have intensified over the past generation, erosion has increased until close to half the world's croplands are losing topsoil at a debilitating rate.

Brown, L. (1984) The state of the world 1984. London: Norton & Co.

Hall, C., Helsing, R. (1976) The Sahelian drought - experience from a supporting programme in Niger. J. Trop. Pediat. 22: 69-93. (Monograph no. 4).

Brown, L.R., Wolf, E.C. Soil erosion: quiet crisis in the world economy. Washington DC: World Watch Institute. World Watch paper; 60.

The Chinese have lead the way in showing how desert can be reclaimed and repopulated with 26,000 inhabitants. Described by: Lai, H.G. (1985) Commonwealth Forestry Review, **64** (3).

Fig. 11

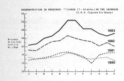

From TALC, PO Box 49, St Albans, UK. From figures in: Segall, M. (1983) The politics of primary health care. In: Institute of Development Studies Bulletin; No. 14. The original source is: Frelimo (1983) Directivas Economicas E Sociais published in tempo no. 662 Maputo: 29-36.

Half to two-thirds of all export earnings are now required merely to pay interest on foreign debt in Argentina, Brazil, Chile, Mexico, Philippines and Turkey. Brown, L. (1984) The state of the world 1984. London: Norton & Co.

Nyerere, J.K. (1982) South-south option. Third World Foundation Monograph No. 10.

Fig. 12

Catholic Relief Service figures made available through UNICEF in: UNICEF (1986) The state of the world's children 1986. Oxford: OUP.

Gopalan, C. (1984) Nutrition and Health Care. Nutrition Foundation of India. (Special Publication; Series 1.)

Fig. 13

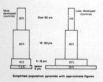

From: Brown, L. (1984, 1985, 1986) The state of the world. London: Norton & Co.

For further information contact Worldwatch Institute, 1776 Massachusetts Avenue NW, Washington DC 20036, USA.

Fig. 14

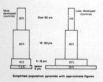

Management in child health. Set of slides available from: TALC, PO Box 49, St Albans, UK.

Morley, D.C. (1973) Paediatric priorities in the developing world. London: Butterworth: 36, 101, 113, 129, 138, 192.

For up to date figures by country on numbers under five mortality, etc, see: UNICEF (1986) The state of the world's children 1986, Oxford: OUP. Available from: TALC, PO Box 49, St Albans, UK.

For a detailed study of population change and development see: (1984) Democratic change and public policy. In: World Development Report 1984. Chapter 4. New York: OUP.

Fig. 15   From: TALC, PO Box 49, St Albans, UK.

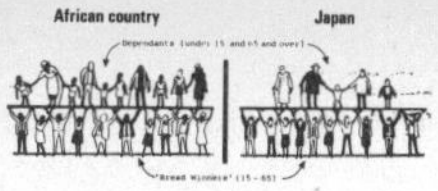

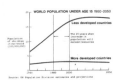

Overseas Development Administration (1984) Dependency ratios in Africa, Asia and Europe, 1985 and 2005 (graphs) second report of population activities.

Fig. 16   Figures from the United Nations Population Division. ESA/P/WP. 65. New York, 1980.

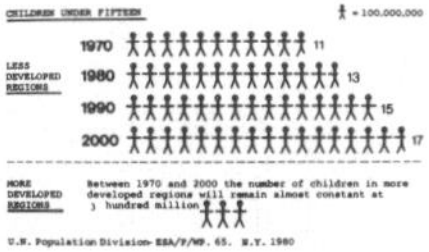

Those responsible for teaching students in health and other fields are strongly recommended to obtain the annual sheets of statistics on world population, children and women available from Population Reference Bureau, 1337 Connecticut Avenue NW, Washington DC, 20036, USA. Similar figures are to be found in: UNICEF (1985, 1986) The state of the world's children. Oxford: OUP.

Fig. 17   United Nations Population Division estimates and predictions.

Ebrahim, G.J. (1976) A model of integrated health care. Trop. Geogr. Med. **28**: S6–S52.

McEvers, N.C. (1980) Health and the assault on poverty in low income countries. Social Sci. Med. **14C**: 41–57.

Labouisse, H.R. (1979) Children and the New International Development Strategy. Assignment Children **47/48**: 41–51.

Fig. 18   This is a modification of a diagram from The New Internationalist, 42 Hythe Bridge Street, Oxford, OX1 2EP. In many large cities two-thirds of the population cannot afford the cheapest accommodation available. World Bank (1975) Housing. Washington DC: World Bank. (Sector Policy paper).

Court, S.D.M. (1977) Conclusion. In: R.H. Jackson (Ed) Children, the environment and accidents. London: Pitman: 154–159.

Fig. 18
(continued)

In some cities children don't go out to play.

Lozells Social Development Centre (1975) Wednesday's children: a report on under-fives provision in Handsworth. Birmingham: Community Relations Commission.

Lipton, M. (1977) Why poor people stay poor: a study of urban bias in world development. London: Temple Smith.

Martin, L.G. et al (1983) Covariates of child mortality in the Philippines, Indonesia and Pakistan: an analysis based on Roz and models. Population Studies 37: 417-432.

Trussell, J., Hammerslaugh, C. (1983) A hazard model analysis of the covariates of infant and child mortality in Sri Lanka. Demography 20: 1-26.

Fig. 19

Figures from: WHO (1984) Report of World Health. Geneva: WHO: 234.

Lagerberg, D. (1978) Child abuse: a literature review. Acta Pediatr. Scand. **67**: 683-90.

Steele, B.F., Pellock, C.B. (1974) A psychiatric study of parents who abuse infants and small children. In: Helfer, R.E., Kempe, C.H. (Eds) The battered child. Chicago: University of Chicago Press.

Grantham-McGregor, S.M., Desai, P., Buchanan, E. (1977) The identification of infants at risk of malnutrition in Kingston, Jamaica. Trop. Geogr. Med. **29**: 165-71.

Rutter, M. (1973) Why are London children so disturbed. Proc. R. Soc. Med. **66**: 1221-5.

Desai, A.R., Pillai, S.D. (1972) A profile of an Indian slum. University of Bombay.

Davis, K. World-Urbanisation 1950-1970. Rev. Ed. California: Berkeley Institute of International Studies, University of California. (Population Monograph Series 4, 9.)

Chandler, T., Fox, G. (1974) 3,000 years of urban growth. New York: NY Academic: 440. (Studies in population).

The growth of cities, the facts. New Internationalist, June 1978.

The difficulty of bringing effective health services to city slum populations is well set out in: Ransome-Kuti, O. (1985) The development of a comprehensive peri-urban child care service. Article in: Prevention of infant mortality and morbidity. Falkner, F. (ed) Karger Basel (Child Health and Development Series Vol. 4).

Morch, Jasper. (1984) Latin America: Abandoned and Street Children. Ideas Forum (UNICEF) Issue No. 18.

STREET CHILDREN Information available from ICRRB, International Catholic Child Bureau, 65 Rue de Lausanne, 1202 Geneva, Switzerland.

Fig. 20

Original source for this figure: Population and Development Review. September 1977.

(1977) Children, the cost to the rich, the benefit to the poor (summarises Java study). New Internationalist. June: 16-17.

Lovering, K. (1984) Cost of children in Australia. Melbourne: Institute of Family Studies. (Working paper no. 8). Totals for a year are $868 for a 2 year old, $1113 for a five year old, $1365 for an 8 year old and $1449 for an 11 year old (all in low income families). Teenagers cost ranged from $2157 for low income families to $3589 for the medium income group.

Bringing up two children "can cost mothers $70,000 (including lost earnings)". Guardian, 19 February 1985.

Fig. 21

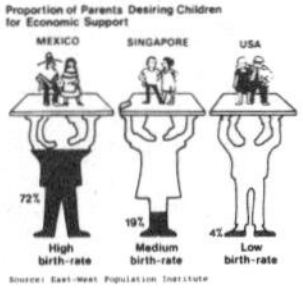

Figure modified from the East/West Population Institute publication.

Fig. 22

Source: UNICEF

McKeown, T. (1979) The role of medicine – dream, mirage or nemesis? Oxford: Blackwell.

Fig. 23

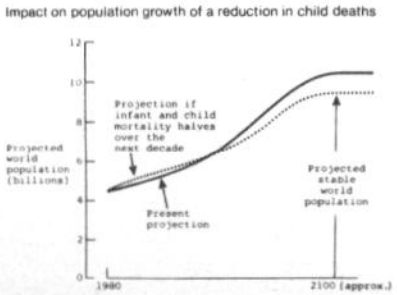

Modified from: UNICEF (1985) The state of the world's children. Oxford: OUP.

Fig. 24

From: Maine, D. in a publication produced by Center for Population and Family Health, 60 Haven Avenue, New York, 10032, USA.

Information on population and the introduction of family planning in different societies available from the International Planned Parenthood Federation (IPPF), 18-20 Lower Regent Street, London, SW1Y 4PW; their publication People is strongly recommended.

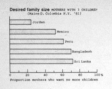

Fig. 25

Source: UNICEF

Kenya 1979 Census. Death per 1,000 births by age 2 months with no education 163; 1-7 years education 104; 8+ years education 61. Kenya Central Bureau of Statistics (1969) Population Census Vol. IV. Analytical Report. Kibet, M. (1982) District level mortality differentials in Kenya, based on 1979 census data. Thesis Population Studies and Research Institute, University of Nairobi.

THE EDUCATION OF GIRLS IS CLOSELY ASSOCIATED WITH A FALLING INFANT MORTALITY AND BIRTH RAT AND IMPROVED NUTRITION

For illiterate mothers there was no improvement in nutrition at high income levels.

Bairazi, R. (1980) Is income the only constraint in child nutrition in rural Bangladesh? Bull. WHO. **58**: 767-772.

Caldwell, J.C., McDonald, P. (1981) Influence of maternal education on infant and child mortality - levels and causes. In: Liege. International Population Conference. Manila 1981, Vol. 2: 79-96 (IUSSP).

Caldwell, J.C. (1979) Education as a factor in mortality decline: an examination of Nigerian data. Population Studies **33**: 395-413.

Caldwell, J.C. Maternal education as a factor in child mortality. World Health Forum **2** (1).

Cochrane, S.H. (1980) The effects of education on health. Washington DC: World Bank (Working papers No. 405).

Gaisie, S.K. (1969) Dynamics of population growth in Ghana. Legon, Accra: University of Ghana, Demographic Unit. (Ghana Population Studies; 1).

Pool, D.I. (1975) Upper Volta. In: Caldwell, J.C. (Ed) Population growth and socio-economic change in West Africa. New York: Columbia University Press.

Ruzicka, L.T., Kanitkar, T. (1972) Infant mortality in an urban setting: the case of Greater Bombay. In: Vidyanathan. K.E. (Ed) Studies on mortality in India. Gandhigram: The Gandhigram Institute of Rural Health and Family Planning. (Monograph series; 5)

Ram, E. (1979) The training of health auxiliaries for basic health services. In: De Souza, A. (Ed) Children in India - critical issues in human development. New Delhi: Manohar Publications.

Fig. 25
(continued)

Grosse, R.N. (1980) Interrelation between health and population: observations derived from field experience. Social Sci. Medicine. **14C**: 99–120.

UNESCO Features (1984) No. 801: 21. (This describes how to combat the relapse into illiteracy.)

Fig. 26

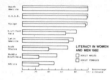

UNESCO. (1978) Estimates and projections of illiteracy. Document CSR-E-29. Paris: UNESCO.

Fuglesang, A. (1973) Applied communication in developing countries. Sweden: The Dag Hammarskold Foundation: 44.

Fig. 27

Kenya 80–90% population within 2 kilometres of school. (1979) CBS Statistical Abstract 1979, Table 105. Government of Kenya.

Figures for number of teachers/1,000 primary school children from UN Statistical Year Book 1981.

Ahmed, S. (1978) Potential contribution of primary school teachers to the health of a developing country. Lancet: 307–308.

Fig. 28

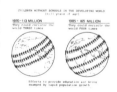

From: TALC, PO Box 49, St Albans, UK.

For information on schooling and literacy write: UNESCO, 7 Place de Fontenoy, Paris 75700, France.

Fig. 29

From a drawing by David Kyungu, a Tanzanian artist.

(1979) Rural Development: whose knowledge counts? IDS Bulletin 10 (2).

All those who wish to understand why we never reach the very poor should read: Chambers, R. (1983) Rural development: putting the last first. London: Longman.

For 20 years Dumont has been foretelling where education was taking Africa. Dumont, R. (1980) Stranglehold on Africa. Dumont, R. (1966) False Start in Africa. London: Ebenezer Baglis.

Bunch, R. Two ears of corn. A guide to people-centred agricultural improvement. World Neighbours 5116 North Portland, Oklahoma City, Oklahoma, 73112, USA.

Chambers, R. (1980) Rural poverty unperceived: problems and remedies. Washington DC: World Bank (staff working paper No. 400).

Fuglesang, A. (1982) About understanding - ideas and observations on cross-cultural communication. Sweden: Dag Hammarskjold Foundation.

Fig. 30

New Internationalist, 42 Hythe Bridge Street, Oxford, OX1 2EP. June 1973: 14.

For those who want to keep abreast with the problems of third world countries in the development process, the New Internationalist is essential reading.

Rural development: whose knowledge counts? IDS Bulletin (1979) 10 (2). Institute of Development Studies, Andrew Cohen Building, Brighton, Sussex, UK.

Fig. 31

Source: The preference of parents in the Punjab for the source of advice and childhood disease. Duplicated document from Narangwal studies.

Mosley, W.H. (1983) Will primary health care reduce infant mortality. Critique of some current strategies with special reference to Africa and Asia. Mimeographical document from CDC Atlanta, USA.

Effectiveness of PHC depends on the community acceptance of scientific basis of disease causation. Caldwell, J.C., Reddy, P.H., Caldwell, P. The social component of mortality decline: An investigation in South India employing alternative methodologies. Mimeo. Canberra: Australia National University, Department of Demography.

WHO (1979). World Health, November.

WHO (1977). WHO Chronicle 31 (11): 428-32.

Fig. 31
(continued)

Harding, T.W. (1975) Traditional healing methods for mental disorders. WHO Chronicle **31**: 436-40.

Lovel, H.J., de Graff, J., Gordon, G. (1984) Mothers measuring growth. Assignment Children **65/68**: 275-291.

(1979) Rural Development: Whose knowledge counts? IDS Bulletin **10** (2).

Fig. 32

Gurney, J.M. Food supply and primary health care in the Caribbean. Cajanus 15(4):220

From Gurney, J.M. Food supply and primary health care in the Caribbean. Cajanus **15** (4): 220.

Lovel, H.J., Feuerstein, M.T. (eds) (1985) Women, poverty and community development. Special issue of the Community Development Journal, Vol. 20 (3): 156-254.

Fig. 33

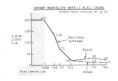

Sources: (1983) Studies in Family Planning **14**: 297
Hsiao, W.C. (1984) Transformation of health care in China. New England Journal of Medicine **310** (14): 932-936

China is taken as the classical example of a truly effective application of the PHC strategy in controlling disease and reducing mortality on a national scale. "... the Chinese have usually taken a holistic, 'causal web' approach to solving disease control problems ... their apparent success in these battles can largely be attributed to their pattern of attacking simultaneously on several fronts, usually in a labour intensive pattern, without a great deal of prior attention paid to which aspect of the attack will be most cost effective". Worth emphasises (see below) that disease control programs were evolved from a modern scientific base of information but the key element to success was mass mobilisation, health education and "social engineering".

Worth, R.M. (1975) The impact of new health programs on disease control and illness patterns in China. In: Medicine in Chinese Cultures: 477-485.

Hillier, S.M., Jewell, J.A. (1982) Health care and traditional medicine in China 1800-1982. Routledge & Kegan Paul.

Fig. 34

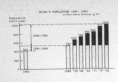

From: (1983) Studies in Family Planning **14**: 295

Hippocrates Unbound. An account of China's partial swing back to Western traditional methods of training. Fox, S. (1984) J.A.M.A. **251**: 490–494

Sidel, R. (1972) Women and child care in China. New York: Hill & Wang: 131, 237.

Sidel, V.W., Sidel, Ruth (1974) Serve the People, USA: Beacon Press: 206.

Fig. 35

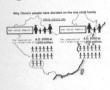

From: Morley, D. (1984) Pregnancy a privilege. Lancet i: 445–446.

Chinese recognise special problems exist with single child families.

Rothleast, M.K. (1971) Birth order and mother-child interaction in an achievement situation. Journal of Personality and Social Psychology. **17**: 113–20.

Xiao Yun (1984) Making 300 million children healthier. Women of China, 4 (April): 26.

Lampton, D.M. (1977) The politics of medicine in China. Folkestone, England: Dawson.

Fig. 36

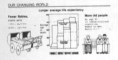

A diagram taken, with some adjustment, from The New Internationalist.

In the UK, to maintain facilities at the present level, a further 20% geriatric beds will be required over the next 20 years. Andrews, K. (1985) Brit. Med. J. **290**: 1023.

(1979) The old in cities. New Internationalist. April: 9.

Seale, J. (editorial) (1985) AIDS virus infection: prognosis and transmission. Journal of the Royal Society of Medicine. **78**: 613–615.

Acheson, E.D. (1986) Aids: a challenge for public health. Lancet i: 662–666.

Hunter, D.J., de Gruttola, V. (1986) Estimation of the risk of outcomes of HTLV-III infection. Lancet i: 677.

Fig. 37

From: Morley, D. (1984) Pregnancy a privilege. Lancet i: 445–446.

Contraceptive usage given on an IPPF visit to China in 1983 from a survey on 1:1,000 women in China, September 1981. Duplicated document.

Chapter 2: Childhood illness in the less developed countries of the world

Fig. 38

Modified from a diagram in: Werner, D. (1977) Where there is no doctor. Palo Alto, California: Hesperian Foundation.

Newell, K. (1975) Health by the people. Geneva: WHO.

Less than 15% of people have true access to health services.

Djukanovic, V., Mach, E.P. (1975)   In: Alternative approaches to meeting basic health needs in developing countries. A joint UNICEF/WHO study. Geneva: WHO.

Finding out about health needs in a district.   Amonoo-Lartson, R., Ebrahim, G.J., Lovel, H.J., Ranken, J.P. (1984) Finding out about helath needs in a district. In: District health care. Chapter 2: 26-66. Macmillan.

The various approaches to how community involvement may take place in primary health care is well analysed in three studies from Asia: Rifkin, S.B. (1985) Health planning and community participation: case studies in south-east Asia. Beckenham, Kent: Croom Helm.

Fig. 39

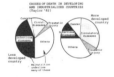

Figures taken from Taylor, Office of Health Economics, 12 Whitehall, London, SW1A 2DY.

Children's deaths represent the end stage of a long period of deterioration.

Puffer, R.R., Serrano, C.V. (1975) Patterns of mortality in childhood. Washington DC: PAHO/WHO.

Between age 15 and 45 female deaths may be 75% higher than males due to childbearing.

El Badry, M.A. (1969) Higher female than male mortality in some countries of South East Asia. Am. Statist. Ass. J. **64**: 1234-44.

Fig. 40

Illustration taken from: Parkin, J.M. (1975) A longitudinal study of village children in Uganda: pattern of illness during the second year of life. In: Owor, R., Ongom, V.L., Kirya, B.G. (Eds) The Child in the African environment. Nairobi: East African Literature Bureau.

There are other mostly unproved factors which may reduce children's ability to resist illness in less developed countries, for example, microtoxins in the food.

The influence of aflatoxins on child health in the tropics with particular reference to kwashiorkor. Hendrickse, R.G. (1984) Trans. Roy. Soc. Trop. Med. Hyg. **78**: 427-435.

Hendrickse, R.G. (1985)   Aflatoxins and Child Health in the Tropics. Proceedings Royal College of Physicians of Edinburgh. **15**: 138-155

For some guidelines on training in care of the sick or injured child and prevention of disease through promotion of environmental sanitation and hygiene, see: Lovel, H.J. (Ed) (1986) Maternal and child health. Teacher training material. An illustrated annotated bibliography. Chapters 6, 7 and 8. WHO/BLAT. Available from TALC, PO Box 49, St Albans, UK.

Fig. 41

TALC figures from a WHO study for the International Year of the Disabled.

Studies in France showed enormous savings by efforts to diagnose conditions such as deafness in early life.

Wynn, A. (1976) Health care systems for pre-school children. Proc. R. Soc. Med. **69**: 340-3.

A new course for teachers and planners of community based rehabilitation programmes has been started at the Institute of Child Health, 30 Guilford Street, London, WC1N 1EH, details sent on request. A resource centre has also been set up there for information in childhood disability and its management in less developed countries.

Information including a well illustrated duplicated resource book for caring for children with disablement in the community is available from Dr Einar Hellander, Consultant in Rehabilitation, WHO, Geneva, Switzerland.

Lovel, H.J. (Ed) (1986) Help for the mother or child with a handicap or disability. Chapter 9 in: Maternal and child health. Teacher training bibliography. WHO/BLAT. Available from TALC, PO Box 49, St Albans, UK.

Fig. 42

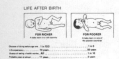

From UNICEF publicity material, 1981, source unknown.

Fig. 43

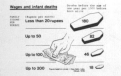

Figure from: Ghosh, S., Ramanujacharyulu, T.K., Hooja, V., Madhaven, S. (1979) Mortality pattern in an urban birth cohort. In. J. Med. Res. **69**: 616-23.

Morris, J.N. (1979) Social inequalities undiminished. Lancet **i**: 87-90.

Grundy, F., Lewis-Fanning, E. (1957) Morbidity and mortality in the first year of life. London: Eugenics Society: 72.

Brenner, M.H. (1979) Mortality and the national economy: a review and the experience of England and Wales 1936-76. Lancet **i**: 568-73.

In the UK we still have a two-fold difference in perinatal mortality depending on social class.

Morris, J.N. (1979) Social inequalities undiminished. Lancet **i**: 87-90

There are 710 million absolutely poor, expected to increase 1 billion by the year 2000.

Galbraith, J.K. (1979) The nature of mass poverty. Harmondsworth: Penguin.

Fig. 43
(continued)

Townsend, P. (1979) Poverty in the United Kingdom. A survey of household resources and the standards of living. Harmondsworth: Penguin.

Elliott, C. (1975) Patterns of poverty in the Third World. New York: Praeger.

Coombs, P.H. (Ed) (1980) Meeting the basic needs of the rural poor – the integrated community based approach. New York: Pergamon.

DHSS Research Working Group (1980). Inequalities in health: report. London: DHSS (Chairman: Sir Douglas Black).

For an excellent study of why we fail to reach the poor.

Chambers, R. (1983) Rural development: putting the last first. London: Longman.

Fig. 44

Occupation of household head and child death rate
Matlab, Bangladesh, 1974–1977

From a Matlab Study (1974–1977). International Centre for Diarrhoeal Disease Research, GPO Box 128, Dhaka 2, Bangladesh.

UK surveys have shown similar differences:

Butler, N.R., Bonham, D.G. (1980) Perinatal and neonatal mortality. Second Report from the Social Services Committee 1979–80. London: HMSO.

Chamberlain, R., Chamberlain, G., Howlett, B., Claireaux, A. (1975) British births, 1970. London: Heinemann,

Preston, S.H. (1975) The changing relation between mortality and level of economic development. Population Studies **29**: 231–248.

Fig. 45

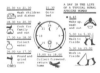

A DAY IN THE LIFE OF A TYPICAL RURAL AFRICAN WOMAN

From Food and Agriculture Organisation (1980) Integration of women into development. In: Ideas and Action No. 137: 16. Original information from: Rogers, B. The Domestication of Women.

ECOSOC (1974) World food conference: resolution VIII on women and food. 22 November 1974:81 (EISS87).

Economic Commission for Africa. The role of women in African development. Background paper. Addis Ababa: Economic Commission for Africa: 10 (E/CONF.66/BP/8).

Where water and fuel have to be carried 5–10 kilometres, energy for child care and preventive measures disappears.

White, G.F., Bradley, D.J., White, A.U. (1972) Drawers of water. Domestic water use in East Africa. University of Chicago Press.

Heavy activities out of home may negate nutrition and medical interventions.

Fig. 45
(continued)

For guidelines on prevention of disease through promotion of environmental sanitation and hygiene, see Chapter 6 in: Maternal and child health. Teacher training illustrated annotated bibliography. WHO/BLAT. Available from TALC, PO Box 49, St Albans, UK.

Taylor, C.E., Sarma, R.S.S., Parker, R.L., Reinke, W.A., Faruqee, R. (1983) Child and maternal health services in rural India: the Narangwal experiment. 2 Vols. World Bank. Baltimore, USA: John Hopkins University Press.

Krishna, Ahooja-Patel (1982) Another development with women. Development Dialogue 1-2: 17.

Basse, Marie-Therese (1984) Women food and nutrition in Africa: perspective from Senegal. Food and Nutrition 10: 65-79.

Gurney, J.M. Food supply and primary health care in the Caribbean. Cajanus 15 (4): 220.

Rutabanzibwa-Ngaiza, J., Heggenhougen, K., Walt, G. Women and Health in Africa. London: London School of Hygiene and Tropical Medicine (Education and Planning Centre Publication; 6).

Fig. 46

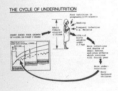

THE CYCLE OF UNDERNUTRITION

Mata, L. (1978) The children of Santa Maria Cauque: A prospective field study of health and growth. Cambridge, Massachusetts: MIT press.

Lechtig, A., Habicht, J.P. (1975) Effect of food supplementation during pregnancy on birthweight. Pediatrics 56: 508-20.

Roberts, S.B., Paul, A.A., Cole, T.J., Whitehead, R.G. (1982) Seasonal changes in activity, birth weight, and lactational performance in rural Gambian women. Trans. Roy. Soc. Trop. Med. Hyg. 76: 668-678.

Iyangar, L. (1974) Influence of the diet on the outcome of pregnancy in Indian women. In: Proceedings of the 9th International Conference of Nutrition, Mexico, 1972. Karger Basel: 48-53.

Andrews, J., McGarry, J.N.F. (1972) A community study of smoking in pregnancy. J. Obstet. Gynaec. Br. Commonw. 79: 1057-73.

Malaria affects growth of the foetus. Robinson, J.S. (1979) Growth of the foetus. Br. Med. Bull. 35: 137-44.

Blondel, B., Kaminski, K., Brerat, G. (1980) Antenatal care and maternal demographic and social characteristics. Evolution in France between 1972 and 1976. J. Epidemiol. Community Health 34: 157-63.

Not all studies correlate mothers' nutrition with birth weight. In the following study fatter mothers had smaller babies:

Abrien, A. (1985) Do maternal energy reserves limit foetal growth. Lancet i: 38-40.

Perinatal mortality rate a sensitive indicator of health care.

Waaler, H.T., Sterky, G. (1984) What is the best indicator of health care? WHO Forum 5: 276-278.

Fig. 47 From Pop. Ref. Bureau 1980.

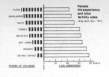

Fig. 48

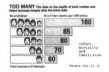

Pregnancy too young.

Infant mortality decline related to improved age/parity of childbearing.

Moseley, W.H. (1980) Biological contamination of the environment. In: Preston, S.H. (Ed) Biological and social aspects of mortality and length of life. Liege, Belgium: Ordina: 39-68.

Baird, D., Hytten, F.E., Thomson, A.M. (1958) Age and human reproduction. J. Obstet. Gynaec. Br. Commonw. **65**: 865.

Ebrahim, G.J. (1980) Cross cultural aspects of pregnancy and breast feeding. Proc. Nutr. Soc. **39**: 13-15.

Harrison, K.A. (1980) Approaches to reducing maternal and perinatal mortality in Africa. In: Philpott R.H. (Ed) Maternity services in the developing world - what the community needs. London: Royal College of Obstetricians and Gynaecologists.

Thompson, B., Baird, D. Sir. (1967) Some impressions of childbearing in tropical areas. J. Obstet. Gynaec. Br. Commonw. **74**: 329.

Friedman, H.L., Edstrom, K.G. (1983) Adolescent Reproductive Health. WHO (Offset Publication; 77).

Acsadi, G.T., Johnson-Ascadi, G. Health aspects of early marriage and reproductive patterns. IPPF Medical Bulletin **19** (4): 2-5.

Fig. 49

Pregnancy too many.

(1980) Biological determination of early life mortality. In: Preston, S.H. (Ed) Biological and social aspects of mortality and length of life. Liege, Belgium: Ordina: 83-112.

Mudkhedkar, S.N., Shah, P.M. The impact of family size on child nutrition and health. Indian Paediatr. **12**: 1073-1077.

Fig. 50

Spurr, G.B., Barac-Nieto, Maksud, M.G. (1977) Productivity and maximal oxygen consumption in sugar cane cutters. Am. J. Clin. Nutr. **30**: 316-321.

Estimates suggest that of those in the third world who are employed, half undertake heavy work and another quarter undertake medium intensity work. Spurr, G.B. (1983) Nutritional status and physical work capacity. Yearbook of Physical Anthropology **26**: 1-35.

Malnutrition will only be prevented when it is understood and managed as a social malady which produces "second class citizens".

Arena, J.M. (1974) Nutritional status of Chile's children: an overview. Nutr. Rev. **32**: 289-95.

Spurr, G.B. (1984) Physical activity, nutritional status and physical work capacity in relation to agricultural productivity. In: Liss, A.R. Energy intake and activity. New York: 207-261.

Basta S.S. et al (1979) Iron deficiency anaemia and the productivity of adult males in Indonesia. Am. J. Clin. Nutr. **32**: 916-925.

Brooks, R.M., Lathom, M.C., Crompton, D.W.T (1979) The relationship of nutrition and health to worker productivity in Kenya. East Afr. Med. J. **56**: 413-421.

For guidelines on action to intervene in the cycle of deprivation see Chapters 2 and 3 in: Lovel, H.J. (Ed) (1986) Maternal and child health. Teacher training material, an illustrated annotated bibliography. WHO/BLAT. Available from TALC, PO Box 49, St Albans, UK.

Fig. 51

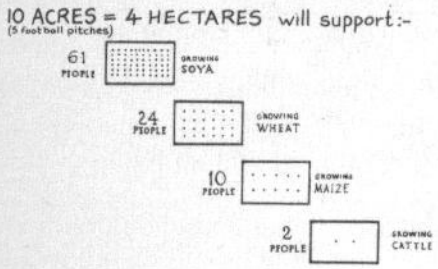

TALC original source unknown.

George, S. (1976) How the other half dies. The real reasons for world hunger. Harmondsworth, Middlesex: Penguin.

Schuftan, C. (1979) The challenge of feeding the people: Chile under Allende and Tanzania under Nyerere. Social Sci. Med. **13C**: 97-107.

Technical information to help farmers reaches the rich but not the poor farmers. Myrdal, G. (1970) Challenge of world poverty. A world anti-poverty programme in outline. Harmondsworth, Middlesex: Penguin.

Kondowe, G. (1980) Farmers' clubs in Jamkhed, India. M.Sc. dissertation. London: London University, Institute of Child Health.

(1984) Guinea Pigs as protein source. In: World Development Forum **2**, (22) 15 December 1984.

Arns, Cardinal of Sao Paulo, reported in: Development as illusion. Guardian, Tuesday 16 July 1985.

Kondowe, G., Tueumuna, T., Ebrahim, G.J., Lovel, H.J., Arole, M., Arole, G. (1983) The role of community groups in furthering primary health care. J. Trop. Paediatr. **29**: 332-336.

Fig. 52

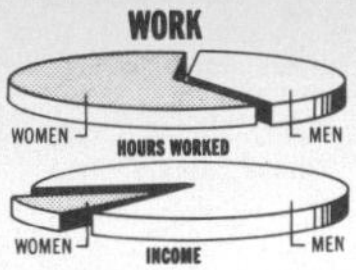

This figure is from Population Reference Bureau 1980.

Rosenfield, A., Main, D. (1985) Maternal mortality – a neglected tragedy. Lancet ii: 83-85.

Baumslag, N. (1985) Women's status and health: World perspectives. In: Advances in international maternal and child health. Jelliffe, D.B., Jelliffe, P., (Eds) Oxford: Clarendon Press.

Fig. 53

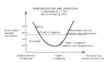

From a UNICEF document.

Fig. 54

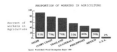

TALC adjusted from Jacobsen, O. (1978) Geographical Journal 2: 355.

Fig. 55

From World Development Report 1984, World Bank, 1818 H Street NW, Washington DC, 20433, USA.

Fig. 56

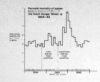

Wynn, M., Wynn, A. (1981) The prevention of handicap of early pregnancy origin. Chapter 19: The prevention of early pregnancy. London: Foundation for Education and Research in Childbearing.

'... men and women make a roughly equal contribution to congenital disorders caused by new mutations during the weeks and months before conception.'

Wynn, M., Wynn, A. (1985) Preconception care of the man. From the First Symposium on Preconception Care (WYETH). London: Charing Cross Hospital.

Wynn, M., Wynn, A. (1983) Effect of nutrition on reproductive capability. Nutrition and Health, Vol 1: 165-178.

Wynn, A., Wynn, M. The importance of nutrition around the time of conception in the prevention of handicap. Applied Nutrition: 1. Bateman, E.C. (Ed) (1981) Proceedings of the British Dietetics Association Study Conference, Exeter 1-7 April 1981. London: John Libby: 12-19.

The National Childbirth Trust (Leeds Branch) (1983). Healthy babies begin before you are pregnant. Leeds: The National Childbirth Trust.

Smithells, R.W., et al (1980) The possible prevention of neural tube defects by periconceptional vitamin supplement. Lancet, 16 February 1980: 339-342.

Wynn A., Wynn, M. (1981) Historical associations of congenital malformation. International Environmental Studies 17: 7-12.

Wynn, A., Wynn, M. (1982) The influence of nutrition on the fertility of women. Nutrition and Health, 1: 7-13

Wynn, A., Wynn, M. (1982) The importance of maternal nutrition in the weeks before and after conception. Birth, 9: (1) Spring.

Barker, W. (1984) Nutritional factors: can they reduce the incidence of mental handicap? Health Visitor, 57 (3): 73-77.

Barr, K. (1984) Early foetal damage - can it be prevented? Health Visitor, 57 (3): 78-80.

Mortimer, P. (1984) Getting fit for a baby. London: BMA (Family Doctor booklet).

Croydon Health Education Centre (1984) Prepare and plan for pregnancy.

Foresight: The Association for the Promotion of Preconceptual Care (1980) Guidelines for future parents. Godalming, Surrey: Foresight, GU8 4AY.

Fig. 57

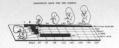

From: TALC, PO Box 49, St Albans, UK.

Tanner, J.M., Whitehouse, R.H., Takaishi, M. (1966) Standards from birth to maturity for height, weight, height velocity and weight velocity: British children 1965. Archs. Dis. Childh. **41**: 454-71; 613-35.

Ferguson, A.C. (1978) Prolonged impairment of cellular immunity in children with prolonged growth retardation. J. Pediatr. **93**: 52-56.

Fig. 58

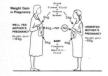

Nutrition both before and during pregnancy are important.

Habicht, J.P., Yarbrough, C., Lechtig, A., Klein, R.E. (1974) Relation of maternal supplementary feeding during pregnancy to birth weight and other sociobiological factors. In: Winick, M. (Ed) Nutrition and fetal development. New York: Wiley: 127-145.

Thomson, A.M., Billewicz, W.Z., Hytten, F.E. (1968) The assessment of fetal growth. J. Obstet. Gynaec. Br. Commonw. **75**: 903-16.

Habicht, J.P., Lechtig, A., Yarbrough, C., Klein, R.E. (1975) Maternal nutrition, birth weight and infant mortality. In: Size at Birth, (CIBA Foundation Symposium 27; New Series). Amsterdam: Elsevier: CIBA Foundation Symposium; Excerpta Medica 27. New series.

In one study the average weight gain was 6 kilograms in pregnancy and 30% of mothers gained no weight at all.

Shah, K.P., Shah, P.M. (1972) Relationship of weight during pregnancy and low birth weights. Indian Pediatr. **9**: 526.

Reinhardt, M. (1980) The effects of malaria, leishmaniasis and trypanosomiasis in pregnancy. J. Trop. Pediatr. **26**: 213-16.

Quereshi, S., Rao, N.P., Madhari, V., Mathur, Y.E., Reddi, Y.R. (1973) Effect of maternal nutrition supplementation on the birth weight of the newborn. Indian Pediatr. **10**: 541.

Fig. 59

From: UNICEF.

Hytten, F.E., Leitch, I. (1971) The physiology of human pregnancy. Oxford: Blackwell.

Aebi, H.G., Whitehead, R.G. (1980) Maternal nutrition during pregnancy and lactation. Berne: Hans Haber.

For guidelines on teaching about appropriate care in pregnancy see: Lovel, H.J. (Ed) (1986) Care of mothers in pregnancy and childbirth. Chapter 1 in: Maternal and child health. Teacher training material, an illustrated annotated bibliography. WHO/BLAT. Available from TALC, PO Box 49, St Albans, UK.

Fig. 60

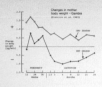

From: Prentice, A.M., Whitehead, R.G., Robert, S.B., Paul, A.A. (1981) Long term energy balance in childbearing Gambian women. Amer. J. Clin. Nutr. **34**: 2790-2799.

Prentice, A.M., Watkinson, M., Whitehead, R.G., Lamb, W.H., Cole, T.J. (1983) Prenatal supplementation of African women and birthweight. Lancet i: 489-491.

National Research Council (1980) Recommended dietary allowances. 9th Ed. Washington: National Academy of Sciences.

Schultz, Y., Lechtig, A., Bradfield, R.B. (1984) Effect of maternal diet and body composition on lactational performance. Am. J. Clin. Nutr. **39**: 296-306.

Fig. 61

From: Development Forum (1984) **12**, (9): 11.

Whitehead, R.G., Paul, A.A., Black, A.E., Wiles, S.J. (1981) Recommended dietary amounts of energy for pregnancy and lactation in the United Kingdom. In: Torun, B., Young, V.R., Rang, W.M. Protein energy requirements of developing countries: evaluation of new data. Tokyo: United Nations University: 259-265.

Also in CAFOD (1984/85) Just food. Includes women in agriculture, Chapter 4, and many other sections relevant to Chapter 1 of this book. CAFOD, 2 Garden Close, Stockwell Road, London, SW9 9TY.

Fig. 62

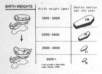

Ghosh, S. 1978 study in New Delhi (from UNICEF report).

Low birth weight affects survival, growth and development of non-verbal intelligence. Neligan, G., Prudham, D., Steiner, H. (1974) The formative years: birth, family and development in Newcastle upon Tyne. London: OUP.

Up to 60% of birth weight variation is due to environmental factors. Of these nutrition is the most important. Polani, P. (1974) In: Size at birth. Amsterdam: Elsevier Excerta Medica: 127-164 (CIBA Foundation Symposium; 27. New series).

Effects of socio-economic factors on birth weight.

Gopalan, C. (1962) Effect of nutrition on pregnancy and lactation. Bull. WHO **26**: 303.

Davies, D.P., Kennedy, J.D. (1985) Insufficient early weight gain in pre-term babies and influence on weight at 12 months. Achives Dis. Child. **60**: 718-721.

Mata, L. (1978) The children of Santa Maria Cauque: a prospective field study of health and growth. Cambridge, Massachusetts: MIT press.

Puffer, R.R., Serrano, C.V. (1975) Birth weight, maternal age and birth order: three important determinants in infant mortality. Washington DC: PAHO (Science Publication; 294).

Fig. 63

Incidence of low birth weight by country. WHO figures 1982.

Low birth weight occurs in around 5% of births in the north and 15-30% in the south. In China, however, only 4.7% of infants weigh less than 2,501 grams at birth.

Chalmers, I. (1980) Better perinatal health: Shanghai. Lancet **i**: 137-139.

Rosa, F.W., Turshen, M. (1970) Fetal Nutrition. Bull. WHO 43: 785-795.

Ciba Foundation (1974) Size at birth. Symposium 27, Elsevier, Excerpta Medica. Amsterdam: Associated Scientific Publishers.

Swedish Agency for Research Cooperation with Developing Countries (1978) Birthweight distribution and indicator of social development. Starky, G., Mellander, L. (Eds) SAREC Report R2.

Fig. 64

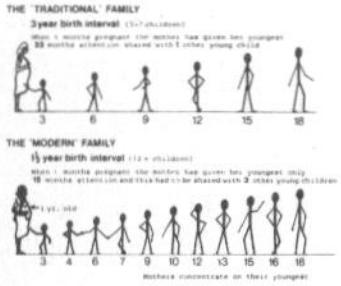

Available from: TALC, PO Box 49, St Albans, UK.

Close spacing can lead to an increase in infection in the family. Aaby, P., Bukh, J., Lisse, I.M., Smits, A.J. (1983) Spacing, crowding and child mortality in Guinea Bissan. Lancet ii: 161.

Traditionally children born too close will 'burn' each other out. Lovel, H., Mkandla, M., Morley, D. (1983) Birth spacing in Zimbabwe a generation ago. Lancet ii: 161.

Fig. 65

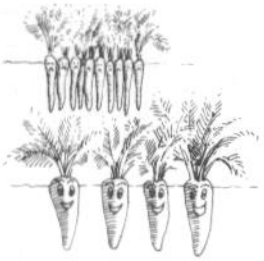

From: Morley, D., Woodland, M. (1979) See how they grow. London: Macmillan. (Drawing by Andrew Crane)

Martin, W.J., Morley, D.C., Woodland, M. (1964) Interval between births in a Nigerian village. J. Trop. Pediatr. **10**: 82.

Morley, D., Woodland, M. (1979) Breast feeding and the birth interval. In: See how they grow. London: Macmillan: 116-137.

For guidelines for teaching see: Promotion of mother and child health through birth spacing and family planning services. Chapter 4 in: Lovel, H.J. (Ed) (1986) Maternal and child health. Teacher training bibliography. WHO/BLAT. Available from TALC, PO Box 49, St Albans, UK.

Fig. 66

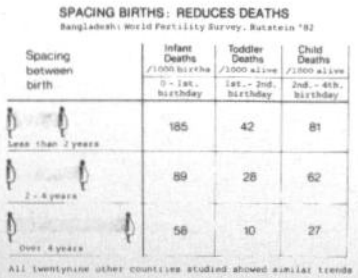

Source: Rutstein Shea (1982): Infant and child mortality: levels, trends and demographic differentials. World Fertility Survey Technical Bulletin: 2001.

Kane, Penny (1985) The impact of birth spacing on child health. Evidence from the world fertility survey. University College Cardiff Press, PO Box 78, Cardiff, CF1 1XL, UK.

Fig. 67

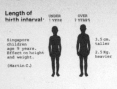

Length of birth interval

UNDER 1 YEAR   OVER 2 YEARS

Singapore children age 9 years. Effect on height and weight.

(Martin C.)

3.5 cm. taller

2.5 Kg. heavier

From figures in: Martin, C.E. (1979) A study of influences on birth interval in Singapore. Monogr. J. Trop. Paediatr. **25**: 46–76. Available from TALC, PO Box 49, St Albans, UK.

'Children are getting 1.5cm taller in the north and 3cms shorter each generation in the south'. Boyd, L.M. (1984) In: World Development Forum Newsletter, 2 (22) 15 December.

Winikoff, B. The effects of birth spacing on child and maternal health. Studies in Family Planning, **14**, (10).

The world fertility survey data provides compelling robust data that the length of inter-birth interval is a stronger determinant of infant and early childhood mortality than any of the other explanatory variable examined. Rutstein, S.O. (1984) Demographic differences in infant and child mortality. World Fertility Survey, Mimeo document.

Fedrick, J., Adelstein, P. (1983) Influence of pregnancy spacing on outcome of pregnancy (UK). Br. Med. J. 29 December: 753–756.

Fig. 68

Short birth interval   TEACHERS ASSESSMENT OF NINE YEAR OLDS (Martin C. '79)   Long birth interval

■ % Brighter than average
□ % Less bright than average

Teachers did not know the length of the childrens birth interval

From figures in: Martin, C.E. (1978) A study of influences on birth interval in Singapore. Monogr. J. Trop. Paediatr. **25**: 46–76.

Hutchison, D., Prosser, H., Wedge, P. (1979) Prediction of education failure. Educational Studies **1**: 73–82.

Fig. 69

Abortion worldwide

Abortions (legal and illegal) per 1,000 live births

■ Over 500
■ 201 – 500
■ 50 – 200
□ Less than 50
□ Unknown

Source: People, Vol 5 No. 2 1978, p. 18

(1978) People **5** (2): 18. Based on IPPF's 1977 unmet needs in family planning survey.

Cook, R.J., Senanayake, P. (1979) The human problem of abortion: medical and legal dimensions. London: IPPF, 18–20 Lower Regent Street, London, SW1Y 4PW.

Lovel, H.J., Bakoula, C. (1985) Lack of family planning services and induced abortion in rural Greece. IPPF Medical Bulletin 17.

Hamand, J. (1985) Abortion in Greece (1 woman in 3). Article in: People 12 (3): 19. Also Lovel, H.J. (1986) Abortion. Follow-up letter in: People 13 (1): 2.

Ock-Kyung, K., (1984) Abortion and fertility control in Korea. IPPF Medical Bulletin 18 (2):6.

Fig. 70

Source: UNICEF.

World Abortion Trends. A briefing paper on issues of national and international importance in the population field, prepared by the Population Crisis Committee, 1120 19th Street, NW Washington DC 20036, USA.

Tietze, C. (1981) Induced abortion. 4th ed. New York: Population Council.

For guidelines for teaching see: Lovel, H.J. (ed) (1986) Promotion of mother and child health through birth spacing/family planning services. Chapter 4 in: Maternal and child health. Teacher training bibliography. WHO/BLAT. Available from TALC, PO Box 49, St Albans, UK.

Potts, M. (1981) More marketing than medicine. People 8: 6-7.

Fig. 71

People **9** (4): 5.

Paxman, J.M. (1980) Low and planned parenthood. London: IPPF, 18-20 Lower Regent Street, London, SW1 4PW.

Fig. 72

Source unknown. Adjusted for TALC, PO Box 49, St Albans, UK.

Fig. 73

From: TALC, PO Box 49, St Albans, UK.

For a good general up-to-date article on population increase see: McNamara, R.S. (1984) Time bomb or myth: the population problem. Foreign Affairs: 1110.

Myrdal, G. (1970) The challenge of world poverty: a world anti-poverty programme in outline. Penguin: 147.

Figures on existing population and growth rates to be found at the end of: State of the World's Children 1986. Oxford: OUP.

Fig. 74

Kenya will double its population in 19 years with a birth rate of 54 per 1,000. This is believed to be the fastest growing rate in the world. See: (1980) World Population Data Sheet. Washington DC. FAO estimates the population of Africa is doubling every 22 years.

Rohde, J., Allmon, J. (1981) Infant mortality in relation to the level of fertility control practice in developing countries. International Population Conference, Manila. 2: 97–112.

Numeiri (Sudan's President) reported in: (1984) Daily Telegraph, Monday 21 May.

Food production in Africa and other countries: Brown, L.R. (1985) State of the world. New York: Norton: World Watch Institute Report.

Fig. 75

From: UNICEF

Fig. 76

Earth watch. People. **11** (Suppl.): 2. Available from IPPF, 18–20 Lower Regent Street, London, SW1Y 4PW, UK.

Africa needs a new strategy for health. This continent contains 29 of the 46 least developed countries. It has also 38 countries with a life expectancy at birth of only 50. (1981) The World Bank World Development Report. Washington DC.

Kehovale, J. (1985) Demographic levels and trends in sub-Saharan Africa. IPPF Medical Bulletin **19** (2): 2.

Brown, L.B., Wolf, E.C. (1985) Reversing Africa's decline. World Watch Paper 65.

'Chirac Population Fear'. Fear of 'terrifying' depopulation in France. (1984) London Times, Wednesday 31 October.

All teachers in health who wish to help their students understand population problems should get the sheets on World Population from Population Bureau, Washington DC, USA.

See also: Chapter 2 (abortion picture). In: Potts, M. (1981) More marketing than medicine. People 8 (2): 6–7.

Fig. 77   From: Gemini News Services Ltd, 40 Fleet Street, London, EC4.

Source: Gemini

Fig. 78

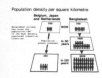

Source: TALC, PO Box 49, St Albans, UK.   Figures taken from: Harrison, P., Rowley, J.   In: Earth watch. People **11** (Suppl.): 2.

For a good brief account of some of the ethical issues in family planning: Camp, S.L. (1985) Ethical issues in family planning. In: Jelliffe, D.B., Jelliffe, P. (Eds) Advances in International Maternal and Child Health; 5. Oxford: Clarendon Press.

McCormack, A. (1983) Roman Catholic perspectives on population ethics. In: Camp, S. (ed) Ethical issues in family planning report **12**. Draper Fund.

Harrison, P., Rowley, J. (1984) Human numbers and human needs.   IPPF, 18-20 Lower Regent Street, London, SW1Y 4PW.

Fig. 79

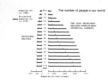

Harrison, P., Rowley J. (1984) Human numbers and human needs.   IPPF, 18-20 Lower Regent Street, London, SW1Y 4PW.

'Sudan plans medals for big families.' Numeiri reported in: (1984) London Daily Telegraph, Monday 21 May.

Fig. 80

Source unknown: TALC, PO Box 49, St Albans, UK.

Kenya moved from a food surplus to a food deficit nation in 1980 with little possibility of reversing this in the next decade. Government of Kenya (1981) National food plan. Sessional paper no. 4.

Fig. 81

(1981) Bulletin UNESCO Regional Asia Office. **22**: June.

Fig. 82

Source: TALC, PO Box 49, St Albans, UK.

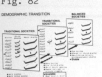

Chapter 3: Opportunity for improving health services

Fig. 83

Original source unknown. From: TALC, PO Box 49, St Albans, UK.

In a more detailed form see: (1973) Bryant's problem solving cycle. In: Morley, D. Paediatric priorities in the developing world. London: Butterworths: 336.

Amonoo-Lartson, R., Ebrahim, G.J., Lovel, H.J., Ranken, J.P. (1984) Making a health plan for the district. Chapter 3 in: District health care; challenges for planning, organisation and evaluation in developing countries. Macmillan.

Lovel, H.J. (ed) (1986) Planning, organisation and evaluation of MCH care. Chapter 10 in: Maternal and child health. Teacher training bibliography. WHO/BLAT. Available from TALC, PO Box 49, St Albans, UK.

Fig. 84

From TALC, PO Box 49, St Albans, UK.

Bryant, J.H. (1969) The gap between biomedical technology and health needs in developing countries. In: Zahlan, A.B., Nader, C. (Eds) Science and technology in developing countries. Cambridge: Cambridge University Press.

King, M. (Ed) (1966) Medical care in developing countries. Nairobi: OUP.

Morley, D.C. (1973) Paediatric priorities in the developing world. London: Butterworth: 36, 101, 113, 129, 184, 192.

Fig. 84
(continued)

Some are critical of the speed with which the implementation of PHC is being attempted: Chabot, H.T.J. (1984) Primary health care will fail if we do not change our approach. Lancet ii: 340. Segall, M. (1983) The politics of primary health care. Institute of Development Studies, University of Sussex, Bulletin **14** (14): 27.

Fig. 85

Figures from de Kadt, E., Segall, M. (1981) Health needs and health services in rural Ghana. Soc. Sci. Med. **15A**: 421–517.

Kenya spends 66% on hospitals, 10% on rural areas. (1979) Government of Kenya Development Plan 1974–1983. Part I: 145. Few countries give such breakdowns. However they are essential for realistic planning of services.

Amonoo-Lartson, R., Ebrahim, G.J., Lovel, H.J., Ranken, J.P. (1984) Building a health organisation in the district. Chapter 4 in: District health care, challenges for planning, organisation and evaluation. Macmillan.

Fig. 86

From: TALC, PO Box 49, St Albans, UK.

Mangudkar, M.P. (1978) Report of a Maharashtra State Commission. Reported in: Health for the millions. **IV** (5): 3. Attempts to get a copy of the original report have been unsuccessful.

The proportion of central government expenditure on health/education/defence in 1982 is given in the tables at the end of: State of the world's children 1986. OUP. The figures for India were: health 2.2%, education 1.9%, defence 20.2%.

Yudkin, J.S. (1980) The economics of pharmaceutical supply in Tanzania. Int. J. Hlth. Series 10 (3): 455–477.

Melrose, D. (1982) Bitter pills, medicines and the third world poor. Oxfam Public Affairs Unit.

Rolt, F. (1985) Pills, policies and profits: reactions to the Bangladesh drug policy. War on Want, 1 London Bridge Street, London, SE7.

Melrose, D. (1981) The great health robbery, baby milk and medicines in Yemen. Oxfam.

Heller, D. (1977) Poor health rich profits: multinational drug companies and the third world. Spokesman Books.

Barnett, A., Creese, A., Ayivov, E.C.K. (1980) The economics of pharmaceuticals, a case study of Ghana. Int. J. Hlth. Services.

Speight, A.N.P. (1975) Cost effectiveness and drug therapy. Tropical Doctor **5** (2): 89–92.

Barker, C., Marzago, C., Segall, M. (1980) Economy in drug prescribing in Mozambique. Tropical Doctor. January: 42–45.

Lall, S. (1977) The political economy of controlling transnationals: the pharmaceutical industry in Sri Lanka (1972–76). World Development **5** (8): 677–697.

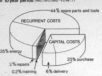

Fig. 87

Breakdown of Lifetime Costs of Cold Chain Equipment
Over 10 year period (WHO/EPI/GAG/'83/WP.1)

From: WHO. Expanded programme of immunisation/GAG/83/WP.1. Perhaps not a very good example of the ratio between capital and current expenditure but the only one readily available in diagrammatic form.

Fig. 88

Figures from (1980) Health Centre Policy Paper. World Bank.

Will primary health care reduce infant and child mortality? A critique of some current strategies with special reference to Africa and Asia. Paper produced for (1984) International Conference on Population. CDC Atlanta, USA: R & D feedback Public Health Service.

Fig. 89

From: UNICEF.

Burki, S.J., Voorhoeve, J.J.C., Layton, R. et al. (1977) Global estimates for meeting basic needs. Washington DC: World Bank (Basic Needs Paper No. 1).

On weapon systems in the US, expenditure on the MX is likely to be $60 billion. Scoville, H. (1980) The MX program. The New York Review, 27 March.

Fig. 90

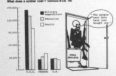

From: TALC. Figures from: Sivard, R.L. World military and social expenditures 1983. Available from: World Priorities, Box 25140, Washington DC, 20007, USA.

Leading article. Military expenditure versus social welfare. (1980) Lancet i: 1225–6.

Barnaby, F. (1980) A 3% rise in military spending. Lancet i: 1231–82.

Who is minding the arms business? Documentation and proceedings of a conference. Netherlands: Pax Christi, PO Box 85627, 2508 CH, The Hague, Netherlands.

Fig. 91

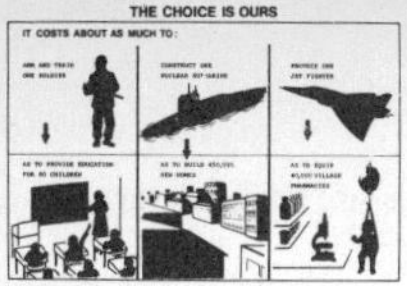

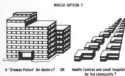

From a UNICEF poster.

World military and social expenditure. Leesburg, V. (1979) WMSE Publications.

Is it sensible for a small country like Britain to devote £1800 million a year to invent tomorrow's defence technology when its armed forces are usually equipped with yesterday's arms and never seem to have enough money to buy today's? Annual review of government funded research (table 2.1). HMSO. 1984.

Carlin, G.T., Chen, L.C., Hussain, S.B. (1976) Demographic crisis: the impact of the Bangladesh Civil War (1971) on births and deaths in a rural area of Bangladesh. Pop. Studies **30**: 87-105.

Fig. 92

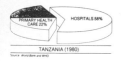

From: Morley, D. (1973) Paediatric priorities in the developing world. London: Butterworths.

Hart, J.T. (1971) The inverse care law. Lancet i: 405-12.

Over a half of the US spending on research, and just under a half of the UK spending goes to arms research. Connor, S. (1984) New calls for Science Ministry. New Scientist, December 20/27: 3-4.

Fig. 93

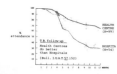

From: Grant, J.P. The state of the world's children 1984. OUP.

Klouda, A. (1983) Prevention is more costly than 'cure': health problem for Tanzania 1971-1981. In: Morley, D., Rohde, J., Williams, G. (Eds) Practising health for all. OUP.

Fig. 94

From: Bulletin, International Union against Tuberculosis, **57**: 152.

Such comparisons are difficult to investigate but are essential to the future planning of health services in less developed countries.

Fig. 95

THE VICIOUS CIRCLE THAT LEADS TO THE OVERUSE OF MEDICINE

From: Werner, D. (1974) Where there is no doctor. Hesperian Foundation, PO Box 1692, Palo Alto, California, 94302, USA.

Mahler, H. Health, a demystification of medical terminology. Lancet ii: 829-33.

Melrose, D. Bitter Pills. Oxfam, 274 Banbury Road, Oxford, OX2 7DZ.

Yudkin, J.S. (1980) The economics of pharmaceutical supply in Tanzania. International Journal of Health Services 10 (3): 455-477.

Lall, S., Bibile, S. (1977) The political economy of controlling transnationals: the pharmaceutical industry in Sri Lanka (1972-76). World Development 5 (8): 677-697.

Barker, C., Marzagao, C., Segall, M. (1980) Economy in drug prescribing in Mozambique. Trop. Doc. 10: 42-45.

Speight, A.N.P. (1975) Cost-effectiveness and drug therapy. Trop. Doc. 5 (2): 89-92.

Creese, A.L., Barnett, A., Ayivor, E.C.K. (1979) The economics of pharmaceutical policy - a case study of Ghana. International Journal of Health Services.

Fig. 96

FACULTY OF MEDICINE — MINISTRY OF HEALTH

Parent, M. French translation of: Morley, D., Woodland, M. (1979) See how they grow. Macmillan. Translation published by Courtejoie, J. Hopital de Kangu-Magumbe, Republic Du Zaire, Africa.

Gish, O. (1979) The political economy of primary care and 'health by the people': an historical exploration. Soc. Sci. Med. **13C**: 203-311.

'Ray to undergo surgery in US'. Reported in: (1983) Hindustani Times, Tuesday 5 June.

Fig. 97

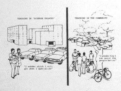

From: Morley, D., Woodland, M. (1979) See how they grow. Macmillan.

Banerji, D. (1974) Social and cultural foundations of the health services systems in India. Jawaharlal Nehru University: New Delhi. Centre of Social Medicine and Community Health.

Ebrahim, G.J., Morley, D.C., Lloyd, J.K., Wolff, O.H. (1974) Can a small group bring about change? UNICEF/WHO Course for Senior Teachers of Child Health. Br. Med. J. **2**: 166-9.

Saunders, D. (1985) Struggle for health. London: Macmillan.

Fig. 98

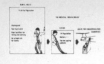

From: Morley, D. (1973) Paediatric priorities in the developing world. Butterworths.

Migration of MDs and Nurses: Mejia, A., Pizuki, H., Royston, E. (1979) Physician and nurse migration: analysis and policy implications. Geneva: WHO.

It would take seven years output from the UK medical schools to replace the 20,000 or more foreign graduates. Editorial. (1980) Update Dec 15: 1457. Journal of post graduate general practice. London: Update Publications Ltd.

Fig. 99

From: TALC, PO Box 49, St Albans, UK.

Abel-Smith, B., Titmus, K. (Eds) (1974) Social policy: an introduction. London: Allen & Unwin.

Abbatt, F., McMahon, R. (1975) Teaching health care workers: a practical guide. MacMillan. TALC, PO Box 49, St Albans, UK.

Fig. 100

Epidemiological studies of the failure of coronary care centres to change mortality rates:

New and inappropriate technology is a serious problem for more developed countries. Doctors and health planners have to develop an informed scepticism towards the marketing of new drugs and technologies.

Smith, T. (1984) Editorial. Br. Med. J. **289**: 393–394.

In child health, there are similar problems with newborn care. Baum, D., McFarlane, A., Tizard, P. (1977) Benefits and hazards of neonatology. Clin. Dev. Med. **64**: 126–38.

Thirty per cent of 800 hospitals equipped for open heart surgery treated no cases over one year. Fein, R. (1980) Social and economic attitudes shaping American health policy. Millbank Mem. Fund Quarterly/Health and Society **58** (3): 349–85.

Fig. 101

A high proportion of doctors in some third world countries (eg. South Korea) are involved solely in private practice, in others almost all doctors in government service also do private practice (Indonesia, South America). World Bank (1975) Health Sector Policy Paper.

Sharpston, M.J. (1972) Uneven geographic distribution of health care: a Ghanaian case study. J. Dev. Studies **8**: 205-222.

Abel-Smith, B. (1976) Value for money in health services. Heineman.

Fig. 102

From the classic 'primary health care' training book: Werner, D., Blake, M. Helping health workers learn. Hesperian Foundation, PO Box 1692, Palo Alto, California 94302, USA.

Eisenberg, L. (1984) Prevention: rhetoric or reality. J. Roy. Soc. Med. **77**: 268-280.

Fig. 103

From: Morley, D., Woodland, M. (1979) See how they grow. Macmillan.

Morley, D., (1981) Distance learning for primary health care. Isr. J. Med. Sci. **17**: 184-191.

For ideas on teaching methods see: Learning how to teach others to provide better MCH care. Chapter 11 in: Lovel, H.J. (ed) (1986) Maternal and Child Health. Teacher training bibliography. WHO/BLAT. Available from TALC, PO Box 49, St Albans, UK.

Fig. 104

From: Morley, D. Information on distance learning in the less developed countries, and a "programmed text" on writing distance learning material is available from: The International Extension College, 18 Brooklands Avenue, Cambridge, CB2 2HN. They also produce a newsletter.

The Open University, Milton Keynes, UK, has a series of non-degree short courses in a distance learning form.

Lovel, H.J. (ed) (1986) Maternal and Child Health. Teacher training bibliography. WHO/BLAT. Available from TALC, PO Box 49, St Albans, UK.

Fig. 105

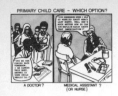

From: Morley, D., Woodland, M. (1979) See how they grow. Macmillan.

Gwatkin, D.R., Wilcox, J.R., Wray, J.D. (1980) Can health and nutrition interventions make a difference? Washington DC: Overseas Development Council Monograph No. 13.

Dissevelt, A.G., Vogel, L.C. (1971) An analysis of the operations of the medical assistant in an out-patient department, with emphasis on administrative procedures. In: Gould, E.C. (Ed) Health and disease in Africa. Proceedings of 1970 East African Medical Research Council Scientific Conference. Nairobi: East African Literature Bureau.

Fendall, N.R.E. (1972) Effectiveness and efficiency. Nuffield Provincial Trust.

Van Etten, G.M. (1976) Rural health development in Tanzania. Van Gorcum and Comp. (21, 205).

Fig. 106

Thomstad, B., Cunningham, N., Kaplan, B.H. (1975) Changing the rules of the doctor-nurse game. Nursing Outlook **23**: 422-427.

Powell, M. (1970) The eternal triangle. Br. Med. J. **ii**: 416.

Morley, D. (1973) Paediatric priorities in the developing world: 341-363. London: Butterworths.

Fig. 107

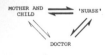

Morley, D. (1973) Paediatric priorities in the developing world: 316-340. Butterworths.

Cunningham, N. (1978) The under-fives clinic - what difference does it make? (Thesis for a doctorate of Public Health, Johns Hopkins University, USA) J. Trop. Paediatr. Dec 1978: 239-334.

Communication in health. Set of slides available from TALC, PO Box 49, St Albans, UK.

Fig. 108

From: TALC, PO Box 49, St Albans, UK.

Abbatt, F., McMahon, R. (1985) Teaching health care workers: a practical guide. Macmillan. Available from TALC, PO Box 49, St Albans, UK.

Werner D., Bower, B. Helping health workers learn. Hesperian Foundation, Box 1692, Palo Alto, California 94302, USA.

Management in child health. Set of slides available from: TALC, PO Box 49, St Albans, UK.

Fig. 109

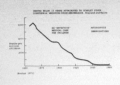

Figures from the Office of Health Economics, 12 Whitehall, London, SW1.

Saunders, D. (1985) Struggle for health. London: Macmillan.

Ebrahim, G.J. (1984) Child health in a changing environment. London: Macmillan.

Gale, A.H. (1945) A century of changes in the mortality and incidence of the principal infections of childhood. Archs. Dis. Childh. **20**: 2-21.

McKinlay, J.B., McKinlay, S.M. (1977) The questionable contribution of medical measures to the decline of mortality in the USA in the 20th century. Millbank Mem. Fund Q. **55**: 405-428.

Fig. 110

Adjusted from McDermott, C. (1982). WHO Forum 1: 123.

Roberts, D. (1960) Victorian origins of the British welfare state. New Haven, Yale.

Hill, M. (1980) Understanding social policy. Oxford: Basil Blackwell and Martin Robertson.

Open University Course Team (1985) Caring for health. Dilemmas and prospects. Open University Press, Milton Keynes, MK7 6AA, UK.

Fig. 111

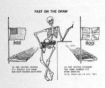

Figures from UK Sunday Observer, December 29th 1980.

Bewley, B.R., Halil, T., Smith, A.H. (1973) Smoking by primary school children: prevalence and associated respiratory symptoms. Br. J. Prev. Soc. Med. **27**: 150-3.

Royal College of Physicians of London (1971) Smoking and health now: a report of the Royal College of Physicians. London: Pitman.

United States Department of Health, Education and Welfare. Office of Smoking and Health. (1977-78) The health consequence of smoking. DHEW, Rockville, Maryland.

Martin, F.M. (1977) Social medicine and its contribution to social policy. Lancet **ii**: 1336-8.

Gray, J.A.M. (1977) The failure of preventive medicine. Lancet **ii**: 1338-9.

In the US it is estimated that 30% of all cancer deaths are due to smoking and world wide is responsible for 15% of cancer deaths: United States Public Health Service (1982) The health consequences of smoking: cancer. A report of the Surgeon General, United States Department of Health and Social Services. Office of Smoking and Health, Washington. United States Government Printing Office.

Fig. 112

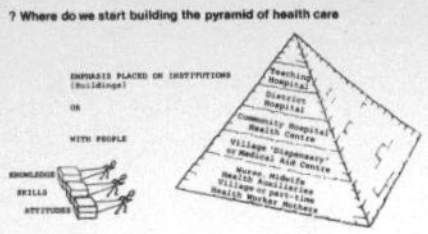

From: Morley, D.C. (1973) Paediatric priorities in the developing world. London: Butterworths.

Newell, K.W. (1975) Health by the people. Geneva: WHO (62, 207).

Chambers, R. (1983) Rural development: putting the last first. London: Longman.

Amonoo-Lartson, R., Ebrahim, G.J., Lovel, H.J., Ranken, J.P. (1984) Building the health organisation in the district. Chapter 4: 67-101 in: District Health Care, challenges for planning, organisation and evaluation. Macmillan.

Fig. 113

From: Morley, D., Woodland, M. (1979) See how they grow. London: Macmillan.

Statement taken from Janus Yen, founder of the mass education movement that took place in China in the 30's. Developed from a statement by Lao Tsu, Tao Te Ching, Book XVII. Translated by: D.C. Lan (1963) Penguin Classics.

Chapter 4: The changing of health workers

Fig. 114

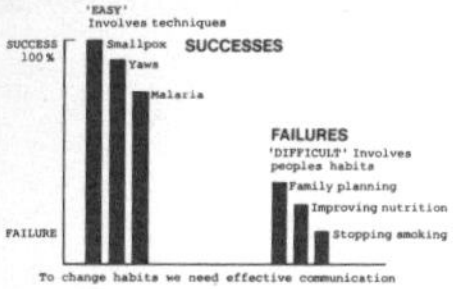

From: Morley, D.C., Woodland, M. (1978) See how they grow. London: Macmillan.

Wray, J.D. (Guest ed) (1974) Expanded MCH programs. J. Trop. Paediatr. 20 (1): 1-3.

Hardiman, M., Midgley, J. (1982) The social dimensions of development. Chichester, UK: Wiley.

Bossert, T. (1979) Health policies in Africa and Latin America: adopting primary care approach. Soc. Sci. Med. **13C**: 65-68.

De Miguel, J.M. (1977) Policies and politics of the health reforms in Southern European countries. Soc. Sci. Med. **11**: 379-393.

Dimmock, S. (1977). In: Barnard, K., Lee, K. (Eds) Conflicts in the NHS. Croom Helm.

Dunlop, D. (1980) Health planning, what about demand? Soc. Sci. Med. **14**: I-III editorial.

Fig. 115

From: TALC, PO Box 49, St Albans, UK.

Newell, K. (Ed) (1975) Health by the people. Geneva: WHO.

(1978) International conference on primary health care, Alma Ata. 11 September 1978. Final report. WHO/UNICEF.

Rifkin, S. (1985) Health planning and community participation. London: Croom Helm.

Fig. 116

Belloc, N.B., Breslow, L. (1972) Relationship of health practices and mortality. Prev. Med. **1**: 409-21.

Belloc, N.B. (1973) Relationship of health practices and mortality. Prev. Med. 2: 67-81.

Foster, G.M. (1977) Medical anthropology and international health planning. Soc. Sci. Med. **11**: 527-534.

Stacey, M. (1976) Concepts of health and illness: their relevance for health and health policy research. In: Health and health policy, priorities for research 1977. Social Scientific Research Council, UK.

Fig. 117

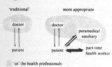

From: Morley, D.C., Woodland, M. (1978) See how they grow. London: Macmillan.

Villod, M.T., Guerin, N. (1974) Why rehabilitate traditional medicine? Children in the Tropics **122**: 13-30.

Fig. 118

From: Werner, D.B. (1974) Where there is no doctor. Hesperian Foundation, PO Box 1692, Palo Alto, California 94302, USA.

Chabot, H.T.J. (1984) Primary health care will fail if we do not change our approach. Lancet **ii**: 340-341.

Werner, D. (1978) The village health worker - lackey or liberator. In: Elliott, K., Sheet, M. Health auxiliaries and the health team. London: Croom Helm.

Werner, D.B. (1976) Health care and human dignity. Proceedings of a symposium on appropriate technology and delivery of health and welfare services for the disabled in developing countries, The Commonwealth Foundation, Occasional Paper No. XLI: 75 (202, 207).

Molina-Guzman, G. (1979) Third World experience in health planning. Int. J. Health Services **9**: 139-150.

Fig. 119

Morley, D.C., Woodland, M. (1978) See how they grow. London: Macmillan.

Abbatt, F., McMahon, R. (1985) Teaching health care workers. London: Macmillan.

A community health project in Africa. Set of slides on achievements and problems of a primary care project in Guinea Bissan. TALC, PO Box 49, St Albans, UK.

Jamkhed. Set of slides on an innovative agricultural and health project in India. TALC, PO Box 49, St Albans, UK. Also a set from Africa: A community project in Africa.

Kromberg, M. (1978) New music – old harmony. Development Forum **6**: 6.

Vaughan, J.P. (1980) Barefoot or professional? Community health workers in the Third World. J. Trop. Med. Hyg. **83**: 3–10.

Molina, G. et al (1980) Colombia: how to select community health leaders. World Forum **1**: 57–61.

Fig. 120

From: Werner, D. (1974.B) Where there is no doctor. Hesperian Foundation, PO Box 1692, Palo Alto, California 94302, USA.

Fuglesang, A. (1973) Applied communication in developing countries. Sweden: The Dag Hammarskold Foundation.

Lovel, H.J. (ed) Maternal and Child Health. Teacher training bibliography. WHO/BLAT. Available from TALC, PO Box 49, St Albans, UK.

Fig. 121

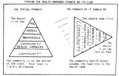

From: Werner, D. (1974.B) Where there is no doctor. Hesperian Foundation, PO Box 1692, Palo Alto, California 94302, USA.

Amonoo-Lartson, R., Ebrahim, G.J., Lovel, H.J., Ranken, J.P. (1984) Building the health organisation in the district. Chapter 4: 102–120. In: District Health Care, challenges for planning, organisation and evaluation in developing countries. London: Macmillan. Available from TALC, PO Box 49, St Albans, UK.

Fig. 122

How much are health professionals taught about management? The General Practitioner controls £80,000, the consultant £530,000 expenditure each year in the UK. Have they been trained in the management of resources? Owen, D. (1984) Medicine, mortality and the market. Lancet ii: 30.

Amonoo-Lartson, R., Ebrahim, G.J., Lovel, H.J., Ranken, J.P. (1984) District health care. London: Macmillan.

Fig. 122 (continued)

Learning how to teach planning, organisation and evaluation. Chapter 10 in: Lovel H.J. (ed) (1986) Maternal and Child Health. Teacher training illustrated annotated bibliography. WHO/BLAT. Available from TALC, PO Box 49, St Albans, UK.

Fig. 123

Conventional 'two box' view of health care

The 'four-box' system of health care

Gray, Lancet '83.ii.1185

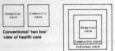

Muir Gray, J.A. (1983) Four box health care: development in a time of zero growth. Lancet November 19: 1185-1186.

Practical management. Chapter 5 in: Amonoo-Lartson, R., Ebrahim, G.J., Lovel, H.J., Ranken, J.P. (1984) District health care, challenges for planning, organisation and evaluation. London: Macmillan.

In the UK the Committee on Health Service - the Court report - attempted to integrate child health services. Great Britain Committee on Child Health Services. (1976) Fit for the future; report. (Chairman S.D.M. Court). 2 vols. London: HMSO.

Segall, M. (1983) The politics of primary health care. In: Health, society and politics. Institute of Development Studies Bulletin **14** (4): 27-37.

Bryant, J. (1980) WHO program of health for all by the year 2000: a macrosystem for health policy-making - a challenge to social science research. Soc. Sci. Med. **14A**: 381-6.

Taylor, R. (1977) The local health system: an ethnography of interest groups and decision making. Soc. Sci. Med. **11**: 583-592.

Fig. 124

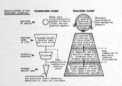

Health bureaucracies are locked into an urban biased, hospital based, high technology system that self perpetuates. (1980) Policies of Developing Countries. Chapter 4. World Bank Health Sector Policy Paper. Washington DC.

Ebrahim, G.J. (1981) Paediatric practice in developing countries. Chapter 1. London: Macmillan.

Smith, A. (1985) The functions of a health service. Lancet i. Examines this in relation to the UK national health service.

Amonoo-Lartson, R., Ebrahim, G.J., Lovel, H.J., Ranken, J.P. (1984) Building the health organisation in the district. Chapter 4 in: District health care: challenges for planning, organisation and evaluation in developing countries. London: Macmillans. Available from: TALC, PO Box 49, St Albans, UK.

Gish, O. (1978) Primary health care. Planning strategy. UNICEF. Carnets de l'enfants. **42**: 46-56.

Gish, O. (1979) The political economy of primary health care and health by the people. An historical exploration. Soc. Sci. Med. **13C**: 203-211.

Fig. 125

Cripwell, K.R. (1981) Community health worker and the need for training in communication skills. Trop. Doc. **11**: 86–88.

Morley, D., Rohde, J., Williams, G. (1983) Practising health for all. OUP.

Lovel, H.J., Feuerstein, M.T. (eds) (1983) Community development and primary health care. Special issue of Community Development Journal, Vol 18 (2): 97–208. OUP.

Lovel, H.J., Feuerstein, M.T. (eds) (1985) Women, poverty and community development. Special issue of Community Development Journal, Vol 20 (3): 156–254. OUP.

Tandon, R. (ed) (1982) Adult education and primary health care; special report. Converzence Vol 15 (2): 1–94. International Council for Adult Education, 29 Prince Arthur Avenue, Toronto, Canada, M5R 1B2.

Fig. 126

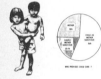

Aarons, A., Hawes, H., Gayton, J. (1979) CHILD-to-child. London: Macmillan.

Shah, P.M., Walimbe, S.R., Dhole, V.S. Wage earning mother, mother substitute and care of the young children in rural Maharashtra. Indian Pediatr. **16**: 167.

Garber, H., Heber, F.R. (1977) The Milwaukee project: indications of the effectiveness of early intervention in preventing mental retardation. In: Mittler, P. (Ed) Research to practice in mental retardation. Vol. 1. Care and intervention. Baltimore: University Park Press.

Knight, J., MacGregor, S. (1981) A pilot study of CHILD-to-child in a rural Jamaican school. Abstract paper from CCMRC, 26th Scientific Meeting, Nassau, Bahamas. CHILD-to-child documentation available from CHILD-to-child, Institute of Child Health, 30 Guilford Street, London, WC1N 1EH.

Abeje, H.Y. (1979) A link between like learning and work. Learning and being: education beyond the schoolroom. UNICEF News, New issue: 112/2.

Rohde, J.E., Sadjimin, T. (1980) Elementary school pupils as health educators: role of school health programmes in primary health care. Lancet **i**: 1350–1352.

Fig. 127

From: TALC, PO Box 49, St Albans, UK.

Lovel, H.J. (ed) (1986) Maternal and child health. Teacher training illustrated annotated bibliography. WHO/BLAT. Available from TALC, PO Box 49, St Albans, UK.

Network of International Council of Adult Education, 29 Prince Arthur Avenue, Toronto, Canada, M5R 1B2.

Fig. 128

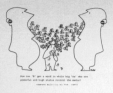

From: UNESCO (1977) Features No. 716. Feature is a free newsletter.

UNESCO, 7 Place de Fontenoy, 75700 Paris, France, have material in relation to education and health.

A list of free newsletters is available from AHRTAG, 85 Marylebone High Street, London, W1M 3DE, UK. Particularly recommended are: Contact from CMC, Route de Ferney, 1211 Geneva 20 Switzerland; and Salubritas from APHA, 1015 Street NW, Washington DC 20036 USA.

For a useful source of material on health education, etc: World Neighbours, 5116 North Portland, Oklahoma City, Oklahoma 73112 USA.

See also references to fig. 114.

Fig. 129

Original source unknown. Available from TALC, PO Box 49, St Albans, UK.

International Development Research Centre. Canada (1975-1980) Low cost health care and manpower training. Vols 1, 2, 3, 4, 5, 6.

Free newsletters available from NFE (non-formal education) Exchange Information Centre, 513 Erickson Unwin, E. Lancing, Michigan 48824 USA, and Development Communication Report, 1414 22nd Street NW, Washington DC 20037 USA.

Fig. 130

Modified from an original drawing from New Internationalist.

Satoto, W.G. (1980) Socio-political constraints on primary health care. Development Dialogue 1: 85-101.

Fig. 131

This drawing is modified from: Werner, D., Bower, B. Helping health workers learn. Hesperian Foundation, PO Box 1692, Palo Alto, California 94302, USA.

Heggenhougen, H.K. (1984) Will primary health care efforts be allowed to succeed? Soc. Sci. Med. **19**: 217-224.

Sidel, V.W., Sidel, R. (1977) Primary health care in relation to socio-political structure. Soc. Sci. Med. **11**: 415-419.

McKinlay, J.B. (1979) Epidemiological and political determinants of social policies regarding the public health. Soc. Sci. Med. **13**: 541-558.

Mburu, E.M. (1979) Rhetoric – implementation in health policy and health services delivery for a rural population in a developing country. Soc. Sci. Med. **13**: 577-583.

See also references to fig. 114.

Fig. 132

Morley, D.C., Woodland, M. (1978) See how they grow. London: MacMillan.

McKay, H., McKay, A., Sinisterra, L. (1974) Early malnutrition and mental development. Swedish Nutrition Foundation Symposium. Uppsala: Almqvist & Wiksell.

McKay, H., Sinisterra, L., McKay, A., Gomes, H., Lloreda, P. (1978) Improving cognitive ability in chronically deprived children. Science 200: 270-78.

Birch, H.G., Gussow, J.D. (1970) Disadvantaged children: health, nutrition and school failure. New York: Grune & Stratton.

Birch, H.G., Richardson, S.A. (1972) The functioning of Jamaican school children severely malnourished during the first two years of life. In: Nutrition, the nervous system and behaviour. Washington: Pan American Health Organization: 64-72 (Scientific Publication No. 25).

Lovel, H.J. (ed) (1986) Maternal and child health. Teacher training bibliography. WHO/BLAT. Available from TALC, PO Box 49, St Albans, UK.

Cravioto, J., Delicardie, E. (1972) Environmental correlates of severe clinical malnutrition and language development in survivors from kwashiorkor or marasmus. In: Nutrition, the nervous system and behaviour. Washington: Pan American Health Organization: 73-94 (Scientific Publication No. 25).

Differences between different ethnic groups with different child rearing ability in London.

Pollack, M. (1972) Today's three year olds in London. London: Heinemann.

Pollack, M. (1979) Nine year old. Lancaster: MTP Press Ltd.

Fig. 133

From: TALC, PO Box 49, St Albans, UK.

Grant, J. (1984) State of the world's children. Oxford: OUP.

For a detailed study from 15 countries of the political and social problems of introducing primary health care. Morley, D., Rohde, J., Williams, G. (1983) Practising health for all. Oxford: OUP.

Newell, K. (Ed) (1975) Health by the people. Geneva: WHO.

Walsh, J.A., Warren, K.S. (1979) Selective primary health care. An interim strategy for disease control in developing countries. N. Engl. J. Med. 30: 967-74.

Gwatkin, D.R., Wilcox, J.R., Wray, J.D. (1980) Can health and nutrition intervention make a difference? Washington DC: Overseas Development Council. (Monograph No. 13).

Stuart, K. (1984) Health for all: its challenge for medical schools. Lancet 25 February: 441.

Fig. 134

Multiple episodes of diarrhoea and growth faltering. Cole, T.J., Parkin, J.M. (1977) Infection and its effect on the growth of young children: a comparison of the Gambia and Uganda. Trans. R. Soc. Trop. Med. Hyg. **71**: 196-198.

Training programmes for those concerned with the management of oral rehydration are available from: Diarrhoeal Disease Control Unit, WHO, Geneva.

Fig. 135

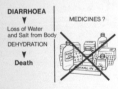

Black, R.E., Brown, K.H., Becker, S., Alim, A.R.M.A., Merson, M.H. (1982) Contamination of weaning foods and transmission of enterogenic E. coli diarrhoea in children in rural Bangladesh. Trans. R. Soc. Trop. Med. Hyg. **76**: 259-264.

Information on many aspects of diarrhoea and its management from: International Centre for Diarrhoeal Disease Research (ICDDRB), GPO Box 128, Dhaka 2, Bangladesh; and Appropriate Health Resource Technology Action Group (AHRTAG), 25 Marylebone High Street, London, W1M 3DE. Both produce regular free newsletters giving up-to-date information.

Fig. 136

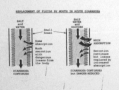

Diarrhoea management. Set of slides and script. TALC, PO Box 49, St Albans, Herts, UK.

The discovery that sodium transport and glucose transport are coupled in the small intestine, so that glucose accelerates absorption of solute and water, was potentially the most important medical advance in this century. (Editorial) (1978) Lancet ii: 300-301.

Cash, R., McLauglin, J. (Eds) (1984) Proceedings of International Congress on Oral Rehydration (ICORT). Washington: Agency for International Development.

Pan American Health Organization (1980) Oral rehydration therapy: an annotated bibliography. Washington: PAHO (116 pages).

Fig. 137

From: TALC, PO Box 49, St Albans, UK.

Chung, A.W., Viscorova, B. (1948) The effect of early oral feeding versus early oral starvation on the course of infantile diarrhoea. J. Paediatr. 33: 14.

Mandgal, D.P., Bradshaw, J., Wansbrough-Jones, M.H., Lambert, H.P. (1985) Management of acute gastroenteritis in children. Br. Med. J. **290**: 1287.

(1980) Oral rehydration therapy (ORT) for childhood diarrhoea. Pop. Rep. **8**: 41-75.

Hirschorn, N. (1980) The treatment of acute diarrhoea in children. An historical and physiological perspective. Am. J. Clin. Nutr. 33: 637-643.

Fig. 138

From: TALC, PO Box 49, St Albans, UK.

The Voluntary Health Organisation of India (VHAI), C14 Community Centre, Safdorjung Development Area, New Delhi 110016, India, have a wide variety of excellent teaching material for various levels including villages. They have a small booklet describing oral rehydration in simple terms.

Fig. 139

Diarrhoea management. Set of slides and script. TALC, PO Box 49, St Albans, UK.

Population Information Programme. Oral rehydration therapy (ORT) for childhood diarrhoea.   Pop. Rep. series 2, no. 2.

(1983) Oral rehydration therapy: an annotated bibliography. 2nd ed. Washington: PAHO/WHO. (Scientific Publication no. 445).

(1983) The management of diarrhoea and use of oral rehydration therapy – a joint WHO/UNICEF statement. Geneva: WHO.

Cutting, W.A.M. (1979) Can village mothers prepare oral rehydration solution? Trop. Doc. **9**: 195–199.

Fig. 140

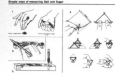

Plastic salt and sugar measuring spoon. Available from TALC, PO Box 49, St Albans, UK.

Church, M.A. (1972) Fluids for the sick child. A method of teaching mothers. Trop. Doc. 2: 119–121.

Hendrata, L. (1978) Spoons for making glucose salt solutions. Lancet i: 612.

Cutting, W.A.M., Harpin, V.A., Lock, B.A., Sedgewich, J.R. (1979) Can village mothers prepare oral rehydration solution? Trop. Doc. **9**: 195–199.

Steinhoff, M.C., Srilatha, V.L., Thilaikarari, R., Abel, R., Mukarji, D.S. (1985) Finger or spoons to make oral rehydration solution? Trans. R. Soc. Trop. Med. Hyg. **79**: 366–368.

Fig. 141

Conteh, S., McRobbie, I., Tompkins, A.M. (1982) A comparison of bottle tops, teaspoons and WHO glucose electrolyte packets for home-made oral rehydration solutions in the Gambia. Trans. R. Soc. Trop. Med. Hyg. **76**: 783–785.

Fig. 142

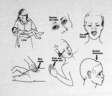

From: TALC, PO Box 49, St Albans, UK.

Colleagues in education recommend that the signs of dehydration will be better learnt if separated into single illustrations.

Fig. 143

Diarrhoea management. Set of slides. TALC, PO Box 49, St Albans, UK.

For further ideas on teaching health workers and parents see: Lovel, H.J. (ed) (1986) Care of the sick child with diarrhoea. Chapter 7 in: Maternal and child health. Teacher training illustrated annotated bibliography. WHO/BLAT. Available from TALC, PO Box 49, St Albans, UK.

Fig. 144

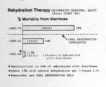

Pape, J.W., Mondestin, B., Jasmin, L., Kean, B.H., Rohde, J.E., Jonson, W.D. (1984) Management of diarrhoea in Haiti. In: Cash, R., McLaughlin, J. (eds) Proceedings of International Congress of Oral Rehydration Therapy. Washington: Agency for International Development.

(1984) Impact of oral rehydration therapy on hospital admissions and care-fatality rates for diarrhoeal disease: results from 12 hospitals in various countries. WHO Wkly. Epidem. Rec., **59** (47): 361–363.

Samadi, A.R., Islam, R., Huq, M.I. (1983) Replacement of intravenous therapy by oral rehydration solution in a large treatment centre for diarrhoea with dehydration. WHO Bulletin **61**: 471–476.

Fig. 145

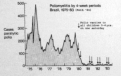

Source: Rissi. (1984) Decline of polio in Brazil. Paper presented to EPI World Advisory Group, EPI. Geneva: WHO.

Wyatt, H.V. (1984) The popularity of injections in the third world: origins and consequences for poliomyelitis. Soc. Sci. Med. **19**: 911–915.

Ofosu-Amaah, S., Kratzer, J.H., Nicholas, D.D. (1977) Is poliomyelitis a serious problem in developing countries? Lameness in Ghanaian schools. Br. Med. J. **1**: 1012–1014. See also accompanying article on polio prevalence in Danfa study area. Br. Med. J. **1**: 1009–1012.

Shattock, F.M. (1976) Workload v. community good: the concept of the protected child. Environmental Child Health **23**: 179–183.

Fig. 146

Egyptian illustration: The doorkeeper Ruma 18th Dynasty NY Carlesberg Glyptotheka Copenhagen. Children's illustration from: '... by the year 1990' No. 2 (1983). A newsletter for the supporters of immunisation, published by the Disabilities Study Unit, Wildhanger, Amberley, Arundel, West Sussex, BN18 9NR, UK.

Nicholas D. et al (1977) Is poliomyelitis a serious problem in developing countries? Br. Med. J. **1**: 1009-12.

Sabin, A.B. (1986) Strategy for rapid elimination and continuing control of poliomyelitis and other vaccine preventable diseases of children in developing countries. Br. Med. J. **292**: 531-533.

Pollard, R. (1983) Whooping cough in Fiji. Lancet **i**: 1381.

Fig. 147

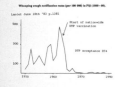

From: (1983) Lancet, 18 June: 1381.

Morley, D.C., Martin, W.J., Woodland, M. (1966) Whooping cough in Nigerian children Trop. Geogr. Med. **18**: 169.

Bwibo, N.O. (1971) Whooping cough in Uganda. Scand. J. Infect. Dis. **3**: 41.

(1984) Report of the expanded programme on immunisation global advisory meeting 21-25 October. Alexandria: WHO (EPI/Gen/85/1).

Fig. 148

From: Berggren (1983) Trop. Doc. **13**: 79-87. Two newborns are dying every minute from this preventable disease. Those wanting up-to-date information on undertaking neonatal tetanus surveys and on efforts to control the disease should write to: Neonatal Tetanus Research Group, WHO, Geneva, Switzerland.

Gwatkin, D., Wilcox, J.R., Wray, J.D. (1980) Can health and nutrition intervention make a difference? Washington: Overseas Development Council.

Schofield, F.D., Tucker, V.M., Wetbrook, G.R. (1961) Neonatal tetanus in New Guinea: effects of immunisation in pregnancy. Br. Med. J. **2**: 785-9.

Kielman, A.A., Vohra, S. (1977) Control of tetanus neonatorum in rural communities - immunisation effects of high-dose calcium phosphate adsorbed tetanus toxoid. Indian J. Med. Res. **66**: 906-16.

Woodruff, A.H. et al (1984) Neonatal tetanus: mode of infection, prevalence and prevention in Southern Sudan. Lancet **i**: 378-379.

Bytchenko, B.D. (1966) Geographical distribution of tetanus in the world. Bull. WHO **34**: 71-104.

Stanfield, J.P., Galazka, A. Neonatal tetanus in the world today. Bull. WHO **62**: 647-669.

Henderson, R.H., Sandarason, T. (1982) Cluster sampling to assess immunisation coverage: a review of experiences with a simplified sampling method. Bull. WHO **60**: 253-60.

Fig. 148
(continued)

Newell, K.W., Lehman, A.D., Leblanc, D.R., Osorio, N.G. (1966) The use of toxoid for the prevention of tetanus neonatorum. Final report of a double-blind controlled field trial. Bull. WHO **35**: 863-71.

Chen, P. (1976) The traditional birth attendant and neonatal tetanus: the Malaysian experience. Environmental Child Health **22**: 263-264.

Fig. 149

From: Centre for Disease Control (1982) Eradication of indigenous measles. United States Morbidity and Mortality Weekly Report **31**: 517-519.

In South and Central America measles in the second year of life caused 20% of all deaths and in two localities 30% of all deaths. Puffer, R.R., Serrano, C.V. (1973) Patterns of mortality in childhood. Report of the Inter-American Investigation of Mortality in Childhood. Washington: Pan American Health Organization.

Global measles eradication, arguments in its favour. Foege, William H. (1984) Banishing measles from the world. World Health Forum **5**: 64.

Henderson, R.H. (1984) Vaccine preventable diseases. Protecting the world's children: vaccines and immunisation. Report of Bellazio Conference, 13-15 March. New York: Rockerfeller Foundation.

Fig. 150

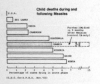

Source: Grant, J. (1985) State of the world's children. Oxford University Press: 46.

Hull, H.F., Williams, P.J., Oldfield, F. (1983) Measles mortality and vaccine efficacy in rural West Africa. Lancet i: 972-975.

Fig. 151

From: TALC, PO Box 49, St Albans, UK.

For information on cold boxes, refrigerators, temperature indicators and vaccines, contact Expanded Programme of Immunisation, WHO, Geneva, Switzerland.

For ideas on teaching see: Lovel, H.J. (ed) (1986) Prevention of infectious disease by immunisation. Chapter 5 in: Maternal and Child Health. Teacher training illustrated annotated bibliography. WHO/BLAT. Available from TALC, PO Box 49, St Albans, UK.

Creese, A.L., Sriyabbaya, N., Casabal, G., Wiseso, G. (1982) Cost-effectiveness appraisal of immunisation programmes. Bull. WHO. 60 (4): 621-632.

Fig. 152

Breast feeding. Set of slides. TALC, PO Box 49, St Albans, UK.

(1981) Breast feeding and health. Special issue of Assignment Children. Vols 55/56. Geneva: UNICEF.

Jelliffe, D.B., Jelliffe, E.F.P. (1978) The volume and composition of human milk in poorly nourished communities. A review. Am. J. clin. Nutr. **31**: 492–515.

McClelland, D.B.L., McGrath, J., Samson, R.R. Acta. paediatr. scand. Suppl. 271.

MacFarlane, J.A. (1975) In: Parent–infant interaction. Amsterdam: Elsevier (Ciba Found. Symp. 33).

Condon, W.S., Sander, L.W. (1974) Neonate movement is synchronised with adult speech: interactional participation and language acquisition. Science **183**: 99–101.

Brazelton, T.B.B., Tronick, E., Adamson, L., Als, H., Wise, S. (1975) Early mother–infant reciprocity. In: Parent–infant interaction. Amsterdam: Elsevier (Ciba Found. Symp. 33).

Klaus, M.H., Kennell, J.H. (1976) Parent to infant attachment. In: Hull, D. (Ed) Recent advances in paediatrics; 5. Edinburgh: Churchill Livingstone.

Brimblecombe, F.S.W. (Ed) (1978) Separation and special care baby units. Clin. dev. Med. **68**: 1–113.

Klaus, M.H., Kennell, J.H. (1976) Maternal–infant bonding. St Louis, USA: C.V. Mosby.

Breast feeding is not a cause of iron deficiency as 50% is absorbed compared with 10% from cows milk. Saarinen, V.M., Simes, M.A., Dallmon, P.R. (1977) Iron absorption in infants. J. Pediatr. **91**: 36–39

Plank, S.J., Milansi, M.L. (1973) Infant feeding and infant mortality in rural Chile. Bull. WHO **48**: 203–210.

Fig. 153

Information taken from: Konner, M. (1980) Science **207**: 788. Available from TALC, PO Box 49, St Albans, UK.

Harfouche, J.K. (1970) The importance of breast feeding. J. Trop. Pediatr. **16**: 135.

Jelliffe, D.B., Jelliffe, E.F.P. (1978) Human milk in the modern world: psycho–social, nutritional and economic significance. Oxford: OUP.

Fig. 154

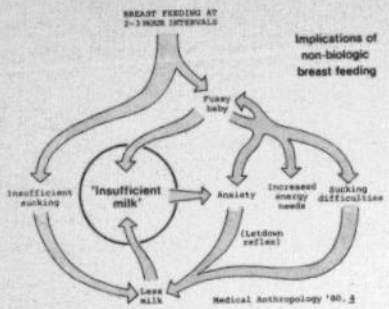

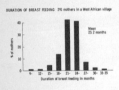

This drawing is modified from: Gussler, J.D., Briesemeister, L.H. (1980) Med. Anthropol. **4** (2): 3-24.

Helsing, E., Savage-King, F. (1982) Breast feeding in practice. A manual for health workers. Oxford: OUP.

Savage-King, F. Helping mothers to breast feed. African Medical and Research Foundation, Wilson Airport, PO Box 30125, Nairobi. Also available from TALC, PO Box 49, St Albans, UK.

Fig. 155

Breast feeding. Set of slides. TALC, PO Box 49, St Albans, UK.

Martin, W.I., Morley, D.C., Woodland, M. (1964) Interval between births in a Nigerian village. J. Trop. Paediatr. **10**: 82.

Whitehead, R.G., Rowland, M.G.M., Hutton, M., Prentice, A.M., Miller, E., Paul, A.A. (1978) Factors influencing lactation performance in rural Gambian mothers. Lancet **ii**: 178.

Jelliffe, D.B., Jelliffe, E.F.P. (1978) The volume and composition of human milk in poorly nourished communities. A review. Am. J. Clin. Nutr. **31**: 492-515.

Fig. 156

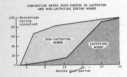

From: Wall Chart on Human Lactation. IPPF, 18-20 Lower Regent Street, London, SW1Y 4PW.

Hytten, F.E., Leitch, I.L. (1971) The physiology of human pregnancy. Oxford: Blackwell.

The findings suggest that contraception, as it is presently practised, is an inadequate substitute for breast feeding. Smith, D.F. (1985) Breast feeding, contraception and birth intervals in developing countries. Studies in Family Planning **16**: 154-163.

McNeilly, A.S. Effects of lactation on fertility. Br. Med. Bull. 35 (2): 151.

Fig. 157

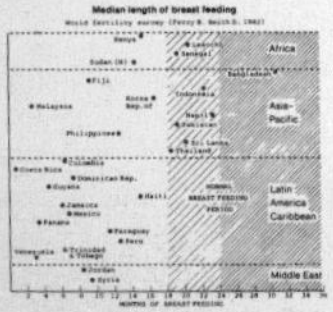

Figures taken from: Ferry, B., Smith, D. (1982) World Fertility Survey. Available from TALC, PO Box 49, St Albans, UK.

For an excellent book giving practical help: Savage-King, F. (1985) Helping mothers to breast feed. Nairobi: African Medical and Research Foundation. Available from TALC, PO Box 49, St Albans, UK.

Biddulph, J. (1981) Promotion of breast feeding: experience in Papua New Guinea. In: Jelliffe, D.B., Jelliffe, E.F.P. (Eds) Advances in international maternal and child health; 1. Oxford: OUP.

Fig. 158

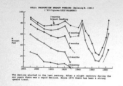

Source: Helsing, E. (1981) Additional figures for 1983 from Leifsolberg. Personal communication.

Jones, D.A., West, R.R. (1985) Lactation nurse increases duration of breast feeding. Arch. Dis. Child. **60**: 772-774.

Fig. 159

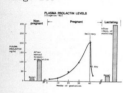

From: Clugston, G. WHO duplicated paper, South East Asia Regional Office, New Delhi.

McNeilly, A.S. (1979) Effects of lactation on fertility. Br. Med. Bull. **35**: 151-4.

Fig. 160

TALC, PO Box 49, St Albans, UK.

Cunningham, A.S. (1979) Morbidity in breast fed and artifically fed infants. J. Paediatr. **95**: 685-9.

Ebrahim, G.J. (1978) Breast feeding: the biological option. Macmillan.

Greiner, T., Almroth, S., Lathom (1979) The economic value of breast feeding. New York: Ithaca (Cornell International Nutrition Monograph Series no. 6).

Fig. 161

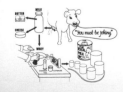

Ebrahim, G.J. (1978) Breast feeding: the biological option. Macmillan.

Chetley, A. (1980) The baby killer scandal. London: War on Want.

Ebrahim, G.J. (1982) Child health in a changing environment. London: Macmillan.

Pittard, W.B. (1979) Breast milk immunology. Review article. Am. J. Dis. Child. 133: 83.

Atherton, D.J. (1983) Breast feeding and atopic eczema. Leading article. Br. Med. J. **287**: 775-776.

Schuster, S. (1983) Breast feeding and atopic eczema. Br. Med. J. **287**: 1220.

Mahood, J.M. (1983) Breast feeding and atopic eczema. Br. Med. J. **287**: 1553.

**Fig. 161
(continued)**

Kell, J.G., Shanks, R.G., Devitt, D.G. (1983) Breast feeding and atopic eczema. Br. Med. J. **287**: 1220-1221.

Midwinter, R.E., Moore, W.J., Soothill, J.F., Turner, M.W., Colley, J.R.T. (1982) Infant feeding and atopy. Lancet i: 339.

Fig. 162

A cartoon from 'Pan', a paper produced during the Rome World Food conference illustrating the pressure of Western advertising.

Muller, M. (1975) The baby killer. London: War on Want.

Background papers and themes for discussion meeting on infant and young child feeding. (1979) Document FHE/ICF/79.3. Geneva: WHO.

Dumont, R. (1966) False start in Africa. London: Andre Dutsch.

Fig. 163

Figures from Narayanan (1984) Occurrence of infection in high risk neonates. Lancet ii: 111.

Fig. 164

A set of plastic tubes representing arms of different sizes from 11cm to 16cm is available. A low cost insertion tape, which Zerfas has shown to be more accurate in use, both available from TALC, PO Box 49, St Albans, UK.

Children are on a spectrum from good nutrition and health, to life threatening undernutrition. Relationship between different measurements and probability of mortality has been measured by: Chen, L.C., Chowdhury, A.K.M.A., Huttman, S.L. (1980) Anthropometric assessment of energy-protein malnutrition and subsequent risk of mortality among pre-school age children. Am. J. Clin. Nutr. **33**: 1836-45.

Beiragi, R. (1982) On the best cut-off point for nutritional monitoring. Am. J. Clin. Nutr. **35**: 769-770.

Lovel, H.J., de Graaf, J., Gordon, G. (1984) How mothers measure growth: community dimensions for expanded growth monitoring in Ghana. Assignment Children 65/68: 275-291.

Fig. 165

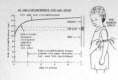

Shakir, A., Morley, D.C. (1974) Measuring malnutrition. Lancet **i**: 758.

Velzeboer, P.H., Selwyn, B.E., Sargent, F., Pollitt, E., Delgado, H. (1983) Evaluation of arm circumference as a public health index of protein energy malnutrition in early childhood. J. Trop. Paediatr. **29**: 135-144.

Shakir, A. (1978) The surveillance of protein-calorie malnutrition by simple and economical means. J. Trop. Pediatr. **21**: 69.

Anderson, M. (1979) Comparison of anthropometric measures of nutritional status in pre-school children in five developing countries. Am. J. Clin. Nutr. **32**: 2339-45.

Fig. 166

Growth charts and teaching material to help in their use. Available from TALC, PO Box 49, St Albans, UK.

An analysis of a collection of around 200 charts was made before designing the present chart. Tremlett, G., Lovel, H.J., Morley, D. (1983) Guideline for the design of national weight-for-age growth charts. Assignment Children Vol. 61/62.

(Editorial) (1984) A measure of agreement on growth standards. Lancet i: 83, 69, 142-143.

Gomez et al. (1955) Malnutrition in infancy and childhood with special reference to kwashiorkor. Advances in Paediatrics **7**: 131.

Morley, D., Woodland, M. (1979) See how they grow. London: Macmillan.

Morley, D.C. (1977) Growth charts - 'curative' or 'preventive'? Archs. Dis. Child. **52**: 395-8.

Morley, D.C. (1968) A health and weight chart for use in developing countries. Trop. Geogr. Med. **20**: 101.

(1978) A growth chart for international use on maternal and child health care. Guidelines for primary health care personnel. Geneva: WHO.

Difference between different ethnic groups if well nourished is minimal. Habicht, J.P., Martorell, R., Yarborough, C., Malina, R.M., Klein, R.E. (1974) Height and weight standards of pre-school children. Lancet **i**: 611-15.

Stephenson, L.S., Lathom, M.C., Jansen, A. (1983) A comparison of growth standards, similarities between NCHS, Harvard, Denver and privileged African children and differences with Kenyan rural children. Ithaca (Cornell International Nutrition monographs series No. 12).

Senanayake, I.P. (1977) Use of home based records in an evaluation of a health care system. Environmental Child Health **22**: 179-183.

Fig. 167

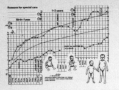

Kielmann, A.A., McCord, C. (1978) Weight for age as an index of risk of death in children. Lancet, 10 June: 1247-50.

Prader, A. (1978) Catch-up growth. In: Barltrop, D. (Ed) Pediatrics and growth. London: Fellowship of Postgraduate Medicine.

Rutishauser, I.H.E. (1975) Growth of the pre-school child in West Mengo district, Uganda. In: Owor, R., Ongom, V.L., Kirya, B.G. (Eds) The child in the African environment - growth, development and survival. Nairobi: The East African Literature Bureau.

Falkner, F., Pernot, Roy M.P., Habich, H., Senecal, J., Masse, G. (1958) Some international comparisons of physical growth in the two first years of life. Courrier 8: 1-11.

Gopalan, C. (1968) Kwashiorkor and marasmus. Evolution and distinguishing features. In: McCance, R.A., Widdowson, E.M. (Eds) Calorie deficiency and protein deficiency. London: Churchill.

Rowland, M.G.M., Cole, T.J., Whitehead, R.G. (1978) Protein-energy malnutrition. Trans. R. Soc. Trop. Med. Hyg. 72: 550-1.

Gopalan, C., Chattejee, M. (1985) Use of growth charts for promoting child nutrition. New Delhi: Nutrition Foundation of India (Special Publication Series; 2).

Gopalan, C. (1983) Small is healthy? New Delhi: Nutrition Foundation of India. Bulletin 5: 33-37.

Fig. 168

A new method of weighing. The TALC spring and scales. Springs may now be made which will stretch up to 14kg, at a centimetre for each kg with an accuracy of 0.5cm. Springs and details on construction of these scales from TALC, PO Box 49, St Albans, UK.

For teaching health workers about measuring growth. Lovel, H.J. (ed) (1986) Promotion of normal growth and development of children and young people. Chapter 3: 188-209 in: Maternal and child health. Teacher training illustrated annotated bibliography. WHO/BLAT. Available from TALC, PO Box 49, St Albans, UK.

Fig. 169

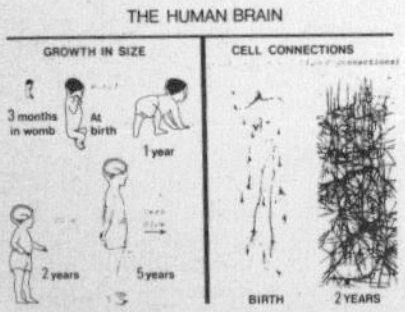

Dobbing, J. (1976) Vulnerable periods in brain growth and somatic growth. In: Wright, E.V., Roberts, D.F., Thomson, A.M. (Eds) The biology of human fetal growth. London: Taylor & Francis.

Dobbing, J. (1976) Malnutrition et development du cerveaux. La Recherche 7: 193-145.

Fig. 170

Drawn from: Davies, T.P., Parkin, J.M. (1972) Catch-up growth following early childhood malnutrition. East Afr. Med. J. 49: 672.

Harvard Institute for International Development (1981) Nutrition intervention in developing countries. Cambridge, Mass: Oelgeschlager, Gunn & Hain.

Fig. 171

Source: TALC, PO Box 49, St Albans, UK.

McLaren, D.S. (1974) The great protein fiasco. Lancet ii: 93-96.

Gopalan, C. (1968) Kwashiorkor and marasmus: evolution and distinguishing features. In: McCance and Widdowson. Colour deficiencies and protein deficiencies. London: Churchill Livingstone.

Waterlow, J.C., Payne, P.R. (1975) The protein gap. Nature **258**: 113-117.

Fig. 172

Church, M. (1979) Dietary factors in malnutriton: quality and quantity of diet in relation to child development. Proc. Nutr. Soc. **38**: 41-9.

Sukhatme, P.V. (1972) Protein strategy and agricultural development. Indian J. Agricultural Economy **27**: 1-24.

Waterlow. J.C., Payne, P.R. (1975) The protein gap. Nature **258**: 113-117.

Weaning foods and energy. Set of slides. Explains with easily understood pictures this concept of energy concentration. TALC, PO Box 49, St Albans, UK.

Fig. 173

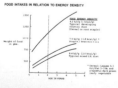

From: Dearden, C., Harman, P., Morley, D. (1980) Eating more fats and oils as a step towards overcoming malnutrition. Trop. Doc. **10**: 137-142.

Food and Agricultural Organisation and World Health Organisation. (1977) Dietary fats and oils in human nutrition. Rome: FAO.

Ljungqvist, B.G., Mellander, O., Svanberg, U.S.O. (1981) Dietary bulk as a limiting factor for nutrient intake in pre-school children. J. Trop Pediatr. **27**: 68-73, 127-35, 184-9.

Hellstrom, A., Hermansson, A.M., Karlsson, A., Ljungqvist, B., Mellander, O., Svanberg, U. (1981) Dietary bulk as a limiting factor for nutrient intake - with special reference to the feeding of pre-school children. J. Trop. Paediatr. **27**: 127-35.

Fig. 173 (continued)

Duggan, M. (1985) MD Thesis. London University. A number of children had food intake studies undertaken under hospital conditions during measles and in the recovery period. The children ate little of a thin low energy concentration porridge (pap) during illness. During recovery many children consumed more than 1.5Kg a day of a more concentrated porridge.

Fig. 174

The "Weanling's Dilemma" should the mother introduce foods which tend to be of low energy concentration and highly contaminated with bacteria. 'TOO EARLY ?' or 'TOO LATE ?'

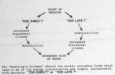

Concept from: Waterlow, J.C. (1981) Observations on the suckling's dilemma - a personal view. J. Human Nutrition **35**: 85-98.

Dugdale, A.E. (1986) Evolution and infant feeding. Lancet **i**: 670-672.

Lovel, H.J. (ed) (1986) Child nutrition and promotion of food supply. Chapter 2: 130-188 in: Maternal and child health. Teacher traiing illustrated annotated bibliography. WHO/BLAT. Available from TALC, PO Box 49, St Albans, UK.

Fig. 175

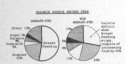

Breast feeding. Set of slides. TALC, PO Box 49, St Albans, UK.

Rutishauser, I.H.E. (1975) Growth of the pre-school child in West Mengo district, Uganda. In: Owor, R., Ongom, V.L., Kirya, B.G. (Eds) The child in the African environment - growth, development and survival. Nairobi: The East African Literature Bureau.

ICDDR Study reviewed in 'Glimpse', April 1983, confirms that weaning foods in Bangladesh do not make up for the shortfall in breast milk.

Fig. 176

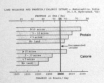

From: (1982) Hyderabad: National Institute of Nutrition. Nutrition newsletter.

Gross food shortage in Bangladesh, 1974, led to a 45% increase in crude death rate in Matlab area. Chen, L., Chakrabortz, J., Sadar, A.M., Yunus, M.D. (1984) Estimating and partitioning the mortality impact of several modern technologies in basic health services. In: Matlab, B-Desh. (1981) International Population Conference, Manila. **2**: 113-142.

India in her sixth five year plan has given priority to exploit oil seeds. Examination is being made of less conventional sources of oil. Hyderabad: Nat. Inst. of Nutrition. Nutrition News 6 (No. 1).

Fig. 177   Figures from FAO, in a private communication.

CONSUMPTION OF OILS AND FATS *

	grams per day	Proportion of total calories consumed
INDUSTRIALISED COUNTRIES	126	34 %
DEVELOPING COUNTRIES	41	16 %

* F.A.O. Provisional figure, Av.'79-'81

Fig. 178   Outcome for children discharged following keratomalacia.   Menon, K., Vijayraghavan, K. (1980) Sequelae of severe xerophthalmia - a follow-up study. Am. J. Clin. Nutr. **33**: 218-20.

Xerophthalmia. Set of slides (code EyX). TALC, PO Box 49, St Albans, UK.

A free newsletter is available from Xerophthalmia Club, Nuffield Laboratory of Ophthalmology, Oxford, UK.

Information leaflets on blinding malnutrition from: Helen Keller International, 15 West 16th Street, New York, NY 10011, USA. Also a free newsletter from Department of Preventive Ophthalmology, City Road, London, EC1.

WHO (1982) Control of vitamin A deficiency and xerophthalmia. Geneva: WHO (Tech. Rep. Ser. 672).

Sommer, A. (1982) Nutritional blindness. Xerophthalmia and keratomalacia. OUP.

Ophthalmology is one of the specialties where effective steps towards primary health care have been taken.   Barrie, R., Jones, J.   Social responsibilities in ophthalmology.   J. R. Soc. Med. **78**: 358-366.

Fig. 179   Source: Indian Ministry of Agriculture. Food and Nutrition Board (1981) Iron in salt. New Delhi: Indian Ministry of Agriculture.

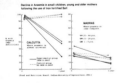

Iron status among school-aged children correlated positively with education achievement and efficiency in problem solving. Pollitt, E., Soemantri, A.G., Yunis, F., Scrimshaw, N.S. (1985) Cognitive effect of iron deficiency anaemia. (Letter) Lancet i: 158.

Crompton, D.W., Neisheim, M.C. (1984) Malnutrition's insidious partner. World Health, March 18-21.

INACG (1979) Iron deficiency in infancy and childhood. Washington: International Anaemia Consultative Group, Nutrition Foundation Report.

Baker, S.J. DeMaeger, E.M. (1979) Nutritional anaemia: its understanding and control with special reference to the work of WHO. Am. J. Clin. Nutr. **32**: 368-417.

Fig. 180   TALC, PO Box 49, St Albans, UK.

Fig. 181   Source: (1985) Heart beat. J. International Society and Federation of Cardiologists, July (No. 2).

Fig. 182   Source: Weaning Foods. Set of slides. TALC, PO Box 49, St Albans, UK.

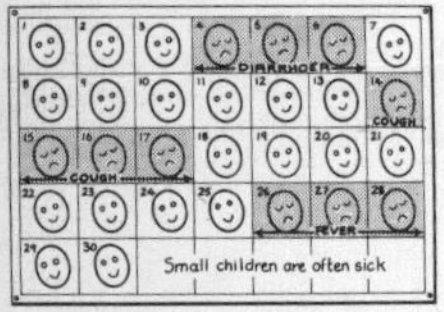

Documentation of social behaviour and contamination of water and food. Rowland, M.G.M., McCollum, J.P.K. (1977) Malnutrition and gastroenteritis in the Gambia. Trans. R. Soc. Trop. Med. Hyg. **71**: 199–203.

Rohde, J. (1978) Preparing for the next round: convalescent care after acute infection. Am. J. Clin. Nutr. **31**: 2258–68.

Stephenson, L. et al (1980) Relationship between Ascaris infection and growth of malnourished pre-school children in Kenya. Am. J. Clin. Nutr. **33**: 1165–1172.

Briscoe, J. (1979) The quantitative effect of infection on the use of food by young children in poor countries. Am. J. Clin. Nutr. **32**: 648–676.

Fig. 183   Fibre in human diet. Set of slides. TALC, PO Box 49, St Albans, UK.

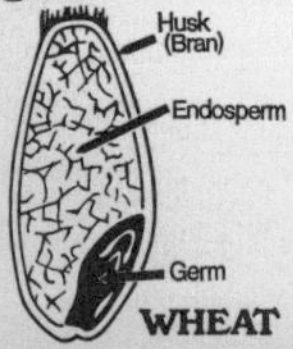

Doll, R., Peto, R. (1981) Stopping smoking and passing 'floating stools' as major ways to reduce cancer. Journal National Cancer Institute **66**: 1192. The causes of cancer: quantitative estimate of avoidable risks of cancer in the USA today.

Cummings, H. (1985) In: Trowell, H.C. et al (ed) Dietary fibre, fibre depleted foods and disease. New York: Grune & Stratton.

Fig. 184   Cycle of malnutrition and infection. From: TALC, PO Box 49, St Albans, UK.

Fig. 185

Illingworth, R.S. (1972) The normal child. 5th ed. London: Churchill.

Effects of social class in UK. Neligan, G., Prudham, D., Steiner, H. (1974) The formative years: birth, family and development in Newcastle-upon-Tyne. London: OUP.

Butler, N., Bonham, D. (1963) Perinatal mortality. Edinburgh: Churchill Livingstone.

In Guatamalan villages nutrition is marginal for all families. Children destined for malnutrition and retarded development are those reared by passive and unresponsive mothers in homes which provide low levels of stimulus. Gravioto, J. (1981) XII International Congress of Nutrition, San Diego.

Kagan, J. (1977) The child in the family – Daedalus. J. Am. Acad. Art Sci. Spring: 57-50.

Donaldson, M. (1979) Children's minds. New York: Norton.

For ideas on teaching see: Lovel, H.J. (ed) (1986) Promotion of normal growth and development of children and young people. Chapter 3 in: Maternal and child health. Teacher training annotated illustrated bibliography. WHO/BLAT. Available from TALC, PO Box 49, St Albans, UK.

Fig. 186

Original from a Quaker poster. Available from TALC, PO Box 49, St Albans, UK.

For information on agriculture contact World Neighbours, 5116 North Portland, Oklahoma City, Oklahoma 73112, USA.

Fig. 187

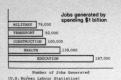

Jobs generated by
spending $1 billion

MILITARY 76,000
TRANSPORT 92,000
CONSTRUCTION 100,000
HEALTH 139,000
EDUCATION 187,000

Number of Jobs Generated
(U.S. Bureau Labour Statistics)

Source: US Labour Bureau. Redrawn for TALC, PO Box 49, St Albans, UK.

Sivard, R.L. (1983) World military and social expenditures. World Priorities, Box 25140, Washington DC 20007, USA.

For a source of information on programmes to assist in national and international cooperation: Friends House, Euston Road, WC1.

The illustrations in this book will be available as transparencies from:

TALC, PO Box 49, St Albans, UK.